LEGAL ASPECTS OF CODE ADMINISTRATION

INTERNATIONAL CODE COUNCIL®

Legal Aspects of Code Administration

ISBN: 978-1-60983-731-0

Project Head:	Stephen Van Note
Contributing Author:	Robert Church
Publications Manager:	Mary Lou Luif
Project Editor:	Daniel Mutz
Production Technician:	Cheryl Smith
Cover Design:	Carmel Gieson

T028390

Table of Contents

Preface

The effective and proper administration of a building department demands that its building official and staff know the legal ramifications of the action taken or not taken by the building department. This book, *Legal Aspects of Code Administration*, is designed to inform the building official of the legal aspects of his or her profession. It is not to be used in place of the advice of a municipal attorney.

The text is written in a logical order with explanation of legal terms that building officials, fire marshals, and their staff must have familiarity in while performing their jobs. It also serves as an excellent refresher to those preparing to take the Legal Module of the ICC Certified Building Official (CBO) and/or Certified Fire Marshal (CFM) certification examination as this book is a required resource for these examinations.

Because of the nature of the subject matter, it is necessary to refer frequently to provisions of the state constitution, state statutes, and building code regulations. It is desirable that the user have access to specific state and municipal laws relating to the specific jurisdiction for which he or she is responsible.

Recognition must be given to the original author of the text, George Dean. Dean practiced law with Metropolitan Nashville Government with specific assignments as legal counsel to the codes administration and planning department. Dean received his A.B. degree from Vanderbilt University.

Recognition is also given to the coauthors of the previous edition: Jennifer Shapiro and Linda S. Pieczynski. The addition of original case law was the result of Jennifer Shapiro's extensive research.

Linda S. Pieczynski is a former assistant state's attorney and the author of *Illinois Criminal Practice and Procedure* (West Publishing) and an instructor of training on legal aspects for the International Code Council.

Robert Church updated the 2002 edition resulting in this updated and refreshed 2017 publication by adding new information, new case law, and revising some of the dated information. He is the Director of the Utah Prosecution Council and has prosecuted for a midsize municipality in Utah for nearly 18 years. He prosecuted all code violations in his city. He has taught Legal Aspects of Code Administration for ICC for over 15 years.

Chapter 1 – Introduction

This chapter briefly describes the concepts discussed in the next twelve chapters.

Topics

Litigation Wave
Legal Concepts and Factual Situations
Subsequent Chapters
Appendix
Index of Terms

Terms

adjudication
liability

Litigation Wave

Within the past 35 years, there has been a tremendous increase in litigation across the United States. This explosion of litigation has affected local governments and their officials. When the 1984 edition of this book was published, there was a trend that placed building code officials at the forefront of exposure to **liability**. Fortunately, this trend was not borne out in the case law of the past 17 years.

Although liability does not often apply to building officials, lawsuits continue to be brought against them. Given some of the tragedies of past years, the public can see the value of a strong local building department. As society becomes more technologically advanced, cities and towns become more populated, buildings become more complex, and new construction materials and techniques become available. Consequently, as the role of code enforcement becomes increasingly more visible to the public, building officials need to be concerned with the legal consequences of their actions. It is crucial that building officials learn to cope with the public scrutiny that results from being forced to defend legally their official activities.

Building officials who familiarize themselves with the law can then use it as a tool to aggressively prosecute code offenders. In recent years, the public has become much more aware of its legal rights, constitutional and otherwise. It is particularly important for a building official to understand how a property owner's new-found awareness of these rights influences both postures of litigation. Indeed, even though they have little chance of prevailing, many property owners now take the offensive and sue the building official, while others more actively defend lawsuits against them. This use of a formal legal process to resolve a dispute is called **adjudication**. Adjudication by the court produces a decision, judgment, court decree, or determination based on a hearing of the factual issues presented by both parties to a dispute. This book discusses some of the defenses raised by the alleged code offenders in response to an official's attempt to enforce judicially a building code. Knowledge of these defenses will help building officials know what to expect.

Legal Concepts and Factual Situations

This book examines general tendencies in the law relating to building codes. It does not specifically cover the law of each individual state; rather it discusses, in general, the state of the law on a national level. Remember, each state's laws may be slightly or radically different from laws in other states. If a question arises concerning the law in a particular state, an attorney from that state must be consulted. This book is not binding law. Do not refer to it in a court of law. Rather, use this book as a starting point for further research or for help in forming questions to pose to the municipal attorney in the applicable jurisdiction. It is important to verify that the consulted attorney has some expertise in municipal law.

Along with the discussion of relevant legal concepts are some of the factual situations that may give rise to important legal consequences. Of course, a multitude of factual situations may occur that have different legal ramifications depending on the law of the home state. A seemingly minute nuance in a particular set of facts can strongly impact a judge's decision. If a situation arises that is similar to one described in this book, consult a municipal attorney immediately for further advice. This course of action will save much time, aggravation, and money.

Legal Aspects of Code Administration will not turn a building official into an attorney; nor will it provide all of the solutions to every situation. It will, however, help the building official become more attuned to several legal and factual issues and promote a better understanding of the judicial process. This increased sensitivity to the possible consequences will help the building official temper his or her actions with caution and good sense. After reading this book, the building official should be aware of situations in which it is imperative to consult an attorney before acting.

Subsequent Chapters

Chapter 2 provides a brief historical overview of the development of building codes as legally binding rules governing the construction of buildings. Chapter 3 discusses the law of local governments and, more particularly, the relationship between local and state government. Chapter 4 briefly discusses state legislative law, while Chapter 5 addresses federal legislative law. Chapter 6 describes the administration and enforcement of the building code from a legal perspective. Chapter 7 discusses administrative law. Chapter 8 addresses the constitutional provisions that directly affect how a building code official performs his or her duties. Chapter 9 looks at related property law concepts, such as easements, restrictive covenants, the transfer of real estate property, as well as property rights that are shared by one or more owners and/or occupants. Chapters 10 through 12 explore the liability of a building official: first for intentional wrongdoing, second for negligent wrongdoing, and third for violations of civil rights. Finally, Chapter 13 offers some practical tips on being an effective courtroom witness.

Appendix

Information included in the appendix has been prepared as reference data for the Management module of the ICC Certified Building Official examination. To provide accurate, concise information regarding federally mandated treatment of issues relative to municipal management, these topical summaries were obtained directly from the US Equal Opportunity Commission.

Index of Terms

Many of the words and phrases used within the text may seem foreign. The use of legalese is intended to acquaint building officials with the legal concepts, jargon, and procedures inherent in the daily workings of a building department. To make learning these terms as painless as possible, this edition includes an expanded Index of Terms with more detailed and easy-to-understand definitions. A term appearing once in **bold** type signals that its definition can be found in the Index of Terms. It is hoped that additions to the text will make the judicial process less threatening, therefore encouraging the building official to use this knowledge to accomplish the goals of the building code.

Chapter 2 – Historical Overview

This chapter illustrates the consequences that occur when building construction and materials are not vigorously regulated.

Topics

Early Building Codes

Development of Modern Codes

Introduction

The evolution of modern building began over 5,000 years ago. Over time, there has been a growth of regulations that have served to govern the methods by which buildings are constructed. While early codes were rudimentary, they underscored the increasing concern of civilization and society with the safety of the buildings in which people lived and worked. This brief, and by no means conclusive, overview of the history of code development is designed to illustrate the consequences that occur when building construction and materials are not vigorously regulated.

Historically, building codes have developed in cycles. Usually when a civilization begins to develop and build, it fails to realize the importance of regulating modes of construction and building materials. The failure to regulate and provide standards leads to extremely poor construction techniques. Eventually the density of the population, especially in urban areas, increases drastically. The combination of shoddy structures and high population density inevitably leads to conditions where a major fire or other disaster spreads through the community. It is only after such a disaster that the survivors realize the necessity and desirability of building codes.

This cycle can be seen in smaller versions in various cities in the United States today. After a tragedy, the public understands the necessity of a strong program of enforcement. The city is able to move more easily against code offenders. The real tragedy is that this mood of compliance and enforcement frequently does not endure. For example, the aftermath of the 1989 earthquake in California revealed that many lives could have been saved if the buildings were more structurally sound. Structural engineers blamed poor workmanship and lapses of code enforcement for much of the devastation. A widespread call for stricter building codes and enforcement was reflected in the news media. In 1994, when California suffered yet another massive earthquake, the newspaper articles surrounding the event read almost identically to those published after the 1989 earthquake. The earthquake of 1994 showed, obviously, that very little had been done after 1989 to protect Californians from another quake. Likewise, this cycle can be seen in some southeastern sections of the United States following hurricane devastations. Failure to enforce codes aggressively to mitigate the effects of natural disasters is all the more lamentable given modern society's early detection capabilities, as well as its access to lifesaving technology.

Early Building Codes

One of the earliest and most rudimentary of building codes was developed in the Babylonian Empire around 2000 BC and was attributed to the king, Hammurabi. The law provided that:

> If a builder built a house for a man and completed it, that man shall pay
> him two shekels of silver per say [approximately 12 square feet] of house
> as his wage. If a builder has built a house for a man and his work is not

strong, and if the house he built falls in and kills the house holder, that builder shall be slain. If the child of the house holder should be killed, the child of that builder shall be slain. If the slave of the house holder should be killed, he shall give slave to the house holder. If goods have been destroyed, and because the house was not made strong, and it has fallen in, he shall restore the fallen house out of his own material. If a builder has built a house for a man, and his work is not done properly and a wall shifts, then that builder shall make that wall good with his own silver.

The Roman Empire also recognized the desirability of building codes. The collapse of an amphitheater, killing or injuring approximately 50,000 people, prompted the governing body of Rome to enact regulations for the safety of public places. This occurred in approximately 27 AD; however, Rome burned only 37 years later in 64 AD. The cause of the fire has been debated for hundreds of years, but poorly constructed buildings were certainly part of the problem.

In London, one of the earliest building codes, the *Assize of Buildings,* was promulgated by Mayor Henry Fitz-Elwyne in 1189. This law regulated the method of building party walls and their use. The code placed a high value on stone construction, which obviously acted as fireproofing. Nevertheless, whether the *Assize of Buildings* was enforced is speculative at best. A fire broke out in London in 1212 and caused partial destruction of the city. Then in 1666, the great fire of London broke out. The fire was out of control for five days and caused partial destruction of 15,000 buildings. After the fire, the English Parliament considered legislation to control the construction of buildings within the city. The London Building Act, as it was named, applied only to that city, but was out of date almost as soon as it was written. It took a number of years for Parliament to act, and by that time, London had begun reconstruction. The reconstruction effort, however, was not regulated because again there was no effective enforcement of the previously adopted code provisions.

On this side of the Atlantic, the most infamous fire in the United States was the Chicago Fire of 1871. The fire lasted for almost two full days, killed 250 people, and destroyed 17,000 buildings. Close to 100,000 persons were left without homes. In 1875 the city enacted a building code and a fire prevention ordinance. Notice once again the historical cycle of ignorance and freewheeling construction, followed by emergency and tragedy, and then finally ending with adoption and promulgation of a building code. The cycle is all too familiar. Unfortunately, the adoption of a building code traditionally comes as the final step rather than the first.

Development of Modern Codes

In 1905 the National Board of Fire Underwriters published the recommended *National Building Code* to serve as a guide to local governments trying to enact legislation regulating construction methods and materials. The code was the result of a number of severe losses suffered by fire insurance companies in the latter part of the nineteenth century and early part of the twentieth century. This recommended *National Building Code* was the only model code in existence until 1927 when the Pacific Coast Building Officials Conference, the immediate predecessor to the International Conference of Building Officials, published its *Uniform Building Code*.

In 1945, the *Southern Standard Building Code*, now known as the *Standard Building Code*, was published by Southern Building Code Congress International, Inc. This code predominated in the southeastern and southwestern portions of the United States. A third model code, the *Basic Building Code*, now known as the *BOCA National Building Code*, was published by Building Officials and Code Administrators International, Inc., in 1950. It was the most widely established code in the northeastern and midwestern United States.

All three of these model codes were similarly structured. Development and changes in the codes themselves were also very similar. These similarities were one of the reasons that the three model code organizations joined efforts and created the International Code Council (ICC).

Conclusion

It is rare today to find a municipality that has not adopted a building code. As noted, the history of building construction throughout civilization demonstrates that any society wishing to succeed must strictly construe and enforce the provisions of applicable building codes. Tragedy has frequently resulted from lax enforcement. It is unfortunate that society is willing to accept the enforcement of an effective building code only after tragedy has struck.

Building officials should be aware of the problems and tragedies of the distant and not-so-distant past. This awareness should help them be articulate advocates of code enforcement in their areas. As has been too often the case, the lack of diligence in this area will likely lead to tragic results.

Chapter 3 – Local Governmental Law

This chapter will give a brief overview of the major types of local governments and the powers that each of them possess.

Topics

Forms of Local Government

Dillon's Rule

Home Rule Municipalities

Local Adoption of a Building Code

Terms

Dillon's Rule

home rule

null and void

statute

ultra vires

Introduction

In the day-to-day administration and enforcement of a building code, building officials need not worry about the power and authority of local governments to enact legislation or to otherwise act. When building officials recommend to the local legislative body the adoption of a particular building code, they must be concerned with the specific power of local government. At that point, the building official is very much concerned with the power of the municipality to enact the desired legislation. This chapter will give a brief overview of the major types of local governments and the powers that each possess. Because the differences between the many forms of local government are vast, the chapter will speak in generalities. To decide the nature of the legislation to be recommended and enacted, each building official must work with his or her own legal advisor to determine the powers and authorities of local government. Be advised that reading this chapter does not take the place of legal advice from an attorney who is familiar with the peculiarities of local governmental law in the state where the building official works.

This chapter will discuss and distinguish municipalities and counties. In most states, they have been the smallest units of government for many years. This chapter will also briefly discuss the different types of municipalities. Additionally, the power of home rule municipalities will be analyzed in some depth. The chapter will close by looking at the process of adopting a building code, along with some pitfalls that must be avoided.

Forms of Local Government

Local governments exist in a variety of forms. Each form generally has different characteristics and, while the specifics may vary from state to state, some general observations can be made about three forms of local government: counties, municipalities, and home rule.

Counties

The great dividing line in local government is between the county and municipal forms. A county is usually considered an arm of the state that has been created by the state for governmental purposes. It may be seen as a unit of state government—a part of the state itself. As part of the state, a county is entitled to many of the privileges of the state, particularly the doctrine of sovereign immunity. This doctrine will be examined in more detail in Chapter 4, but for now it should be understood to mean that the state cannot ordinarily be sued for any wrongdoing of which it may be guilty. A state is immune from suit; therefore, because the county is considered an arm of the state, a county is also immune from suit. Even today, as the U.S. Supreme Court chips away at the doctrine of sovereign immunity, the county, through its relationship with the state, is usually immune.

Municipalities

A municipality is very different from a county. Generally, a municipality is viewed as a corporation established by the state legislature for the good of inhabitants who live in a prescribed area. In most cases, a municipality is created by the incorporation of the people who live in a certain area, and it is invested with subordinate powers of legislation so that it may assist in the civil government of the community. It is created by charter, which is often adopted in a public referendum. The charter, like that of a private corporation, establishes the powers and duties of the municipal government. A municipal government may not act beyond the scope of that authority.

Unlike counties, municipalities do not have the full protection of sovereign immunity. Because they are considered public corporations, they are responsible under the law for their corporate acts. The theory for this reduced immunity is that in many respects the municipal corporation undertakes activities that are similar to, if not the same as, those taken by a private corporation or business. To impose legal liability on those activities is, therefore, seen by the courts as no different than ordinary, nonpublic cases. Naturally, there are some municipal activities that have no analog in the private sector. As to those "governmental" or "discretionary" activities, the doctrine of sovereign immunity does indeed apply and no liability may be imposed.

Municipalities exist in great variety today. Cities, towns, townships, villages, and boroughs are all different forms of municipalities. Many states also distinguish between classes of municipalities. For example, New York and Indiana have cities of the first, second, and third classes. Class differentiation is important. Frequently, different classes of municipalities have different powers and authorities under state law. In the same way, the county form of local government may also have authority totally different from the municipalities. The class of local government must always be accurately identified before examining the power or authority of a particular governmental entity to undertake a specific action. Because they differ from state to state, it is not possible in this limited space to describe any of the intrinsic differences between these municipal classes. The laws of each state must be explored to determine the limits of the powers of law.

Home Rule

Finally, in some states one very special type of local government is known as **home rule**. This form of government enjoys greater latitude and discretion in enacting legislation than do other forms of municipalities. While there are certainly very distinct limits to its authority, home rule government may act in areas without specific authorization from the state. This freedom enables a home rule government to act in any area it deems appropriate. Home rule municipalities are discussed in greater length later in this chapter.

Dillon's Rule

One important rule governs all municipal law, and municipal attorneys must constantly refer to it in advising clients as to the extent of the power and authority of any local government. It is **Dillon's Rule**. It states that a municipal corporation has only those powers which are: (a) expressly granted to it by charter or other state legislation; (b) implied or necessarily incident to the express powers; and (c) essential and indispensable to the declared objects and purposes of the corporation. Almost every power and function of a municipal corporation must be traceable, directly or indirectly, to some state authorizing (enabling) legislation. If no authorizing legislation can be found, then the local government most likely lacks authority to undertake the operation.

Expressed Power

An expressed power under Dillon's Rule is one that has been "set forth and declared exactly." These powers may and do form the basis for direct municipal actions insofar as they are consistent and within the bounds of other higher laws. Examples of those laws are the state and federal constitutions and the state and federal laws of general application. Frequently, state law expressly authorizes or mandates the adoption of a building code by a local governmental entity. For example, in New Jersey a statute expressly states it is required for all localities to adopt a building code. This authorizing **statute** is a classic example of the exercise of an expressed power.

Implied Power

Implied powers either arise from those powers expressly granted or essential to the operation of the powers that are expressly granted. For example, in the context of building codes, the legislation may not specifically authorize the issuance of a certificate of occupancy, but its issuance may easily be viewed as necessarily implied in the powers granted.

Essential and Indispensable

Powers that are "essential and indispensable to the declared objects and purpose of the corporation" may be seen either as a subset of the implied powers or some kind of inherent power of the municipality. For states that use the first approach, the difficulty arises in determining what is essential and indispensable. For example, in some states, the authority to adopt a building code is viewed as essential and indispensable, but in others it is not. Because an attorney can never be sure that the state courts will uphold a municipal legislative enactment that is not based on an express authority, the best advice is always to enact enabling legislation prior to the adoption of municipal legislation affecting any topic.

Enabling Legislation

In the area of building code adoption, many states have held, notwithstanding the general application of Dillon's Rule, that there are certain inherent municipal powers and that no enabling legislation need exist in order to justify the enactment of such legislation. The adoption of a building code appears to be one of those inherent municipal powers. The courts have ruled that if the adoption, administration, and enforcement of a building code are of such fundamental importance to the health and welfare of a community, it is not necessary for that community to have special and express legislation permitting it to regulate the construction of buildings in the area. It still must be emphasized, however, that if the municipality or other form of local government has a choice between attempting to enact a building code in the absence of express authority, and the possibility of gaining expressed authority from the legislative body of the state, the local government should first attempt to gain approval from the state before proceeding with the adoption of the local building code. (Further discussion of enabling legislation may be found in Chapter 4.)

Ultra Vires Legislation

If a building code must be enacted in the absence of any express legislation, the opposing lawyer will undoubtedly argue that the legislation is ***ultra vires***, which means that the local governmental entity has acted beyond the scope of its powers. The phrase is customarily applied to private corporations, but it may be and often is employed in analyzing the actions of public corporations, such as a municipality. *Ultra vires* is defined as the "modern legal designation, in the law of corporations, of acts beyond the scope of the powers of the corporation, as defined by its charter or acts of incorporation." For example, if a municipality attempts to adopt a building code in the absence of enabling legislation in its charter or otherwise, and, if upon challenge, a court is not convinced that the adoption of a building code is one of the municipality's implied or inherent powers or functions, the court would most probably declare the building code an *ultra vires* action and therefore **null and void**. Something that is null and void has no legal force or binding effect. The law in question is therefore unable to support the purpose for which it was intended. Most often this type of challenge will arise in a lawsuit by the municipality to enforce some provision of a building code. As a defense the alleged building code offender will challenge the validity of the enactment of the code itself. If there is no enabling legislation authorizing the adoption of the building code, the probability of this defense being raised increases. The reasoning is that the defendant cannot be guilty of violating the code as law because the code was never actually the law in that municipality. Therefore, it pays to be careful when adopting a building code. Not only must proper enabling legislation be in place at the state level, but all other procedural requirements must be met and documented by the municipality. It is normally not the job of the building official to ensure that these conditions be met. For greater peace of mind, however, the building official should keep a sharp eye out for the details involved in the process.

Zoning ordinances are good examples of *ultra vires*. Most states have enacted a standard state-zoning enabling act developed by the U. S. Department of Commerce in 1926. Zoning law is, as a result of this standard act, uniform in many respects from one state to another. Under the act, the powers of the board of zoning appeals are broken into three parts. If a municipality enacting a zoning ordinance attempts to vest the board with a power beyond that authorized by its state's version of the act, the action is *ultra vires* and subject to being declared unenforceable by the courts. This, of course, holds true of a board of building code appeals as well.

In the majority of the United States today, Dillon's Rule still survives intact. There is at least one state, Utah, that has explicitly done away with Dillon's Rule. The supreme court of that state has ruled that Dillon's Rule no longer applies there. It will be some time before the ramifications of this decision are fully understood.

Home Rule Municipalities

The county form of government was briefly described at the beginning of this chapter. Municipalities were also discussed along with enabling and *ultra vires* legislation. The third form of government has been reserved for special attention because if building officials happen to live in a home rule municipality, certain special rules apply. Generally these rules make it easier for the government to enact legislation to protect the public welfare. This section will briefly discuss some of these differences. Unfortunately, there are probably as many different types of home rule municipalities as there are home rule municipalities. The focus here will be on the two most important categories and their impact on building code enactment and enforcement.

The home rule municipality is distinguished from the other types of local government in that its charter is constitutionally derived from an authorization in a state's constitution. A state whose constitution contains a provision authorizing home rule municipalities allows the people of a city to establish their own charter by referendum. Most municipal charters are acts of the state legislative body. In other words, the state legislature enacts the charter and grants the powers to the local communities under which they must govern. A charter in a home rule municipality is directly passed by the people who live in the community. The home rule is adopted directly by the citizenry of the affected locale. In fact, one of the main reasons for the development of this type of municipality was the desire to stop the state legislative bodies from interfering with purely local affairs of which the state had limited knowledge. Interference from the state level was the decisive factor in the rise of many home rule municipalities. The provisions of the state constitution allowing the direct adoption of the city charter are of prime importance when examining the powers of the home rule city.

Legally, the effect of a home rule charter is the same as if it were passed by the state legislature. It is considered a state law. It has the same force and effect as a law directly enacted by the state legislature. Generally, when viewed from this perspective, the home rule charter is seen as a grant of virtually unlimited powers to the municipality over local affairs. Essentially, this means that where there is no provision in the local charter granting the authority to the municipality to enact a law in a certain area (for example, building codes), the city may go ahead and enact legislation; therefore, a building code could be adopted even without state-authorizing legislation. Of course, if the charter did specifically provide for the adoption of a particular type of law, the city could pass it just as in any other ordinary municipality. The only area in which the city would lack authority to enact legislation would be where the state had previously enacted legislation and specifically denied the city the right to enact similar legislation. In those areas the city is powerless to control its own affairs. But in all other areas, whether expressly provided for in its charter or not, the city is free to act as it deems appropriate within the limits of state and federal constitutional law.

Other home rule charters are deemed limitations on the exercise of municipal power. In those areas specific authority, in the charter or elsewhere, must be found for the exercise of a specific legislative action. It cannot be emphasized enough that given the multiplicity of constitutional provisions, reference must always be made to the particular state constitution involved, as well as to the local charter that is the subject of scrutiny.

Home rule was theoretically a great advance in the law of municipal corporations and has freed local governments to regulate their own affairs as they see fit. In practice, the result is somewhat more mixed. Generally, the local government must be somewhat careful as to how freely it acts in any given area. In many states there is a constant ebb and flow as to areas in which the home rule municipalities may adopt legislation without garnering state approval. This should be of little consequence to building officials, at least in the area of the adoption of a building code itself. Some of the more peripheral codes, such as storm water management ordinances and solar access ordinances, may be controlled more tightly by the state general assembly, and thus the municipality may not have as much discretion. Even so, home rule offers great advantages to those municipalities that are fortunate enough to have it.

Local Adoption of a Building Code

The creation and enactment of a building code by a local governmental entity is an important legal step requiring caution and the advice of an attorney. While the selection or development of a building code is usually the task of a building official, responsibility for getting it legally operative must rest with a municipal attorney. There must be a close working relationship between the attorney and the building official in both areas in order to pass successfully an ordinance adopting a particular code.

As has been previously discussed, there must be some authority for the enactment of a building code at the state level. This is particularly true if the municipality does not have home rule or if the state does not recognize this power as one of the inherent powers of a municipality. The municipal attorney should be requested to ensure there is ample authority for the adoption of such a code by the local government before proceeding. If there is no such authority, it should be garnered from the state before any code is adopted.

The provisions of the enabling legislation must be followed precisely. Most states that have express provisions allowing the adoption of a building code, and even those states that do not, have legislation that permits the adoption of the various codes by reference. In order to obtain the benefit of adoption by reference, instead of publishing the entire code, great care must be taken to follow exactly the procedural steps established in the state's statute.

A notice of intent must frequently be published in a newspaper of general circulation in the municipality. This is to inform the public of the pendency of an adoption of a building code. The code itself must normally be filed with the clerk of the municipality or county prior to the adoption. This is for the purpose of public reference. If someone is interested enough to examine the code in detail, a number of copies must be available at some public place for the purpose of that review. Although a specified number of copies must normally be provided, some deviation here may be permitted so long as the availability of the document is not substantially decreased. If, for example, the procedural requirement is to provide five copies at the city recorder's office and only four copies are provided, this is not a deviation from the procedure that would ordinarily void the enactment of the building code; however, great care should be taken in this area. From a practical viewpoint, it is precisely in this phase of the enactment of a building code that not enough care is taken. Frequently no copies are provided for the purpose of public reference, or a number of copies are initially provided, but are somehow misplaced in the clerk's office prior to the time of enactment. It is a good idea for the building official to inspect periodically the copies at the clerk's office to ensure that they are still available to the public.

The normal legislative process must be strictly followed in the case of the adoption of a building code. Many municipalities require a number of "readings" prior to effective passage; the caption of the bill and its effectuation clause must all be in proper order. Any referrals to other governmental units, such as planning commissions, that are required by the state law or local charter, must also be observed. Again, these procedural requirements must be observed strictly. Any deviation from the requirements may mean the voidance of the entire building code as passed.

All too often once the code is passed very little care is taken to observe the requirements of the ordinance. At any given time, if a citizen were to walk into a city recorder's office and demand to see a copy of the current building code, it would be unlikely that an accurate copy of the code could be produced. This failure to observe the requirements of the code may also lead to a dismissal record of code prosecutions against alleged offenders. (These procedural matters will be discussed more in Chapter 6.) It is prudent, however, to ensure that all required copies of the code are on file at the place of public reference at all times.

Any requirement that a public hearing be held is also of great importance. Failure to hold a public hearing or the mishandling of a public meeting in a manner that prevents the public from effectively voicing its views on the adoption of a building code would condemn the code in the eyes of virtually any court. Once again, great care must be taken in the adoption process.

Conclusion

The powers of a local government are unfortunately quite narrow as compared to the powers of a state government. The state is the ultimate repository of legislative power, and, unless the state has granted the right to a municipality to enact legislation on a given topic, the municipality simply cannot act. Fortunately building codes often fall outside of this general rule. Usually the courts will find that the adoption of a building code is of such paramount importance to the health, safety, and welfare of the populace, that no special or express enabling legislation at the state level is necessary. Building officials and attorneys must examine carefully and thoroughly the limits of power of the governmental unit within which they operate, be it a municipal or county government. If it is a municipal government, officials must carefully determine what class or category it falls under. Each of these different forms and classes can have special limitations on their powers, and the necessary legal research must be done in order to ascertain whether that will have any impact on the adoption of a building code. When adopting a building code by reference under general legislation allowing such enactments, an official should exercise a great deal of care in attending to the details required by the statute. All procedural requirements must be met meticulously in order for the passage to be valid and lawful. It is primarily the responsibility of the attorney for the legislative body to see that those details are met, but the building official should always be alert so that he or she may help the attorney in the process and oversee the actions of the attorney. Sometimes a friendly suggestion can save an ordinance from being struck down by a court of law as invalidly enacted. The two professionals must work together, closely, in order to pass successfully and then, even more importantly, administer and enforce the adopted building code.

Chapter 4 – State Legislative Law

This chapter discusses the control that state governments exercise over building officials and the code enforcement process.

Topics

Enabling Legislation

State Building Codes

Related Legislative Provisions

Preemption

Sovereign Immunity

Terms

declaratory relief

enabling legislation

injunction

preemption

regulation

reverse

sovereign immunity

statute

statute of limitations

Introduction

This chapter provides a brief overview of state laws that deal with the functions and responsibilities of the building official. It examines characteristics of state **enabling legislation** to give building officials an understanding of the overall building code process. The impact of mandatory statewide building codes on local authority and other related legislation emphasizes the integral function of building officials in the overall code process. Finally, the chapter discusses the doctrines of **preemption** and **sovereign immunity**. These two doctrines illustrate the level of control the state has over the functions of local officials with whom building officials must deal.

This chapter should give the building official an appreciation for the degree of control that state governments exercise over municipal officers in general, and over the building code process in particular. A clear understanding of the impact of proposed state legislation will empower the building official to avert potential trouble.

Enabling Legislation

Chapter 3 pointed out that many states have some form of legislation in place, which enables local governments to enact building codes. These **statutes**, which are prepared and enacted by a local, state, or federal government, must be followed to the letter when establishing a local government codes enforcement system. They must also be read in accordance with any state statutes that permit by reference the adoption of building codes. It is important for code officials to be familiar with the statutes of their respective states to ensure proper enforcement procedures. For example, the **statute of limitations** sets forth time limits for bringing various legal actions.

Most enabling legislation requires that buildings and other structures be divided into identifiable classes and that an official of some type be appointed to implement and enforce the provisions of the local ordinance. This official is generally known as the Building Official or by some similar title. Generally, an administrative board is set up to hear appeals of the building official's decisions. Although administrative procedures will be discussed in Chapter 7, the board usually has three general powers. First, the board is authorized to hear any appeal of a building official's decision. If it concludes that the building official has made an incorrect decision, the board may **reverse** the decision of the building official. Usually, such reversals arise in situations involving the building official's interpretation of the building code. Reversals may also occur if the board weighs the evidence differently or makes new findings as to the facts of the case.

Second, the board may have the power to modify the provisions of the code itself when the intent of the code is ensured. When doing this, the board must be careful to remember that it is not the local legislative body and that the power to enact law should rest exclusively with the legislators. There is a very minimal distinction between granting an appeal in the code provisions for a special reason and amending the code outright. The board is allowed to grant an appeal but is not allowed under any circumstances to amend the code.

Third, the board may also be empowered to consider new and innovative building techniques and may permit or prohibit such techniques in its jurisdiction. Once again, the line dividing this power from the power held by the local legislature is often hard to discern.

The state enabling legislation may also spell out the method by which an appeal may be taken to court from a decision of the board. In some states, the board's finding of facts and evidence is accorded great deference by the courts making it unusual for the board's determination to be reversed. In other states, the courts hear all the evidence over again and accord the board's position very little weight. Not surprisingly, in these states, reversals of board decisions are much more common. The method of appeal will be discussed in Chapter 7.

State Building Codes

Rather than allow local governments to control construction, some states regulate it themselves. When states do this, there is no local building code department and no local control.

A number of states now prescribe minimum code standards. In these states, the local government must meet a set of minimum standards in the code it adopts if it wishes to regulate building construction. A **regulation** is a rule established by a government agency having the force and effect of law even though the rule is not set forth explicitly in the statute. Where the local code does not meet the minimum specifications, the state controls the construction industry.

The state imposes a building code or a requirement of a building code on a local government, whether it wants one or not. To enforce the code, the local government has the option to set up its own department or to allow the state to regulate the local activities.

Generally, these mandatory state building statutes do not apply to home rule municipalities. As stated in Chapter 3, the home rule government has the power and authority under its charter and the state constitution to adopt its own police power regulations. Because home rule provisions can vary widely, local counsel should be consulted to see if mandatory state legislation has been introduced at the state capitol. In many cases, such legislation can be amended prior to passage to provide specifically for the exemption of home rule municipalities. It is better to provide expressly for this exemption in the legislation itself rather than fight a court battle over it after passage.

Related Legislative Provisions

Since many building officials are also responsible for other areas of codes enforcement, and because related code provisions usually impact the building code, it is worth dedicating a few paragraphs here to examine some standard provisions.

The Fire Code

Although the fire and building codes often play against one another, they should actually complement each other. While the building code is designed to mandate the most current building construction techniques, the fire code (or fire prevention code) is designed to maintain the structure against the threat of fire during its existence. The building code is a construction code; the fire code is a maintenance code.

To best enforce and administer all codes, it is necessary for the fire marshal's office and the building and code enforcement departments to cooperate. Sometimes it is common for procedures followed by the fire marshal to conflict or differ from those required by the building or code enforcement official. Despite these differences, the fire department and building department can work together successfully by avoiding turf issues and cooperating jointly in plan reviews and investigations. In new construction, the building department will usually be the primary party, whereas the fire department and the code enforcement department will be concerned with existing structures. By doing joint plan reviews or inspections where appropriate, the expertise of all parties is fully utilized. Furthermore, the property owner will not get conflicting directions from two different agencies if they cooperate from the beginning of a project.

Zoning Ordinances

Zoning ordinances divide the local government into different classes and land uses into different categories. The underlying purpose is to separate and regulate land uses that are not compatible with one another. Naturally, it does very little good for a builder to get a building permit only to learn that the type of building he or she intends to build is not permitted under the zoning ordinance. To avoid this, building officials must have a close relationship with the zoning officials in their jurisdictions. Because many building officials also work as zoning officials, this should not be difficult to achieve. (For a more complete discussion of zoning ordinances, see Chapter 9.)

Storm Water Management

State storm water management was initiated by the states' desire to participate in the National Flood Insurance Program. Storm water management regulation was intended to protect against the possibility that a serious flood would ever threaten proposed construction. Ideally, the legislation should achieve this goal by identifying areas that lie in the floodplains and floodways. More specifically, protected development is permitted in the floodplain, but no development is allowed in the floodway. These regulations usually require that any development contains its own runoff so that the drainage remains similar to that which existed prior to the new construction.

Preemption

Preemption is a judicially created doctrine that says that a state may not pass a law that is inconsistent with federal law. If a state enacts such a law, the federal law will take precedence over the state law to the extent that there is conflict. Preemption allows the federal and state governments to regulate activities that would otherwise be subject to local control. Usually, there is a strong state or federal policy being served that cannot be met adequately by the imposition of municipal regulations. (For an example of federal preemption, see the discussion of the Consumer Product Safety Act in Chapter 5.)

The most obvious illustration of preemption arises in those states where the state has adopted a building code and prohibits the adoption of a code by its local governments. This type of state building code entirely preempts the regulation of building construction. Preemption does not always need to be comprehensive. The state or federal government may select some types of occupancies to regulate, leaving all other types to the local governments. For example, in some states, all schools and hospitals are inspected by state officials and the local building official has no authority whatsoever. Those officials working in states using this type of building code must be aware of which occupancies are subject to preemption and which are not.

The state building code need not expressly state that it intends to preempt the local government's authority to enforce and administer its own building code. If the state regulations are detailed and comprehensive, a court of law should determine that the state intended for the local government to have no authority in that area.

All inclusive state regulations of day care centers and homes for the mentally and physically handicapped are examples of state preemption that are not explicitly stated in the state legislation.

It is important that building officials keep abreast of the actions of their own state legislatures. It is likely that the municipal attorney in any jurisdiction will be unable to keep up with all the legislation introduced; therefore, it is up to the building code official to shoulder the burden. The state organization of building code officials, however, will most likely be aware of any relevant legislation. If the building official or the building code organization becomes aware of the introduction of legislation that appears to be preemptive in nature, the municipal attorney should be alerted. The sooner an attorney is consulted, the better the likelihood that an amendment will be added to clarify that the legislation is not intended to oust local regulations from their proper place. Also, if the legislation does not pass in its present state, the attorney may be able to secure an administrative or judicial determination that the legislation is not preemptive. If that fails, the building official should consult with his or her attorney concerning what can be locally regulated.

Sovereign Immunity

In its broadest terms, **sovereign immunity** stipulates that the state may not be held liable for any wrongdoing that it or any of its agents may commit. This ancient doctrine originated in England, where it was widely accepted that the king could do no wrong. In England, the king and all of his men were not held responsible for their actions. Sovereign immunity applies not only in the area of tort liability, which will be discussed later, but also in the field of regulation. Generally, local building regulations do not apply to the construction and maintenance of state buildings. Therefore, if the state decides to build an office building within the jurisdiction of a local building official, that official has no right to require that a building permit be obtained prior to the initiation of the project. Furthermore, the official has no right to inspect the premises during the construction process, and no right to inquire that a certificate of occupancy be obtained prior to occupancy of the building.

There are some exceptions to the general rule. First, some states have expressly waived this immunity from local regulation. If the state has waived its immunity, then the local government not only has every right to require the state to comply with its local code, but it also has the duty to do so. Second, the state may have waived its immunity with respect to certain types of buildings. State office buildings are an example. Again, the local building official would have a duty to require compliance with the local code. Finally, state officials may request the help of the local building official on particular projects. Provided that this request is made at the start of a project, the building official should not worry about agreeing to this request. When such a request is made after the building has been completed, however, the local official's ability to inspect the structure comprehensively has been compromised. To be safe, postconstruction requests should always be declined.

An experienced building official will usually know what types of state buildings are subject to local control. If the official is unsure, however, the best course is to sue the state for declaratory and injunctive relief. **Declaratory relief** is an interpretation by a court of law as to whether the state has immunity in this particular field. If the court holds that the state is not immune from local inspection, it could issue an **injunction** requiring the state to stop performing any work on the project until it has obtained a permit and is in compliance with all other code provisions.

Chapter 5 – Federal Legislative Law

This chapter discusses federal legislation that may impact the administration and enforcement of local building codes.

Topics

Role of the Federal Government
The Consumer Product Safety Act
Immunity

Terms

act
common law
police powers

Introduction

Federal legislation is law in the form of statutes, acts, or rules, which are enacted by Congress. This type of law, like state legislation, prescribes what the law will be in cases arising under its provisions. This is different from **common law,** which is, generally speaking, the body of law that emerges from judicial decisions. Unlike federal constitutional law, federal legislative law has very little impact on the day-to-day work of a building official. This is because the enactment and enforcement of the building code is for the most part a purely local concern, and it is therefore rarely affected by federal statutes. Some federal legislation exists that may impact the administration and enforcement of local building codes. This chapter provides an overview of the federal system of government and briefly discusses the relevance of the Consumer Product Safety Act (CPSA) to the building official. Finally, the chapter will discuss how the power of the federal government provides the buildings it owns with immunity to inspection by the building official.

Role of the Federal Government

Within the last few years there has been growing sentiment among the voters in the United States that the federal government has become too big and unmanageable. The vast growth of the federal government could not have been foreseen by the framers of the Constitution. Much academic debate exists regarding the intended scope and power of the federal government, as opposed to the power held by the states. One side argues that the federal government was originally conceived to possess distinctly limited powers, while another side argues that the flexible structure of the Constitution reflects the framers' view that the role of the federal government could change and grow along with the growth of society. Regardless of which view is correct, the states have been given some authority through the Tenth Amendment to the Constitution: "The powers not delegated to the United States by the Constitution, nor prohibited by it to the States, are reserved to the States respectively, or to the people." This power of the states to adopt laws to protect and promote the health, safety, morals, and general welfare of its citizens comes from the Tenth Amendment of the U.S. Constitution and is known as the state's **police powers.**

Theoretically, any authority not expressly given to the federal government should belong to the states. Remember from Chapter 3, however, that each state has relinquished a portion of what little power it has left by expressly delegating some of its regulatory power to local governments within its jurisdiction. Generally, the federal government plays a very limited and indirect role in the area of local building codes. For the most part, the states have divested themselves of jurisdiction and authority over building codes. Therefore, administration and enforcement of building codes remains primarily the concern of local jurisdictions. The Consumer Product Safety Act is an exception to this generality.

The Consumer Product Safety Act

The Consumer Product Safety Act (CPSA)[1] is an example of federal legislation that can affect the building official. It was enacted because Congress felt that state and local governments could not adequately protect consumers from the various dangers presented by many products in commerce. An **act** is just another name for a statutory law, and thus has the same power as a statute. This particular act was based on a Congressional finding that "an unacceptable number of consumer products which present unreasonable risks of injury are distributed in commerce." Congress further found that consumers, many of whom are unable to anticipate or safeguard themselves adequately, must be protected against such risks. The CPSA also sought to help consumers evaluate the comparative safety of consumer products and to develop uniform safety standards. To that end, CPSA would work to minimize conflicting state and local regulations. Finally, CPSA sought to "promote research and investigation into the causes and prevention of product-related deaths, illnesses and injuries."

Consumer Product Safety Commission

To effectuate these goals, the CPSA provides for the creation of the Consumer Product Safety Commission (CPSC). The CPSC is an independent regulatory commission consisting of five commissioners. These commissioners are appointed by the president of the United States with the advice and consent of the Senate, and they serve a term of seven years. The commissioners all have backgrounds in areas related to consumer products and protection. No more than three of the commissioners may belong to the same political party, nor can any of them be related to or employed by a manufacturer of consumer products, nor can any of them have any financial ties to producers of consumer products. One of the five commissioners is appointed Chairman of the Commission and exercises all of the executive and administrative functions of the CPSC. The president can remove a commissioner or the chairman from his or her post only for neglect of duty or malfeasance in office. (See Chapter 11 for these legal concepts.)

The CPSC has the power to create standards that ban from commerce those products it finds hazardous. Specifically, it is directed to maintain an injury information clearinghouse to collect, investigate, analyze, and disseminate information relating to the causes and prevention of death, injury, and illness associated with consumer products. It must also conduct continuing studies and investigations relating to injuries and illnesses involving consumer products, and follow proper rule making procedures with the goal of creating and enacting effective safety standards, which will be known as consumer product safety rules. These rules serve to ban unsafe products or to provide manufacturers with safety standards.

In promulgating these rules, the CPSC follows a comprehensive rule-making procedure that is laid out in the CPSA. This procedure is initiated by the publication of a notice of the proposed rulemaking in the *Federal Register*, a periodical that publishes information regarding proposed regulations. The notice must identify the product and the nature of the risk of injury associated with it, summarize the regulatory alternatives available to and under consideration by the CPSC, and invite comments from interested persons, including the general public and building officials. The CPSC must then specify the time for comment; this time period may not be less than 30 days nor more than 60 days.

After the comments have been gathered and analyzed, the CPSC may then develop a proposed rule to reduce the risk of harm associated with the product. The text of the proposed rule must be published in the *Federal Register*, along with an analysis of the potential benefits and costs of the proposed rule, a description of reasonable alternatives, and a brief explanation as to why those alternatives should not be published as a proposed rule.

Within 60 days of the publication of the proposed rule, the CPSC must either adopt the proposed rule or withdraw the notice of proposed rulemaking. Under the CPSA, a withdrawal is appropriate if the proposed rule is not "(i) reasonably necessary to eliminate or reduce an unreasonable risk of injury associated with the product, or (ii) in the public interest." In order to adopt, the CPSC must make certain findings, including the degree and nature of the risk the rule is designed to reduce or eliminate; the number of products subject to the rule; the need of the public for the products; the impact of the rule on the utility, cost, or availability of the products; and other means of achieving the objective without disrupting ongoing commercial practices. The CPSA prohibits the sale or manufacture of any product that does not conform to the applicable rule. Likewise, it prohibits the manufacture or sale of any banned hazardous product so declared by a consumer product safety rule.

CPSC and the Building Official

How does the CPSA affect the building code official? Unfortunately for the building official, there is a preemption provision in the CPSA:

> Whenever a consumer product safety standard under this chapter is in effect and applies to a risk of injury associated with a consumer product, no state or political subdivision of a State shall have any authority either to establish or to continue in effect any provision of a safety standard or regulation which prescribes any requirements as to the performance, composition, contracts, design, finish, construction packaging, or labeling of such product which are designed to deal with the same risk of injury associated with such consumer product: unless such requirements are identical to the requirements of the federal standard.[2]

Most of the building codes in effect across the country, however, often contain safety standards or regulations regarding dangerous designs that have already been covered, or that will be covered in the future by the CPSA. When this occurs, all of those local provisions are preempted. The local regulation or standard will not be preempted if it is more stringent than the analogous consumer product safety rule and protects the public more than does the standard promulgated by the CPSA. Unless the difference in protection between the two standards is great, it is very difficult to judge when a higher degree of protection is afforded. Therefore, in most cases, the federal standard will preempt the field.

Preemption (defined in Chapter 4) recently arose with regard to kerosene heaters. In *National Kerosene Heater Association v. Commonwealth of Massachusetts*, a manufacturer of unvented kerosene heaters sued the state of Massachusetts claiming, among other things, that its state and local ordinances banning unvented kerosene heaters must be preempted by the fact that the CPSC investigated the possible danger of kerosene heaters and found that because of the low incidence of injury arising from these heaters, it did not have to initiate rulemaking. CPSC reasoned that the voluntary standards adopted by the states and localities were sufficient to address the risk of any fire hazards that may be associated with the heaters. The court determined that there was no preemption because CPSC's recognition of the voluntary standards adopted by the states did not involve CPSA's prescribed rulemaking procedures. It did not go through the proper rulemaking procedure; therefore, a building official who finds an unvented kerosene heater during a routine inspection can cite a code violation and may report the owner of this product to the proper authorities. If, in the future, the CPSA promulgates a much less stringent rule than the one adopted in Massachusetts, the Massachusetts building official may continue to enforce the Massachusetts rule. If the CPSA properly promulgates a safety standard that is similar to or possibly more stringent than the Massachusetts standard, then the building official must follow the CPSA.

Immunity

Much like state governments, the federal government is immune from the effect of municipal police power regulations such as building codes and zoning ordinances. Therefore, local building code regulations have no impact on the construction of federally owned buildings. Consequently, federal buildings, such as federal courthouses, post offices, and federal office buildings, do not have to comply with the provisions of the local building codes.

Conclusion

The federal government exercises little control over the administration and enforcement of local building codes. It does, however, regulate certain types of products that it considers to be dangerous to members of the general public. If properly enacted, federal regulations are more stringent than those enacted by states or municipalities. The federal regulations will preempt the state and local regulations. For the most part, the federal government is not involved in the enforcement and administration of building codes.

Chapter 5 Endnotes

1. 15 U.S.C. §2058.

2. *National Kerosene Heater Ass'n Inc. v. Com. of Mass,* 653 F. Supp. 1079 (Mass. 1986).

Chapter 6 – Administration and Enforcement

This chapter discusses legal concepts relative to the administration and enforcement of codes.

Topics

Permit Issuance

Permit Revocation

Inspection

Administrative Search Warrants

Plans Examination

Civil Prosecutions

Injunctive Relief

Handling Complaints

Evidence

Administrative Guidelines

Terms

complaint	injunctive relief	summary action
discretionary authority	ministerial act	temporary injunction
due process	permanent injunction	temporary restraining order
equitable estoppel	probable cause	vested rights
equitable powers	return of the warrant	writ of mandamus
hearsay	statute of limitations	

Introduction

This chapter will examine concepts that relate to the enforcement and administration of the building code. Initially, the chapter will describe the issuance of permits and discuss the importance of that function to the overall enforcement scheme of the building code. Specifically, it will discuss the ways in which an inspector carries out, investigates and inspects for potential violations. This overview is not the final word on inspection and investigatory techniques; however, building officials all have their own way of performing their jobs. Technical discussions of the code itself will not be included. The legal implications arising from such investigations and inspections are the central concern of this chapter. We will examine the handling of citizens' complaints and suggest methods of dealing with them efficiently.

This chapter will also address some methods of enforcing the code against potential violations. In particular, administrative guidelines are important in this regard. The chapter will describe situations in which a judicial order prohibiting specific conduct is appropriate, as well as, discuss the criteria by which such an order may be granted.

This chapter will also outline the various defenses to building code enforcement. Potential building code offenders may use these defenses to defeat attempted code enforcement. It is advantageous for building officials to be able to predict how code offenders might defend their violations.

Permit Issuance

The issuance of the building permit is the most important step in the enforcement and administration of building codes. The application for the building permit and the permit itself are the two most important documents a building code official has to determine what the builder or contractor is doing on the job site. It is crucial, that the building permit be issued in a prescribed fashion and that all the necessary steps be taken to ensure that the permit is issued properly.

Prior to the issuance of the permit, a written application is required from either the owner of the building or from the agent of the owner. Keep in mind that in many cases, the type of documentation required by the issuer of a permit is dictated by the type of structure being built. For example, when applying for a permit to construct a single-family unit, it may not be necessary to submit complete architectural plans of the individual structure. The builder of a large commercial office building in a downtown area, however, will always be required to submit complete plans in order to be eligible for a building permit. Building officials should be thoroughly aware of what is required for the issuance of a particular permit. Regardless of how simple the proposed construction, it is important that the applicant be required to describe, as specifically as possible, what he or she is attempting to do on the job site. It is also crucial that the permit applicant sign the application attesting to the truth of the statements made in it.

The permit should require complete information as to ownership or which contractor is doing the job. If prosecution later becomes necessary because of a violation, the information on the permit may be used to prove ownership of the property or who is the responsible party. The permit should require the names of the owners and any contractors, addresses for everyone so they can properly be served, and dates of birth in case arrest warrants are issued. If the property is in a trust, the application should require a disclosure of the identity of all beneficiaries, along with addresses and dates of birth.

To best prepare for possible litigation, an application should be extremely specific and comprehensive. In many cases, it is not practical to require lengthy documentation about every step in the building process. To return to the above example of a permit for a single-family residence, the building department will usually not require complete architectural diagrams, although it would be logical, from a legal standpoint, to require such documentation. It would be overly burdensome for most large building departments to keep abreast of permits for these types of structures. Most departments do not have the time or manpower to closely review each application. Even if not required, however, it is always desirable for every applicant to spell out as clearly as possible his or her intentions for the proposed construction.

The person whose job it is to approve or reject permit applications must be carefully instructed regarding his or her duties. An error in the issuance of a permit may affect the safety and well-being of the inhabitants of those mistakenly approved structures. To minimize possibly fatal mistakes, the permit examiner should always have his or her decisions double-checked.

Once an application is approved, and a permit is granted, and construction has begun on a building site, it becomes difficult to revoke the issued permit. This is true even if a mistake exists on the permit itself. Courts frequently lean toward not enforcing the code rather than revoking a permit on which a builder has mistakenly relied, through no fault of his or her own.

Permit Revocation

This does not mean that a building official cannot revoke a building permit. If a permit is mistakenly issued and it is obvious that the issuance was a mistake, the building department will be able to revoke the permit without much trouble if, for example, it is obvious that allowing the permit to stand would pose tremendous danger to the safety of the general public. The courts will likely use a common-sense approach to determine whether or not a permit should be revoked. So if the omitted consideration is one that poses a serious safety threat to members of the general public, the harm that will be suffered by the builder as a result of revocation is far outweighed by the harm that might be suffered by the public at large.

It is often difficult to determine whether a code violation is serious enough to warrant revocation of a mistakenly issued permit. Because the entire building code relates to safety and construction, any violation of a code provision might result in tremendous harm to members of the public, or it might not. As one might imagine, attorneys are not very useful in determining which code violations are serious enough to fight actively for permit revocation. Here is where the building official's expertise comes into play. The building official bears the responsibility of determining whether or not a violation is of such magnitude that it poses an immediate threat to the safety of others. If it is, he or she has a duty to take immediate steps to prevent continued construction. Further work on the building can be prevented by a stop-work order or by instituting a lawsuit directly against the builder in order to obtain a court order to prevent further work on the project.

Theories

Two basic theories exist regarding whether or not a building permit can be revoked. The traditional rule holds that after the building permit has been issued, work has begun on the project, and if a substantial amount of work has been done, the permit may not be revoked, even if an error was made in its issuance. This rule is subject to the exception discussed earlier where there is an immediate public safety factor involved. Assuming that there is no such public safety factor involved, if substantial work has been done under the permit, it may no longer be revoked. The rationale for this can be explained by the doctrine of **equitable estoppel**. This is a doctrine by which the municipality may be precluded by its actions, or by its failure to act, from asserting a right that it otherwise would have had. If another party has justifiably relied on the action or lack of action of the municipality and this reliance has changed his or her position so that he or she would suffer injury if the municipality is allowed to repudiate its actions, then the court will not allow the municipality to do so under the principle of equitable estoppel.

The builder has **vested rights** in continuing the project as planned. If an insubstantial amount of work has been done, the mere fact that the permit was issued and some work accomplished on the project does not vest any particular rights in the builder. The rights become vested only when a substantial amount of work has been completed. As is always the case in the law, there is no set measurement of what constitutes "substantial." In *G.J.Z. Enterprises v. City of Troy*,[1] the court found that a substantial amount of work had been done. Here, the plaintiff bought land in Troy believing that the land was zoned for multiple-family dwellings when it was actually zoned for single-family dwellings. The City of Troy mistakenly issued a building permit to the plaintiff to build multiple-family apartment buildings. One month later, the city realized its mistake. By the time the mistake was realized, however, the apartments were already about 70 percent completed. It was at this point that the city issued a stop-work order and withdrew the building permit. The plaintiff filed a complaint to enjoin the city from revoking its permit and also filed a motion for a preliminary injunction to enjoin the city from enforcing the stop-work order.

The court held for the plaintiff and affirmed the lower court's decision to issue the preliminary injunction. In deciding to uphold the injunction, the court listed four requirements a plaintiff is required to show: (1) a clear, protectable right of that party; (2) an irreparable injury to this right if the injunction is not issued; (3) an inadequate legal remedy; and (4) the likelihood of success on the merits.[2] After applying these requirements to the facts of the case, the court determined that the plaintiff expressly conditioned its purchase of the land upon it being zoned for multiple-family dwellings, and that it was more than reasonable to assume that the plaintiff would rely on the representations of the city clerk and the building inspector when it began to build on the land. In fact, the court concluded that the city induced the plaintiff to purchase the land. It held that an injunction was necessary to avoid the irreparable injury that would befall the plaintiff if the city was allowed to enforce the stop-work order.

In the Minnesota case of *Snyder v. City of Minneapolis*,[3] the plaintiff brought suit against the city for damages caused when the city issued him a building permit to build a new building and a permit to demolish his existing building, but the city then revoked the building permit after the existing building was demolished. In his complaint, he alleged negligence, estoppel, and a deprivation of his constitutional rights in violation of Section 1983,[4] and sought an injunction to compel the city to grant him a variance (negligence and variance are defined in the Index of Terms). The court rejected his Section 1983 claim but held for him on the estoppel and negligence claims. In so doing, it rejected the city's defense of discretionary immunity from liability for its negligent issuance of the building permit. In spite of this finding of liability, however, the court allowed Minnesota's cap on tort liability to stand, thus limiting the amount of monetary damages the plaintiff could collect.

In the recent Connecticut case of *Gallicchio Bros. Inc., v. Zoning Board of Appeals of the Town of Newington*,[5] however, the court upheld the building department's revocation of a permit, even though the plaintiff had relied on it and begun construction. In this case, the plaintiff applied for and received the zoning and building permits necessary to construct single-family housing on its property. Soon after receiving the permits, the plaintiff began construction. The lot was cleared, excavation begun, and a foundation poured. A few weeks later, the building official realized he had made a mistake in issuing the permit. He ordered the plaintiff to stop work, backfill the foundation, secure the site, and cease and desist from further activity. About a week later, the building department notified the plaintiff that the building permit had been revoked. The plaintiff appealed the building department's revocation, but their appeal was denied. Even though substantial work had been done under the permit, it did not equitably estop the building department from asserting its right to revoke. The court seemed to rely heavily on the plaintiff's knowledge that the issuance of the permit was improper at the time it was obtained, as well as other contributory behavior by the plaintiff.

The second theory has only recently begun to appear in some jurisdictions. This rule permits the revocation of the permit, but at the expense of the building code official. The courts, such as those in the State of Washington, adhere to this rule because they feel that while revocation of permits in many instances are necessary for the protection of public health and safety, the burden of the cost of the mistake should fall on the person who negligently issued the permit rather than to the innocent builder or developer. The rationale is that the building official has the requisite expertise and is in the best position to understand what is required. Therefore, if the permit is erroneously issued, the builder should not suffer; so these courts allow a lawsuit by the builder against the building official in his or her personal capacity for the negligent issuance of the permit itself. This theory is not widely accepted. Building officials should check with a local municipal attorney to determine how the courts in their jurisdictions rule.

Disclaimers

In an attempt to avoid liability, the building department can print a disclaimer on the building permit and application to help prevent these kinds of misunderstandings. This disclaimer can state that the applicant warrants the truthfulness of the information in the application, and that if any of the information provided is incorrect, the building permit may be revoked. Furthermore, the application and permit can provide that if the permit is issued wrongfully, whether based on misinformation or an improper application of the code, the building permit may be revoked. Although these disclaimers may not prevent the application of the doctrine of equitable estoppel, they may help the court resolve the issue in the building official's favor. Remember that these disclaimers, however, cannot entirely overrule judge-made law regarding the revocation of permits.

Another benefit of including a disclaimer is that it may prompt the builder to be more candid with the examiner than he or she might otherwise be. Although disclaimers will not give rise to widespread change, anything that promotes communication between the builder and the building official is a move in the right direction. Note that in most states, it is against the law for a building official to refuse to issue a building permit unless there is some reason for that refusal. In other words, the building official cannot refuse to issue a permit for no reason.

For example, Section 105.3.1 of the *International Building Code*® (IBC®) provides that:

> ...If the application or the construction documents do not conform to the requirements of pertinent laws, the building official shall reject such application in writing, stating the reasons therefor.

Therefore, under the IBC, the building official must deny issuance of a permit if the application or the construction documents, or both, does not conform to the requirements of the building code itself, or if they do not conform to the requirements of other pertinent laws. The denial will be put in writing.

Another option for the building official is to use his or her **discretionary authority** to grant a modification to the code when there are practical difficulties encountered. For example, a change of occupancy in an existing building requires accessibility that can be achieved by the use of two risers. The building official uses discretionary authority to replace the steps, which are located a short distance from the property line and public walkway, with a ramp that does not fully comply with the requirements of an accessibility ramp. The granting of the modification to the code due to practical difficulties meets the intent of the code.

If the building code official does not issue a permit and does not include a reason for his or her denial of the permit, the applicant may appeal to the Board of Building Code Appeals.

In most cases, where the application is for a project of some scope or value, the applicant will probably bring suit against the building code official. While the nature of the suit may vary from jurisdiction to jurisdiction, the majority of plaintiffs will seek relief in the form of a **writ of mandamus**. This occurs when the court commands the municipality to perform one of the duties it is responsible for performing. This writ may be issued by a court to an administrative official, who, for some reason, is not performing his or her duties under the code. To be successful in obtaining a writ of mandamus, the plaintiff must demonstrate to the court that he or she is clearly "entitled to the administrative action sought" and that the administrative official has no discretion about whether the action should or should not be taken. If a building official refuses to issue a building permit to a builder for a political reason, or some other reason, despite the fact that the plans are complete, accurate, and in compliance with all laws and ordinances, the builder may ask the court to issue a writ of mandamus.

In the case of *Pigs R. Us, LLC v. Compton Township*,[6] the plaintiffs successfully obtained a writ of mandamus against the township for a denied building permit application. Pigs R Us applied for and received a building permit for a swine facility from the township. After the township received a letter urging it to revoke the permit, the township held several public hearings before the township board. Before the board reached a decision, the plaintiffs filed for a new building permit for the same facility. It is undisputed that the proposed swine facility complied with all of the requisite township zoning ordinances. Contrary to Compton Township's own standard operating procedures, the township made no immediate decision on the second application. Rather, it revoked the plaintiff's first permit, refused to consider the second application, and adopted an interim zoning ordinance. This interim ordinance converted all nonresidential uses, such as the one the plaintiffs were proposing, from permitted to special uses. The board then denied the plaintiff's second application because the interim ordinance now required a special-use permit. Plaintiffs petitioned the court for a writ of mandamus to compel the township to issue the building permit, which was granted. The court found that the board acted arbitrarily when it enacted the interim zoning ordinance and that the plaintiffs were entitled to the building permit based on their first application. In summary, the plaintiff must show that the building official has no discretion as to whether to issue the permit.

In these cases, the attorney would argue that the building official's function here is not merely administrative, and that the building official had to exercise administrative discretion to determine whether or not to issue this particular permit. Unfortunately, if there truly were no good reason for the denial of the application, this argument would fail. If the applicant meets all the requirements of the building code and other pertinent laws and ordinances, then the building official has no justification to refuse to issue the permit.

Another defense an attorney might assert is that the applicant for the building permit has failed to exhaust administrative remedies. More specifically, the attorney might claim that the plaintiff should have appealed the building official's decision to the Board of Building Code Appeals before coming into court, and should be precluded from being heard in court until the plaintiff has appeared in front of the appropriate administrative tribunal. If it appears to the court that the building official had no legitimate reason for failing to issue the permit, the court will be reluctant to deny the writ of mandamus based on this failure to exhaust administrative remedies.

Provisions for the suspension of revocation of building permits are made in the IBC Section 105.6. It provides that:

> The building official is authorized to suspend or revoke a permit issued under the provisions of this code wherever the permit is issued in error or on the basis of incorrect, inaccurate or incomplete information, or in violation of any ordinance or regulation or any of the provisions of this code.

An interesting question develops in light of recent constitutional law decisions. The Supreme Court of the United States requires that where a person has a right that has become vested, prior to the removal of that right by a governmental agency, the person be given notice and an opportunity to be heard. In the case of the issuance of a building permit, once a substantial amount of work has been done on the project, the right to that permit becomes vested, assuming that the applicant constructs the building in the way stated on the permit. The building official, however, may conclude during an inspection that progress on the work is not going according to the plan submitted and may wish to take **summary action** to revoke the permit or issue a stop-work order. A stop-work order is immediate action taken to abate a violation without formal court proceedings. Stop-work orders are authorized by IBC Sections 115.1 and 115.2, which provide that:

> The stop work order shall be in writing and shall be given to the owner of the property involved, or to the owner's agent or to the person doing the work. Upon issuance of a stop work order, the cited work shall immediately cease. The stop work order shall state the reason for the order, and the conditions under which the cited work will be permitted to resume.

A similar concern would be raised when a certificate of occupancy is revoked. In all of the instances, the builder arguably has a right that is vested and that is being taken away by the action of the governmental official. There is no case law on this point, as of yet. Even so, to avoid any possible future liability, it would be prudent to provide the builder with some **due process**. Before issuing a stop-work order, it would be fairly simple to hold an informal hearing before the building official. Assuming the builder is dissatisfied with the building official's decision, an appeal could be taken to the Board of Building Code Appeals (BBCA). To prevent possible constitutional violations, it would be ideal if after the building official has learned that a builder has violated the code in some way that the building department set a time and date for a hearing to determine the accuracy of those charges. A very short period of time, perhaps one or two days, would be necessary. A notice of the violation could be posted at the work site on one day and a hearing could be held in front of the building official the very next day. This would interrupt the process of construction for only a short period of time, and the constitutional requirement of notice and opportunity to be heard would be met.

The building official should reduce his or her decision to writing and include specific reasons for the decision. If aggrieved by the building official's decision, the builder would then be free to appeal to the BBCA. This should protect the building department from any allegations of unconstitutional process. This procedure should be informal. A written record of the hearing should be kept, and a letter summarizing what occurred should be sent to the builder. These records will be useful to the building official if forced into court.

If the applicant is required to post a performance bond, the building official should not release the money to the applicant until all conditions of the permit are met. Sometimes good-hearted inspectors authorize the release of the sum, relying on an applicant's promise to complete a small item, such as landscaping, at a later date. Often, promises are empty and the municipality loses an effective enforcement tool by acting prematurely. The threat of a ticket is not as powerful as the withholding of a large sum of money from the applicant.

The importance of affording a builder his due process rights cannot be stressed enough. As already discussed, it is relatively easy to afford a builder his due process rights. When mailing any form of notice to the builder, be sure to send it certified mail, return receipt requested. The signed, returned receipt can be used to provide proof that the builder was put on notice. The signed receipt can also be used at later administrative and court hearings. By affording the builder his due process rights, the building official is protecting himself and his department from a Court finding that a builder's constitutional rights have been violated.

Inspection

Section 110 of the IBC states that construction or work for which a permit is required shall be subjected to inspections by the building official and that such construction or work shall remain accessible and exposed for inspection purposes until approved. Required inspections set forth in Sections 110.3.1 through 110.3.10 shall be made by the building official upon notification. Section 104.7 requires that official records of applications received, permits and certificates issued, fees collected, reports of inspections, and notices and orders issued shall be retained for the period required for retention of public records. It is essential that such records be kept by all building code departments. Without records of the inspection process, it becomes very difficult for an attorney to prosecute successfully an alleged code offender or to defend the building official. Generally, it is best to have a standard form, which is completed by each inspector either during or immediately following each inspection.

Each inspector should be trained in the manner in which the department performs its routine inspections. A specific process should be adopted by the entire department, and each of the inspectors should be required to adhere to that process. Naturally, the inspection process must be evenhanded and should avoid discrimination against any party. If a building inspector is working under the authority of a building official, this is an example of a **ministerial act**; in other words, it is performed under the authority, policies, and procedures of a supervisor. A ministerial act is performed because the law requires it and does not involve discretion.

The first step in the inspection process should be for the building inspector to check office records and become as knowledgeable about the property as possible before making the actual field inspection. This preparation would include noting any unusual characteristics about the building or its design and prior enforcement attempts by the building official or any other agency. Once the building inspector is familiar with the property characteristics, he or she should make the field inspection. Again, it is important for the inspector to document everything that he or she notices during the inspection. Without written documentation, enforcement of the code becomes very difficult. Courts prefer the official inspection reports over oral testimony. The courts know that building officials inspect many buildings and cannot remember the nuances of each one. They also know that a person's memory of an event changes as time progresses. The power of the written word in court should not be underestimated. Whenever possible, this testimony should be backed up and based on a written document such as an inspection report.

Every inspection must be documented, but only rudimentary information needs to be recorded. This information includes the date, address, and any observed violations or impressions that might not actually amount to a violation. The building inspector should write in common, everyday language. It is not necessary to cite every violation or make every comment in the language of the building code. In fact, the less building code terminology used, the easier it can be understood by others who are outside the construction industry. The building official must clearly state which section of the building code is being violated or noted; a reference to that specific section can be made by number. It is never necessary to copy the entire code provision.

Whenever possible, the building official should take photographs or videos of any violation observed. This one piece of evidence is the most valuable part of the official's file. A defendant will often try to minimize a violation. When confronted with photographic evidence, he or she will usually plead guilty. Photographs or videos can also be used during the sentencing phase of the proceeding as aggravation or to demonstrate what needs to be done to bring the property into compliance with the municipality's ordinances.

It is a good idea for the building official to keep a copy of each inspection report. Often a copy is kept in the property file maintained for that particular parcel of property, another copy is given to the supervisor, and a copy to the contractor.

Administrative Search Warrants

Some states have made provisions via enabling legislation for administrative search warrants. These states make it easier for building officials to inspect property by allowing for administrative search warrants. In these states, enabling legislation will prescribe the rules and procedures to obtain the warrant. Every provision of the legislation must be followed precisely. An affidavit setting forth facts sufficient to issue the warrant must be present and establish **probable cause** to believe there is a violation of the building code. It is important for the building official to work with the municipal or county attorney on these administrative search warrants to ensure all the required procedures are met. They can help in drafting an affidavit that establishes probable cause. They will also help the building official avoid potential liability for violating any federal civil rights acts or state laws. Once the search warrant is issued it is generally the building official who executes, or serves, the warrant and conducts the search. After the search has been completed, the building official may have to comply with specific jurisdictional requirements, such as filing a document known as a "**return of the warrant**." The return of the warrant is a document filed with the court, informing the court that the search warrant was served on the person named in the search warrant and that the search took place on a specific date and time. The building official will want to consult their municipal or county attorney to ensure the rules are followed and all required documentation is filed with the court.

Other states have done away with separate administrative warrants. Rather, they have combined administrative and criminal search warrants into one. In these states a search warrant will be issued if there is probable cause to believe there is a violation of health, safety, building code, or local ordinances or even animal cruelty laws.[7] The building official should consult with their municipal or county attorney to determine which type of warrant should be sought. In Chapter 8, a further discussion will take place on the difference between an administrative warrant and a criminal search warrant. Chapter 8 will also discuss the constitutional requirements to obtain a warrant as well as the limitations on a building inspector's right of entry and search and seizure.

Plans Examination

One of the most frightening areas of potential liability in the enforcement of the building code is the examination of building plans by members of the building code department. If a building collapses, if there is some kind of structural defect, or if inappropriate materials are used in a building, owners are increasingly likely to sue the building code department. Obviously, in major urban areas where skyscrapers with one hundred stories or more are being constructed, the possible liability of a building code official or a plans examiner can be staggering.

To perform the function of a plans examiner, the building code department must have a qualified expert in the area. Although the IBC does not specifically make mention of particular requirements for the position of plans examiner, the importance of the job requires an individual with a background in structural engineering or an architect with experience in the design and construction of buildings. IBC Section 107.3 requires the code official to examine the submitted construction documents. It is sometimes difficult to find well-qualified people to assume these responsibilities. While the private sector can pay more to persons with these qualifications, building code departments are not notorious for high salaries. Even so, it is important that the most highly qualified personnel be employed. Some courts may impose liability on the building department even though Section 107.3.1 of the IBC requires that a licensed professional engineer or architect stamp the plans submitted by the applicant. The reliance by the building code official and his or her department on the stamp of a licensed architect or engineer, however, is insufficient in many states today. The department must have its own qualified personnel determine whether or not plans are acceptable.

The division of plans examination within a building code department must be thorough in everything it does. A small mistake could mean the loss of many lives and the imposition of legal liability. It is very important that every detail be checked and double checked prior to the issuance of a permit. Notes and records should be kept of the plans examiner's impressions as the examination is conducted. Those notes and records should be kept in the master file on the particular property in question. A standard plan review form should be used for every plan review.

Civil Prosecutions

Once a violation has been found, some action must be taken to enforce the code. Ordinarily, if the structure has been completed, the summary procedures of the revocation of a permit or issuance of a stop-work order are not available. Once the construction has been completed, prosecution in the city courts becomes the final method of enforcement. In most jurisdictions, a civil or quasi-criminal complaint may be filed against the owner or occupant of the property. Normally, with a civil **complaint**, the notice of violation may be served either through the mail or physically delivered to the alleged offender. In some jurisdictions, an alleged offender is still required to be arrested under an arrest warrant. A typical complaint in most jurisdictions will require the six elements described on the following pages.

1. Name of person or entity to be charged

The first decision that must be made when a complaint is prepared is, "Who is the party to be charged?" Answering this question correctly will prevent lawsuits for false arrest. The entity, either a person or corporation, that has committed the offense should be charged. If a corporation has committed the offense, the corporate name should be used, for example, Doe Enterprises, Inc. Just because a business name is used does not mean that the defendant is a corporation. It could be that the person is conducting business as a sole proprietor, but using a business name. Such a name is called an alias. In some jurisdictions, persons who operate businesses using alias names must register those names with an agency such as a county clerk. There may be a penalty for failure to register. If a person uses an alias for a business, the proper defendant would be "John Doe, doing business as Doe's Diner."

When the person being cited is the owner of real estate, it is critical that proper ownership be established. The building official cannot rely on the tax records to prove ownership. Anyone can be designated to pay taxes on a parcel of land.

Every jurisdiction has some office that keeps records of ownership, such as the recorder of deeds. Many of those offices are now computerized. With certain information, a list of transactions can be accessed. The most recent deed should be checked for ownership. The person(s), trust, or corporation named in the deed is the owner who should be cited.

Municipal records may also contain information about the identity of the owner or person responsible for a piece of property that is the subject of a code or zoning violation. Municipal records are admissible as business records in court if the person who keeps the records can testify they were made in the ordinary course of business.

An application for a permit might contain the name of the responsible party, or a transfer tax declaration might contain the name of the owners. Records containing information regarding municipal services might contain the name of the responsible party. If all else fails, a tract search can be ordered on the property to determine who the legal owner is. A title company will search the records for a fee. The number of the recorded deed will usually be listed on a title search. Once that is done, a certified copy of the document showing ownership by a particular individual or entity can be obtained from the local recorder of deeds or another governmental agency charged with keeping real estate records.

If the owner of the land is to be charged and the property is in a trust, the trust is charged. Therefore, where the property is held in a bank land trust, the correct party would be, for example, "Peach Grove Bank & Trust, as Trustee for Trust Number 1234." If the search reveals that the property is in a trust, it is necessary to determine who the beneficiaries are. Many states have disclosure statutes, which set forth the procedure for finding out this type of information.

Sometimes more than one person may be responsible for conditions on a piece of property. Depending on the way an ordinance is written, an owner might be cited for a violation along with a tenant or contractor. By naming all responsible parties, the necessary persons will be brought into court, which may expedite a settlement of the case. If there are multiple owners, all persons should be cited.

Whenever an inspector has a question as to whether or not there is enough legal evidence to prove who the responsible person is, then that person should contact the prosecutor handling the case.

2. Designating the charge

Every complaint must contain the section number and the name of the violation. Usually, only one violation section may be used per count in the complaint. If the offender has committed more than one violation, each violation must be described separately. The title of the charge should be descriptive enough so that the defendant understands the charge. For example, if someone has property that is littered with garbage and debris, the charge would be "Failure to Maintain Exterior Property." When deciding which number to use in the ordinance violation section, the charge should be very specific, such as violation of Section PM-303.1. If the ordinance has different sections, the proper subsection should be cited.

3. Body of the charge

Every ticket must contain a description of the violation that is sufficient so that the defendant can defend against the charge and make sure he or she is not charged twice for the same offense. Therefore, the ticket should contain a statement that describes the offense in the language of the ordinance being used. If the language of the ordinance is very general, then a specific allegation and description should be used. Care should be taken, however, to use only words that describe what can be proven by the building official's or other witnesses' testimony. For example, for the above charge the complaint would read, "Said defendant did fail to maintain the exterior property at 123 Waterbury, Peach Grove, Illinois, in a clean, safe and sanitary condition, in that the backyard contains numerous piles of garbage and rubbish." The defendant would know the exact charge. Care must also be taken not to get too specific. In the case of housing code violations, a general description of the problem would be sufficient. For example, "Defendant did fail to maintain the plumbing equipment in the building located at 123 Waterbury, Peach Grove, Illinois," would be better than giving a detailed list of every single plumbing problem contained in a particular building.

4. Date and time of the offense

Each complaint must contain an allegation regarding the date and time of the offense. For ordinance violations, the date must fall within the **statute of limitations**. The date and time in the complaint should be the same date and time that the inspector observed the violation. That way the individual can testify being at 123 Waterbury, Peach Grove, Illinois, on a particular date and time and observing the plumbing problem.

5. Signature of the complaining witness

Each complaint must be signed by an individual, either an inspector or a witness. In some jurisdictions, a complaint may be signed by an officer who receives information from another individual about the offense.

6. Notary or affidavit

Depending on the jurisdiction, a complaint may need to be verified by the person signing it (that is, sworn to under oath that the information contained therein is true and correct).

Taking a defendant to court on a complaint can be effective in terms of compliance and cost. The most important factor in a successful prosecution, aside from the facts of the case, is the competence of the prosecution. Prosecuting violations is different from civil litigation because of the quasi-criminal nature of the charges. The best attorneys are usually those who have had experience in a state's attorney or district attorney's office. Any municipality that retains an attorney should make sure the attorney has a commitment to the area of zoning and code enforcement and views prosecution as a way to gain compliance and assist the municipality in establishing its reputation as a place where code requirements are enforced.

While fines are not usually very high for ordinance violations, the inconvenience of going to court and the fear most people have of it are powerful incentives for a defendant to come into compliance, and often by the first court date.

If a defendant needs more persuasion to correct a problem, he or she can be charged with multiple violations because most codes provide that every day of noncompliance is a new violation. As the amount of potential fines grows, the defendant will usually try to reach an agreement with the prosecutor.

If a defendant needs time to come into compliance, the prosecutor may ask the judge to make it a condition of any sentence imposed. If the defendant violates the sentence, he or she may be subject to re-sentencing or contempt of court charges, which carry with them a possible jail sentence.

There may be situations where filing citations against the defendant does not produce the desired result. For example, the court may not be willing to use its power, or the property may have deteriorated so badly that condemnation proceedings are necessary. If that occurs, the municipality may want to seek an injunction. This type of relief may be sought before a chancery court, which is one with **equitable powers**.

Injunctive Relief

Types

An injunction is sought by the building official. The remedy is, in essence, an order of the court, which requires that the defendant cease and desist from all conduct that amounts to a violation of the building code. In almost every jurisdiction in the United States today, **injunctive relief** is broken into three types: a temporary restraining order (TRO), a temporary or preliminary injunction, and a permanent injunction.

The **temporary restraining order** is an order issued by the court without notice to the other party and without an opportunity for the other party to be heard. A TRO will be issued only in the most extreme circumstances. This should be obvious because, under most circumstances, it would be unconstitutional for a court to take any action without giving notice and an opportunity for the other side unless there is an absolute emergency.

The **temporary injunction** is a judicial order that is issued pending a full hearing by the court. The temporary injunction is issued only after notice is given to the opposing party and a usually brief hearing in front of the court.

Finally, the **permanent injunction** is a judicial order that is issued after the court has heard all of the evidence in the case. It is issued based on a final review of the position of both sides.

All three types of injunctions may be issued in a single case. For example, a building official may determine that the conduct of a building contractor is so dangerous to the public at large that work on a project must immediately be stopped. A lawsuit may be filed asking for injunctive relief, and the attorney for the building official and the building official himself may appear in front of the judge that very afternoon to request a temporary restraining order. Based on the information presented, the judge may issue the temporary restraining order to remain in effect for two or three days. Meanwhile, the judge will set a hearing on the temporary injunction within that two- or three-day period during which the TRO will be in effect. Immediately thereafter, the TRO is served on the alleged building code offender by an agent of the court, thereby giving notice of the lawsuit and of the court's order that the allegedly dangerous activity cease. Two or three days later the hearing on the temporary injunction is held, and the court, after a short hearing, reaches a tentative conclusion as to whether the injunction should be issued or not. After a temporary injunction is issued, all activity ceases until there is a final, full hearing on the merits of the whole case. After that full hearing, a permanent injunction may be issued. A permanent injunction is issued under particular sets of circumstances that are not detailed here.

Seeking a Temporary Restraining Order or Injunction

The factual circumstances and legal standards that must be met in order to receive a temporary restraining order or a temporary injunction should generally be known by building officials so that an educated decision may be made whether to seek either.

Both the temporary restraining order and the temporary injunction are usually subject to four legal requirements. First, the building official seeking the injunctive relief must show that there is a significant threat of irreparable harm to the public if the injunction is not granted. Second, the building official must show that the harm the public would suffer if the injunction is not granted is greater than the harm the other party would suffer if the injunction is granted. Third, the building official must show probable cause that he or she will prevail on the legal merits of the controversy. Fourth, the building official must demonstrate that the issuance of the restraining order or injunction is in the public interest. Usually, when representing the building department, an attorney will reverse the order of those four elements. There is rarely a challenge to the contention that the building official is acting in the public interest. The building official has the responsibility to make sure that building construction within his or her jurisdiction is done in a safe manner. Therefore, generally, the issuance of the injunction will be in the public interest. As to the third element, the probability of success on the merits of the case usually lies strongly in favor of the building official. In most cases, the defendant is in violation of the building code; however, the remaining two elements pose a difficulty to the municipal attorney.

To demonstrate to the court that an injunction should be issued, the building official must prove that some immediate irreparable harm is about to occur. If the construction is not of such a nature that personal injury will occur to members of the public in general, the judge is likely to believe that an injunction should not be issued. Of course, the building official can enforce the code by a civil complaint in municipal court. Thus, the key element in obtaining such an injunction is to demonstrate to the court that immediate, irreparable harm will somehow occur to members of the public in general or to particular occupants of a building.

Some examples of the types of irreparable harm that may be used in order to obtain an injunction are the improper installation of electrical connections, improper installation of fire protective materials, and improper construction techniques. In evaluating whether or not to seek a temporary restraining order, the building official should be aware at all times that it is the immediacy of the harm to the public that the judge is interested in. Consultation with local counsel is of course important in determining whether or not injunctive relief should be sought.

Handling Complaints

A significant portion of time is spent by building code departments responding to complaints regarding parcels of property. Some general guidelines relating to handling those complaints may be useful.

First of all, the person who receives the complaint should obtain as much information as possible. The name of the complainant, his or her address, phone number, the date that he or she viewed the alleged violation, and the nature of the alleged violation are all important. It is also important for the person who handles the complaint to realize that the job of the codes department is made easier when the citizenry of the jurisdiction cooperates. Therefore, the code representative should be as cooperative and polite as possible.

The department should establish a standard procedure for handling the complaint once it is received and reduced to writing. As soon as it is received, the complaint should be routed to the proper inspector. Within a few days an inspection should be made, a report completed, and action taken. Whether or not a violation is found, the citizen who has made the complaint should be notified of the outcome of the department's investigation. A short letter to the citizen who complained is all that is necessary.

While the complaints of local citizenry are probably public records, under the public records act in most states the information need not be revealed over the telephone. If someone calls and asks the name of the person who complained about a specific parcel of property, the building code department can normally refuse to respond. However, it is important to know what information must be disclosed by state law. Many states have freedom of information acts that specify the type of documents that must be revealed. There may be exceptions to the disclosure requirements if an investigation is ongoing, or if the information reveals the identity of persons who file complaints with or provide information to administrative, investigative, or law enforcement agencies. The building department should establish a clear policy based on the advice of counsel regarding this area. Because a complaint becomes a public record once it goes to court, many citizens who complain do not wish their names to be taken. Even if no name is given, a complaint should always be addressed.

Evidence

When a building official takes a case to court, he or she must make sure that there is sufficient evidence to prove the charges against the defendant. Verbal testimony is used to prove most cases. The witness testifies as to what he or she observed about the property during the inspection process. The witness may also testify about any admissions the defendant made regarding the offense. For example, the building official can describe conversations he or she had with the defendant or owner of the property in question and whether the defendant admitted responsibility. Information told to the building inspector by a third party who is not an agent of the defendant is usually not admissible because it violates the rule against hearsay. **Hearsay** is a statement made out of court that is being introduced for the truth of the matter asserted in the statement. A hearsay statement is only admissible if it is an exception to the hearsay rule, such as an admission of a party.

The building official should use any corroborating evidence available to bolster his or her testimony. Photographs, videotapes, or audiotapes are admissible to demonstrate what the witness observed. This evidence should be gathered on the date and time set forth in the complaint.

Business records are admissible if the witness can testify they are kept in the ordinary course of business (things such as warning letters, permits, applications, certified mail receipts). Some records may be automatically admissible because of state law. Others must be certified as official records by the proper governmental agency.

If a case involves more than a witness's testimony substantiated by a photograph, the building official should contact the municipality's attorney to make sure he or she has obtained the necessary items for trial. Furthermore, the official needs to remember to bring the items of evidence to court.

Administrative Guidelines

Every building code department will find that as more and more applications are made under the building code, the department will make certain decisions that are not expressly resolved by the code. Any written set of rules simply cannot cover every single situation that could possibly come up during the construction of buildings. The department should adopt written administrative guidelines to cover those areas not already covered by the code. These may relate to the manner in which inspections are to be made, the manner in which citizens' complaints are to be handled, and the order of authority within the department. In each of these cases, the general rule should be reduced to a written form.

Operation of the department will be more efficient if each employee is given a copy of this administrative rule book to follow. It is particularly important for the person in the building code department who accepts applications and makes decisions regarding granting permits to be familiar with previous department actions on a given type of application. In other words, if the situation is not explicitly covered by the building code, the decision made by the department should be reduced to writing and incorporated into this administrative rule book. Thereafter, if the question comes up again, it can be referred to in the rule book.

Naturally, if a question is not covered by the building code itself or by the rule book, then a new rule needs to be written. It need not be complex. The staff of the building code department should make a decision as to how those applications should be handled in the future, usually in consultation with the staff of the model code organization with which they are affiliated. The decision should be written up, along with an explanation of why it is the best policy, and then placed in the rule book given to each employee.

Once a year, the building code department should have a meeting of the entire staff to go over the various rules that are covered in the book. This type of review session will help the members of the department keep up to date. It may also help correct tendencies toward improper inspection or other incorrect procedures that may have developed during the previous year.

These administrative guidelines are also important because they will help explain the reasoning of the building official regarding actions on any particular building code application. If the building official has reduced the decision to writing and included it in the administrative rule book, even if the particular reason is not included in the building code itself, an application for a building permit can be denied based on these administrative guidelines. The guidelines will generally be upheld by a court of law if challenged via a writ of mandamus. Thus, the guidelines serve a legal function—they make the decision-making process of the building official more legitimate.

Finally, the guidelines facilitate uniform administration of the code. If the decision on the prior application has been written down, the same decision can be easily made in the future applications of the rule.

DeBry v. Noble

Before we end this chapter, let's introduce the cases of *DeBry v. Salt Lake County*[8] and *DeBry v. Noble.*[9] *DeBry v. Salt Lake County* was decided by the Utah Court of Appeals in the summer of 1992. DeBry appealed and the Utah Supreme Court granted certiorari (agreed to hear the case), resulting in the 1995 case of *DeBry v. Noble*. Rather than try and refer to the cases individually, they will both be referred to hereafter by the Utah Supreme Court case name of *DeBry v. Noble*.

Robert J. DeBry, a prominent personal injury and wrongful death lawyer in the state of Utah, and his wife sued Wallace R. Noble in his individual capacity and as the Chief Building Official of Salt Lake County, Utah, as well as Salt Lake County. They are collectively referred to as the Public Plaintiffs.

The DeBrys claimed they were injured by the negligent inspection and issuance of a temporary certificate of occupancy of a building they purchased from a third party. They claim their constitutional rights were violated and that the Utah Governmental Immunity Act (Act) did not provide immunity for the negligent inspection and issuance of the temporary certificate of occupancy. The Utah Court of Appeals and the Utah Supreme Court denied their claims, ruling in favor of the Public Plaintiffs.

In 1985 the DeBrys executed an earnest money agreement for the purchase of an office building from Cascade Enterprises while it was still under construction. Prior to completion of construction, Cascade erroneously represented to Noble that they had obtained all the necessary permits for the building. Noble violated a cardinal rule in the permit issuance process. He did not verify the accuracy of Cascade's claim. He recalled that some kind of inspection had recently been completed by a county inspector but made no further attempt to verify Cascade's assertion. With that recollection and relying on Cascade's statement, Noble issued a temporary thirty-day certificate of occupancy in December 1985.

In fact, however, Cascade had only obtained a footings and foundation permit in November 1984, which a simple check of the file would have revealed. Instead, and without any actual facts to support the decision, Noble concluded that there did not appear to be any significant dangers that would preclude temporary occupancy of the building while construction was completed and brought into compliance with the county building code. He therefore issued the certificate. Shortly thereafter, the DeBrys purchased the building.

After the temporary certificate of occupancy was issued, someone in the Salt Lake County building department discovered that only the footings and foundation permit, not a building permit, had ever been issued to Cascade. Despite discovering this, the county let the temporary certificate of occupancy stand. On March 17, 1986, Salt Lake County performed an inspection and determined that a certificate of occupancy could not be issued due to persisting defects in the building. Two days later the county legally put the DeBrys on notice of the specific defects, giving them thirty days to remedy the defects. After no corrective action had taken place, the County, on May 15, 1986, again legally advised the DeBrys that they were occupying the building without a valid certificate of occupancy, that they needed to correct the defects, and obtain a valid building permit. Again, the DeBrys took no action to correct the defects or obtain a certificate of occupancy. Instead, the DeBrys filed a complaint against Cascade as the seller and contractor, several subcontractors and suppliers, and the architect, designer, real estate company, lenders, mortgage company, and title company.[10]

In November 1986 the County "served" the DeBrys with an order to vacate within ten days because they had not corrected the defects and had not obtained a valid certificate of occupancy. The DeBrys exercised their due process rights and appealed the county's order to the Salt Lake County Board of Appeals. Among other issues raised before the Board, the DeBrys requested an extension of time to vacate the building. After reviewing the DeBry's appeal, the Board denied the request for the extension of time. A more complete discussion of the duties and powers of the Board of Building Code Appeals will take place in the next chapter.

The DeBrys then filed suit against the county and Noble. They claimed the county and Noble were negligent in failing to require the building contractors to correct violations of the building code and in issuing the temporary certificate of occupancy without making any inspections or determining whether a building permit had been issued. The negligence claim will be further discussed in a later chapter.

The DeBrys also alleged that the County and Noble deprived them of their due process rights. Specifically, the notice to vacate deprived them of their constitutional rights of freedom of enterprise and occupation, their right to use their building and their right to equal protection. On appeal, the Utah Court of Appeals disagreed with the DeBrys. The Court noted that the DeBrys had been put on notice through the County requests to bring the building into code compliance but chose to ignore the March and May 1986 notices. The Court went on to state that it was not until the November 1986 notice, nearly six months after the County's last request, that the County served the notice and order to vacate the building.

Furthermore, the DeBrys were afforded an opportunity to be heard and present evidence on the notice and order to vacate before the Salt Lake County Board of Appeals. The Board determined that the DeBrys failed to comply with past orders of the County to cure the defects in the building, no building permit had ever been secured, no certificate of occupancy had been issued, and no required fees had been paid. The Board determined that the DeBrys were illegally occupying the building.

The Utah Court of Appeals ruled that the DeBry's due process rights had not been violated. They were provided with sufficient notice to obtain a building permit, cure the defects, and obtain a certificate of occupancy. Each notice informed them of the consequences for failing to comply. Further, they were afforded a hearing and opportunity to appeal the County's order to vacate. For these reasons, there was no violation of the DeBry's due process rights.

In terms of affording the DeBrys their due process rights, the County got it right. This is why it is so important for building officials to be aware of and afford everyone their due process rights. While it may not have relieved the DeBrys of their obligation to correct the present code violations, it may have delayed the process had the Court ordered Salt Lake County to start the process all over. We'll leave *DeBry v. Noble* for now but come back to it later.

Conclusion

This chapter has described some of the concepts that are legally important to the enforcement and administration of the building code. The legal ramifications surrounding the issuance of building permits was discussed as were the various types of relief a building official might seek through the courts. When seeking any kind of relief, the building official must ensure that due process rights are being afforded to everyone. Finally, the case of

DeBry v. Noble was introduced. This case showcases the mistakes that can occur as well as the right way to proceed when taking any kind of administrative or judicial action.

Chapter 6 Endnotes

1. *G.J.Z. Enterprises, Inc. v. City of Troy.*
2. Id. at 23.
3. *Snyder v. City of Minneapolis.*
4. See Chapter 12.
5. *Gallichio Bros., Inc. v. Zoning Bd. of Appeals of Town of Newington.*
6. *Pigs R Us, LLC v. Compton Township,* 770 N.W.2d 212 (2009).
7. Violation of health, safety, building, or animal cruelty laws or ordinances—Warrant to obtain evidence. Rule 40(k), Utah Rules of Criminal Procedure.
8. *DeBry v. Salt Lake County,* 835 P.2d 891, Ct App. (1992).
9. *DeBry v. Noble,* 889 P.2d 428, Utah (1995).
10. "Largely because of the manner in which the DeBry's [sic] and their attorneys litigated their lawsuit, a relatively simple case was transformed into an unnecessarily protracted and complicated lawsuit. In the four and a half years preceding trial, the DeBry's [sic] amended their complaint nine times, changed attorneys several times, caused one judge to be recused and moved twice to disqualify the trial judge who ultimately sat, obtained at least one continuance of the trial date, and filed numerous motions, many of them repetitive. At the time of their appeal the court file alone contained twenty-eight volumes with over 13,000 pages." The DeBrys ultimately received $22,625 in damages from Cascade. *DeBry v. Cascade Enterprises,* 879 P.2d 1353, Utah (1994).

Chapter 7 – Administrative Law

This chapter discusses the rules of procedure for boards of building code appeals and the boards' powers under model building codes.

Topics

Creation of the Board of Building Code Appeals

Application to the Board

Powers of the Board

Appeals Procedures

Terms

administrative action

burden of proof

de novo

Introduction

This chapter will examine the general concepts of administrative law that are most relevant to the building official. The primary focus will be on the procedures to be used before a board of building code appeals. This board is known by various names, and there are a variety of different tribunals covering different parts of the building process. To avoid confusion, it will be referred to as the Board of Building Code Appeals (BBCA) throughout the chapter. The BBCA usually derives its power from the building code through which it was created. In many cases, situations arise that are not addressed within the code but should nevertheless be considered. Without explicit support from the code, the members of the BBCA are left on their own to determine how they will rule. This chapter will discuss **administrative action**, the process by which the BBCA, or any administrative agency, forms its decisions. The chapter will also discuss the benefits that would arise if the BBCA adopted procedures to govern the hearing process itself. Additionally, the chapter will discuss some aspects of administrative discretion and the necessity of adopting administrative regulations, which should be distinguished from rules of procedure before the BBCA.

Creation of the Board of Building Code Appeals

The *International Building Code®* (IBC®) includes a section dealing with the Board of Building Code Appeals. The board of appeals shall be appointed by the governing body and shall hold office at its pleasure.

The board adopts rules of procedure for conducting its business.

> 113.3 Qualifications. The board of appeals shall consist of members who are qualified by experience and training to pass on matters pertaining to building construction and are not employees of the jurisdiction.

Application to the Board

Someone who wants to construct a building or other structure must apply under the building code to the building official for a building permit. The BBCA will only become involved once the building official denies the issuance of the permit. Upon receiving permit denial, the applicant should be informed of his or her right to appeal to the BBCA. If this is not already printed on building department denial forms, the applicant should be informed in writing of the right to appeal to the appropriate BBCA. Remember that there are a variety of different places to appeal a denial, depending on the reason the permit was denied. They include, but are in no way limited to, the boards of electrical appeals, zoning appeals, building code appeals, and storm water management appeals.

It is important for the municipality to have these boards of appeal in place with members appointed, even if they only exist on paper. All too frequently, a defendant may seek an appeal and the municipality scrambles to create a board for that purpose. If a board of appeals exists in an ordinance, it should exist in reality.

Powers of the Board

It is very important for municipal attorneys who handle appeals from BBCA decisions to know what powers the board wields. Attorneys must know under which circumstances those powers may be exercised. There is a doctrine in the law that states that the legislature cannot delegate to an administrative body the responsibility of making decisions when there is no explicit criteria for making those decisions. Unfortunately, in the area of building code appeals, there exist very few criteria by which the BBCA can judge whether a particular application should be granted or denied. The next pages look at the IBC and the provisions under that code, which grant the BBCA the power and the authority to act. The criteria under which an appeal may be taken are very poorly defined. There might be two reasons for this. First, it may be the case that the types of appeals that are seen by building officials are so broad as to defy categorization; and if something cannot be categorized, it is difficult to adopt criteria by which to judge those issues. Second, it may be the case that the vagueness of the criteria indicates uncertainty about the function of the BBCA.

The *International Building Code*® (IBC®)

IBC Section 113.2 provides that:

> An application for appeal shall be based on a claim that the true intent of this code or the rules legally adopted thereunder have been incorrectly interpreted, the provisions of this code do not fully apply, or an equally good or better form of construction is proposed.

This provision appears to set out three different avenues of appeal to the BBCA. An appeal is allowed: (1) if the true intent of this code or the rules legally adopted has been incorrectly interpreted; (2) if the provisions do not fully apply; and (3) if an equally good or better form of construction is proposed.

Furthermore, Section 113.2 also provides that:

> The board shall not have authority to waive requirements of this code.

Although this section states that the board shall not have authority to waive requirements, the language appears to be somewhat broad since it is difficult to know when the board may safely grant or deny a variation as referred to in Section 104.10.

> Where there are practical difficulties involved in carrying out the provisions of this code, the building official shall have the authority to grant modification for individual cases, upon application of the owner or owner's agent, provided that the building official shall first find that special individual reason makes the strict letter of this code impractical, the modification is in compliance with the intent and purpose of this code and that such modification does not lessen health, accessibility, life and fire safety, or structural requirements. The details of action granting modifications shall be recorded and entered in the files of the department of building safety.

For example, an argument can be made that in establishing the building code in the first place, the legislative body of the municipality thought that it was doing manifest justice and adopting the code in the public interest. Why, then, must there exist a Board of Building Code Appeals that can substitute its judgment of what is good for the public interest as opposed to that of the legislative body? This is not an easy question to answer. As noted before, similar problems have arisen in the area of zoning. In zoning-related situations the courts have usually held that the language similar to that in the *International Zoning Code*® (IZC®) is sufficiently well drawn to affirm the decision of the administrative body. The broad language poses problems not only for those people considering appeals, but also for the members of the BBCA, as well as for building inspectors. The language does not specifically provide for guidelines that the members of the board might use to determine whether a variation may be granted. Nor, for that matter, does the language tell the board how much proof the appellant must demonstrate to succeed in his or her attempt to get a variation or modification.

Again, the operative question is, "How would members of the Board of Building Code Appeals know when to grant a modification?" The conditions stated in Section 113.2 are general guides as to when a modification would be in order.

Impact on Judicial Review

It is very possible that the vague, broad, and general outlines of power for BBCA set out in the model codes are beneficial from a legal standpoint. While it is possible that a court will throw out the entire provision because it is too vague, most courts are very hesitant to do this. Once the board's attorney has crossed that major hurdle, he or she may argue successfully that the board has extraordinarily broad powers and may do almost anything under the provisions of the code. The attorney can be even more assured of success in court if there happens to be a decision in that jurisdiction that affirms the power of a BBCA, or for that matter a similar decision affirming the power of a board of zoning appeals. This makes it very easy for the board's attorney to prevail in any case where the board's decision has been appealed. What may be beneficial for the board, however, may be unfortunate for the building official. If the case law has interpreted the code as granting vast power to the

BBCA, the building official's decisions will be frequently overturned. If the board is pro-builder in its attitude, the public interest may get lost.

Unfortunately, the broad language of the code provisions cited here makes it very difficult to determine whether or not a particular case is properly presented before the BBCA.

Appeals Procedures

This section reviews some of the standard procedures that should be followed by boards of building code appeals. These include establishing rules of procedure; holding open public meetings; giving an appellant notice; presenting proof; granting remedies; ensuring the legality of rulings; rehearing a case; and handing down orders.

Some of these suggested procedures may help to prevent serious damage to particular cases, which may wind up in front of courts after an adverse decision by the board. Most of the procedures are rather simple to put into effect, and they make it very easy for the board's attorney to defend the board's decision. Of course, before implementing any of these procedures, the building official must consult with the municipal attorney. The attorney will be able to warn the building official of those state laws that might prevent him or her from implementing these procedures.

Rules of Procedure

One of the most basic procedures a board may establish is the adoption of rules of procedure for those persons who come before it. These rules need not be complex. It is best to develop a set of rules that reflect the board's current practices and procedures. These rules can help the building official's attorney in court when opposing counsel suggests that the board was playing favorites and made special rules for some special cases. If a set of written rules establishes the guidelines for every case, and are not deviated from without good reason, the court will never find that the decision was made arbitrarily. These rules of procedure are necessary and essential and may even help the board members to refresh their memory regarding problems that rarely arise. The remaining sections of this chapter will deal with certain types of provisions that may be inserted into the rules. To make the rules official, there is usually a legal requirement that municipal boards file their rules of procedure with some central office. Some municipalities might have to file the rules with the building official. In other municipalities, they might be filed in the clerk's office or in a similar office. Naturally, any rules that are written must be adopted by a majority vote of the board following whatever procedures are normally followed by that board.

Open Public Meetings

One of the first things to establish in any set of rules and regulations for the board is that the meetings are open to the public. This does not mean, however, that everyone can participate in the hearings. Generally, under most state laws, a limit may be established on the number of persons who may speak about a given issue in a given case. With the open public meeting laws that have been enacted in the various states across the country in the last twenty years, however, most boards must keep meetings open so that members of the public at large may come in and watch. The board may have a provision that only interested parties, defined as the applicant and surrounding neighbors or some other such definition, may actually participate in the hearings. Of course, that does not mean that someone from across the county could not come in and sit and watch the hearing itself.

Notice

The notice requirement is one of the most crucial requirements in the appeals process. In order for an appellant to get a fair hearing in front of the BBCA, he or she must be informed of the time and place of the hearing within a reasonable period before the hearing takes place. In other words, it would be insufficient notice to inform someone of a hearing the day before the hearing was scheduled to take place. Appellants must be given an adequate amount of time to prepare their materials and argument.

Generally, notice is not given to anyone, aside from the appellant and the members of the board. There is no case law that holds that there is a requirement for notice to be given to other parties. If the drafters of the code believed that adjoining building owners should appear at a hearing concerning their neighbors, there would be explicit language in the code. Notice to surrounding property owners would make the hearings more difficult. There would undoubtedly be neighboring property owners who would appear in opposition if such notice was given. Obviously, if no notice is given, it is more difficult for those property owners to find out about the hearing and raise opposition.

A broader notice requirement would serve the best interest of the building official. If an appeal is filed that the building official finds to be groundless, it would be helpful to have members of the general public at the hearing to openly oppose the application. It also takes some pressure off the board members. The arguments of the opposing building owners will help the board to make a decision about the case. Likewise, notifying the public about the existence of these hearings will ensure that the board's decisions are made in a fair and consistent manner. The board would be less likely to arbitrarily rule on an issue if the public were watching their every move.

The trend is toward more expansive notice requirements. These requirements will likely result in more court cases. The voiced opposition will help to create a more complete record in the event that the case goes into the court system. Furthermore, it would make the hearing appear more legitimate and more easily affirmed.

Burden and Presentation of Proof

Burden of proof refers to who must prove the issue in controversy and how much proof must be presented to an administrative tribunal or to a court of law in order to be awarded the sought-after relief. In any case before the BBCA, the burden rests with the appellant. The appellant must show that he or she is entitled to the relief requested.

Courts that review the BBCA decisions usually employ the substantial evidence standard. This standard provides that if a reasonable person could think that the board's decision was based on evidence sufficient to prove the issue in question, the reviewing court will accept and affirm the board's decision. This is a fairly lenient means of reviewing the evidence presented to an administrative board. Furthermore, because administrative tribunals rarely have attorneys on their board, the federal rules of evidence are not strictly applied. This means that objections based on hearsay, leading questions, and irrelevant evidence do not normally come up. Therefore, the board will hear or allow in any piece of evidence the appellant provides. The chairman of the board can, at his or her discretion, request that the appellant limit the amount of evidence in cases where the appellant has attempted to introduce an excessive amount. For the most part, the board does not have any strict guidelines dictating what can or cannot be admitted. This lenience reflects the general informality of the hearings themselves.

The same informality can lead to sloppiness in the reporting of the proceedings of board meetings. It is a good idea to tape record board meetings so that the board has a record of exactly what happened at the meeting in case an appeal is taken to court. In some states, tape recordings are required.

Before the appellant presents proof, the building official should explain to the board why the appeal was brought, why the building department rejected the initial application, and the exact scope of the relief being requested by the appellant. This presentation will not only prepare the board members for the case in front of them, but it will also help a reviewing court to determine the scope of the proceedings, and why the building official initially refused to issue a permit.

The court system relies generally on two types of review: a *de novo* hearing and one based on the record before the administrative tribunal. A *de novo* hearing is one in which the whole hearing is reheld in front of a court. The court disregards the facts collected in front of the administrative tribunal and gathers its own facts. When the court's review is based on the record before the administrative hearing, it will only consider the facts that were in front of the administrative tribunal. In a state where the appeals are by a *de novo* hearing, it is not important for the building official to explain the reasons for his or her denial of the application in the first place. The building official will have an opportunity later in court if the case is appealed. In those states that have only a hearing on the record, however, the building official must have placed into the record the reasons for denial of the application. He or she must also have placed into the record sufficient information from which the court can conclude that the relief being sought by this applicant could not be granted by the board. In other words, the building official must articulately and comprehensibly present during the hearing before the BBCA gives the reason for the denial.

One way to do this is to write a short, but accurate, explanation for the denial of the application. Further, the building official should provide a written recommendation for the BBCA. That recommendation should be backed up with facts regarding why the board should not grant the relief sought. This written recommendation can then be incorporated into the record before the court if an appeal is taken, and the court will have a very good idea of why the application was denied. These writings should be written in plain language.

Most judges are not sufficiently familiar or knowledgeable about the content of building codes.

Granting Remedies

An earlier section of this chapter discussed the ambiguity found in the three model building code organizations regarding the scope of the board's power to grant remedies. The suggested rules of procedure to be adopted by each local board should clear up much of the confusion through adoption of a statement describing the circumstances under which the board would be inclined to grant certain kinds of relief. This statement should be developed by the building official, probably with the assistance of each of the model code organizations.

Administrative Discretion

Most courts will defer to the administrative officials in the interpretation of a building code. This means that the courts will also defer to the decisions of the local BBCA. As long as the BBCA's decision was not made in an arbitrary or capricious manner, the courts will uphold its ruling. A decision would be found arbitrary or capricious if it were made without reliance on either the law or the facts. If the board is at all unsure about the legality of its rulings, it should consult with a municipal attorney.

Rehearings

The ability of a local administrative body to rehear a particular case varies tremendously from state to state. In many states, rehearings are not available. Once the board has made its decision in writing and gives the reasons for its decision, there can be no reconsideration by that board. In those states, the only recourse the appellant has is in a court of law.

A number of other jurisdictions exists, however, which allow rehearings. Normally, there is a thirty- or sixty-day period within which an appeal must be taken to the courts from the BBCA. During that time period, the BBCA may still be in control of the case. If a party has appealed for a rehearing during that time, the board has the power to grant the motion and rehear the entire case. It is best, obviously, to control the number of rehearings permitted by rule or regulation adopted by the board, and it is also best to control the time period within which such an application for a rehearing may be entertained. For example, in Tennessee, an appeal from a local administrative body must be filed within sixty days. Many local administrative boards in Tennessee have, therefore, adopted regulations that permit them to entertain a rehearing application within sixty days from the time the board made its decision. After the sixty days have elapsed, the case is closed for good.

Orders

The IBC requires that every order and decision of a board of building code appeals be reduced to writing, with copies of the decision provided to the building official and to the appellant. This order should specify as precisely as possible the exact reasons upon which the board based its decisions. Many courts have invalidated grants of applications that do not include a specific reason for the approval. These courts generally feel that it is impossible for them to review a decision of the board without knowing the basis of the BBCA's decision.

It is, therefore, advisable for the building official to draft a tentative order setting out the findings and conclusions of the board. The building official should secure approval of the order at the meeting prior to the time the order is actually filed and sent out to interested parties. This is more difficult than it sounds. In many cases, there is no clear consensus among the board members as to why a particular action was taken. The procedure of having the building official specify the grounds in a post-hearing order will help to validate the board's decision in a court of law. The existence of this written order should be sufficient to uphold any challenge that the board abused administrative discretion, even if members did not seem to have a reason for voting in favor of granting a particular application. A well-written administrative order can win many cases that might otherwise be lost. If the case is especially controversial, it would be beneficial for the building official to enlist the aid of an attorney to help with drafting the tentative order.

Conclusion

The suggestions about rules of procedure before boards of building code appeals given in this chapter, and the observations with regard to the boards' powers under the three model building codes, have been laid out in an effort to protect local boards from reversals by courts of law. The BBCA's responsibilities are great. Its decisions affect large numbers of people, particularly in urban areas. The health, safety, and welfare of the community as a whole can be adversely affected by the wrong rulings. With this difficult task in front of them, the board members need every means of support from those people who work with them, including the building official, the staff of the building department, and their legal counsel. By following some of the suggestions made in this chapter, perhaps the board will be able to administer more effectively and enforce the building codes.

Chapter 8 – Constitutional Law

This chapter will discuss some ways in which federal constitutional law impacts the day-to-day operation of a building department.

Topics

Search and Seizure

Substantive Due Process

Retroactive Code Provisions

Equal Protection Clause

Terms

appeal

appellate court

cause of action

discriminatory enforcement

Equal Protection Clause

facial validity

per se

substantive due process

tenant

writ of certiorari

Introduction

The actions of government officials must be permissible under the United States Constitution. Any state or local legislation that allows government officials to act outside of the boundaries set by the Constitution can be challenged in a court of law and found invalid. The building official, like his or her colleagues in other areas of governmental service, must understand the principles of constitutional law that may affect the building official's work. This chapter will discuss some ways in which federal constitutional law impacts the day-to-day work of a building official. It is possible, for example, that what an official considers to be a simple inspection of a building, can be found to be a violation of the Fourth Amendment to the Constitution. The overview of search and seizure law as it relates to building officials will provide some guidelines regarding how, when, or whether or not it is legal to enter and inspect a premises.

This chapter will also define and discuss substantive due process, a concept that requires that any legislation—including the building code—bear some rational relationship to a legitimate public objective. A code that does not bear such a relationship will be vulnerable to legal attacks.

Finally, there will be a brief examination of the Equal Protection Clause of the Fourteenth Amendment of the Constitution and its relationship to code enforcement. Even a building code, which looks on its face to bear a rational relationship to a legitimate public objective, can be challenged if it is being enforced arbitrarily or in a manner that discriminates against a certain group of protected people. This discussion will strive to impress how extremely important it is for anyone enforcing a code to enforce it consistently.

Search and Seizure

The Fourth Amendment to the Constitution generally prohibits the search or seizure of any property unless a warrant has been issued. The amendment guarantees:

> The right of the people to be secure in their persons, houses, papers, and effects, against unreasonable searches and seizures, shall not be violated, and no Warrants shall issue, but upon probable cause, supported by Oath or affirmation, and particularly describing the place to be searched, and the persons or things to be seized.

The United States Supreme Court has held that a search is *per se* unreasonable if it takes place without a warrant having been issued.[1] There are exceptions to this general rule of law, but in the area of building code enforcement, the Court has steadfastly applied that principle since 1967.

For building officials around the country, routine periodic inspections are one of the most effective methods of code enforcement. Because it is the building official who decides whether or not to obtain a search warrant before inspecting a building, it is very important for he or she to understand the constitutional limits. If a building official acts in violation of the Fourth Amendment, that action could result in the exclusion of evidence of code violations that a building department might bring in any court proceeding in order to enforce the code.

Model Code Provisions and Camara

A building official must understand that the building code can never authorize an unconstitutional inspection. In spite of the fact that virtually every housing and building code enacted across this country contains a provision permitting inspections to be carried out in the line of duty, these provisions do not allow the building official to inspect someone's property in a manner that contravenes the mandates of the Constitution. The first and most important case in this field established that principle.

In *Camara v. Municipal Court of the City and County of San Francisco*,[2] the Supreme Court held that: (1) if an occupant—it need not be the owner—of a residential structure does not consent to an inspection, a warrant must be obtained in order to legally gain entry onto the premises; and (2) an occupant who does not consent to an inspection cannot be prosecuted for a violation of a law requiring obedience to the orders of the municipal officials. In *Camara*, a city housing code inspector came to the lessee's apartment complex to perform a "routine annual inspection." Upon arriving, he was told by the owner of the complex that the lessee of the ground floor was using the rear of his leasehold as a personal residence. The inspector determined that the occupancy permit did not allow residential use of that floor and demanded that the lessee consent to an inspection. The lessee refused, claiming that the inspector did not have a search warrant.

A few days later, the inspector returned to the apartment without a warrant and asked again to be permitted entry in order to inspect the ground floor. The inspector cited a provision of the city code:

> Authorized employees of the City departments or City agencies, so far as may be necessary for the performance of their duties, shall, upon presentation of proper credentials, have the right to enter, at reasonable times, any building, structure, or premises in the City to perform any duty imposed upon them by the Municipal code.

Although this provision clearly gave the inspector the right to search Camara's apartment, he nonetheless refused to permit an inspection without a warrant. A short time thereafter, Camara was criminally charged with refusing to permit a lawful inspection and was arrested.

The trial court sided with the city against Camara by finding that the mandatory inspection provision of the San Francisco city code was not contrary to the Fourth Amendment. This decision was affirmed by a California **appellate court**. Camara once again appealed the decision to the Supreme Court, which agreed to hear the case.

The Court began its analysis by stating the fundamental premise that a search of private property is unreasonable unless consented to or authorized by a search warrant. It then addressed each of the city's three arguments in favor of carving out an exception to that rule in the case of municipal health and safety codes.

To the city's first argument that municipal inspections are not a substantial intrusion into personal privacy, the Court acknowledged that "routine inspection of the physical condition of private property is a less hostile intrusion than the typical policeman's search for the fruits and instrumentalities of crime," but felt that any official disruption of the sanctity of the home gave rise to Fourth Amendment protection. Furthermore, inasmuch as the codes are enforced by criminal processes, the property owner possibly faced much more severe intrusions by his refusal to comply. In fact, imprisonment was permitted under one of the code sections.

The Court likewise rejected the city's second argument that municipal health and safety inspections are filled with safeguards that protect occupants against unreasonable searches by inspectors. The Court, however, felt that the practical effect of this argument would be to leave each decision to the discretion of the official in the field: "This is precisely the discretion to invade private property which we have consistently circumscribed by a requirement that a disinterested party warrant the need to search."

The Court also rejected the City's final argument that:

> ...the health and safety of entire urban populations is dependent upon enforcement of minimum fire, housing, and sanitation standards and that the only effective means of enforcing such codes is by routine systematized inspection of all physical structures.

The City reasoned that the decision to inspect an entire municipal geographical area is based on administrative policies concerning such factors as the age and condition of the majority of the structures. According to the City, a judicial magistrate—a neutral officer of the court charged with issuing warrants—would have grave difficulties in assessing such policies. The Court responded by holding that such policies can be accommodated by reducing the burden of obtaining the warrant. That is, when obtaining a warrant for municipal inspections, some lesser standard would apply than if a criminal search were being authorized. The Court indicated that an inspector need not possess probable cause to believe that a structure contains violations of the code in order to obtain a warrant. This conclusion was based on the important governmental interests involved, such as prevention of fires, epidemics, unsightly conditions, and depression of economic values of real property. It further justified its decision not to apply the probable cause requirement to noncriminal residential inspections by noting that routine periodic inspection is the only effective way to ensure compliance.

The Court finished on a practical note by suggesting standards for the issuance of warrants. Probable cause "must exist if reasonable legislative or administrative standards are satisfied with respect to a particular dwelling." For example, a magistrate might look to the passage of time since previous inspections, the nature of the structure, or the condition of the entire area. Specific knowledge of the condition of a particular structure is not necessary. It then concluded that "warrants should normally be sought only after entry is refused unless there has been a citizen complaint or there is other satisfactory reason for securing immediate entry."

Inspectors should always ask for consent before seeking a warrant. Seeking a warrant should be a last resort. When consent cannot be obtained, there may be exceptions to the warrant requirement, but these exceptions should be exercised *cautiously*. They include violations in plain view, emergency situations, heavily regulated businesses, and abandoned buildings, and are described on the next several pages.

Consent

Both before and after *Camara*, the easiest way for a building official to conduct a lawful inspection of a building is to obtain the consent of the proper person. In general, this is not difficult. There are three factors courts examine when looking at the issue of consent: (1) whether the person had authority to consent; (2) the scope of the consent; and (3) whether the consent was voluntary and intelligent. Building officials should make contact with an occupant of the structure, identify themselves, and inquire as to the identity of the occupant and his or her relationship to the property. Frequently, the occupant is either the sole or the joint owner of the property. When this is the case, a building official may enter the property without violating the Constitution simply by obtaining the occupant-owner's consent.

Authority to Consent

Building officials should always try to make sure that the occupant they are speaking with has authority to consent to a search of the premises.

There may be a problem, however, if the occupant is a tenant. If the owner is an absentee landlord, his or her consent may not be obtainable. In general, the owner's permission need not be obtained if the tenant gives his or her consent. As the occupant of a building, house, apartment, or land that is owned by someone else, a **tenant** typically pays an agreed upon price for the right to occupy the property. The specified period of time the tenant may occupy the property as well as other rights and responsibilities of the tenant are usually spelled out in a legal agreement known as a lease.

In the Tennessee case of *Jackson v. Davis*,[3] two co-owners sued, among other defendants, two "building inspection officials" for an alleged Fourth Amendment violation. Specifically, the tenants of the residential structure, fearing that their electrical wiring was faulty, asked for an inspection of the electrical system. After examining the premises, the inspectors found a defective wiring system that made the residence unsafe and "dangerous to human life." After the tenants moved out, the inspectors had the electricity disconnected. The trial court found that the inspector's search of the property was not in violation of the Fourth Amendment. It reasoned that once the premises had been rented to tenants, those tenants were the only people who had an expectation of privacy. This expectation lasts for the duration of the tenant's lease. During that time period, the tenants were the only parties who had a legitimate expectation of privacy in the property. By requesting the inspection of the electrical system, the tenants had given their consent and thereby waived their Fourth Amendment rights.

In spite of this decision, the building official should still exercise caution when entering a building without a warrant. In the *Jackson* case, the court found that the tenants "had the exclusive right of occupancy and use of the building." In some situations, however, a tenant may not have such rights to the entire building. The building code official should always question the occupant in a detailed fashion about his or her rights to the property. Even if it seems clear that the occupant has total control over the entire premises, it is always better to err on the side of caution.

In *Cranwell v. Mesec*,[4] a 1995 Washington case, the court agreed with the *Jackson* decision and extended its holding to allow a tenant to consent to a search of the common areas of an apartment building such as the laundry room, the hallways, and the entryway. *Cranwell* also stated that a tenant's consent to search both his or her private apartment and the common areas of the apartment structure will override any explicit written refusal of consent on the part of the owner.

In spite of the preceding cases, if a tenant claims to possess the rights to the entire building but there are reasonable indications that this claim is untrue, the building official should find the owner or get a warrant. For example, if the occupant claims the right to use an entire structure but certain portions of it are padlocked and the occupant cannot readily produce a key, a reasonable person might have second thoughts about the accuracy of the information. Ordinarily, if the story is not too far-fetched, the building official will be protected from liability because of this reliance on the tenant's misinformation. Because of the time and cost that must be expended when a code official assumes incorrectly that the property is in the entire control of the occupant, however, it is advisable to contact the owner. If that is not possible, the code official should get a warrant if there is any doubt as to the extent of the occupant's control over the building.

There are other kinds of occupants besides those who have rights under a lease. Sometimes, as in the case of unmarried couples, only one of the parties signs the lease agreement. In this situation, the party who has not signed the lease can consent to a search, provided they both have equal access to the property. The US Supreme Court has said that any person with apparent equal right to use or occupy the property may consent to the search of the property.[5] Evidence discovered during the search may be used against either person. It is important to note, however, that the person giving consent must have "equal rights" in the property.

The Supreme Court of the United States held in *Illinois v. Rodriguez*[6] that an officer may rely on a person who acts like he or she has authority to consent to the search, but in fact does not. The key inquiry will be whether or not the officer was reasonable in believing the person had authority. In *Illinois v. Rodriguez*, the defendant's girlfriend reported that she had been assaulted at "their" apartment. She took officers to "their" apartment, letting them in with her key. Officers observed that she had furniture and others items in the apartment that made it appear that she lived there, even though she had in fact moved out. Officers found evidence of drug use. The defendant was arrested and convicted. On appeal, the Supreme Court ruled that if officers reasonably believe the person has authority to consent, the search will be upheld and the evidence admitted. Cotenants have equal rights to the common areas of the rented property. They may give consent to search those common areas. They may not, however, give consent to search the private areas of a cotenant. For example, two college students share a two-bedroom house, one cannot give consent to search the other's bedroom. However, if two college students share a single bedroom, the consenting roommate may allow a search of the portion of the shared room over which the consenting roommate has control. If, while searching the consenting roommate's half of the room and evidence of a crime or building code violation is seen in plain view (this will be discussed in the next section), the building inspector may not seize the evidence, but the building official may make note of it and use that information as the basis for obtaining a warrant to return later. The other party assumes the risk that the cotenant may consent to a search of the common areas.

If a cotenant is present and denies consent to search, even if another cotenant gives consent, the building official cannot search the premises, not even the common areas of the premises. The US Supreme Court established this rule in *Georgia v. Randolph*.[7]

In *Georgia v. Randolph*, police were called out on a domestic dispute. Officers made contact with the defendant's wife. She told the officers that her husband was a cocaine user and that evidence of his cocaine use was inside the home. While she gave consent to search the home, the defendant told the officers they could not search. Over his objection, officers accompanied the wife into their bedroom where a section of a drinking straw with powdery residue was found. The officers retreated from the home to obtain a search warrant. Upon reentry into the home they found further evidence of cocaine use. The defendant was indicted for possession of cocaine and was found guilty. He appealed to the Georgia Supreme Court arguing that his wife did not have authority to consent to search their shared premises, even though she had an equal right to use or occupy the premises.

The Georgia Supreme Court agreed with him, stating that the wife had "no authority, either in law or social practice to override the present and objecting co-tenant's [*sic*] express denial of consent." The State of Georgia appealed to the US Supreme Court. The US Supreme Court, however, affirmed the decision of the Georgia Supreme Court. The Justices said they did not want to discourage the reporting of crime. They said that a cotenant may enter the premises, retrieve the evidence of a crime, and turn it over to waiting officers outside. A cotenant may also provide statements that can be used to obtain a warrant. Further, there may be exigent circumstances that justify a warrantless entry. But when a potential defendant who has a self-interest in objecting (1) is, in fact, "at the door" and (2) objects, the cotenant's consent does not suffice for a reasonable search. If a search in fact takes place, as it did in *Georgia v. Randolph*, the evidence will be suppressed and cannot be used in court.

The Supreme Court then said that if the potential objector is nearby, but "not at the door," and does not take part in the conversation where permission is sought and given, the objector loses out. It is a fine line the court is drawing. So long as there is no evidence of the police or other government official removing the potentially objecting cotenant from the entrance of the premises for the sake of avoiding a possible objection, consent to search from the other cotenant will be valid. For example, in a case of domestic violence, police officers will separate the perpetrator from the victim and take statements from both individuals. The perpetrator may be placed in a police vehicle for safety reasons or even arrested and taken to jail. In these instances, the perpetrator/cotenant is not "at the door" and not part of any conversation where consent to search the premises takes place. Even if the perpetrator/cotenant would have objected to the search, permission to search granted by the victim/cotenant is valid. However, if it can be shown that the only reason police officers removed the perpetrator/cotenant from the scene was to prevent any objection to the search, any subsequent search will be invalid.

It is important to note that neither court used the term husband or wife but rather referred to them as cotenants. That means this rule applies to all cotenant situations. Going back to our roommate example, if both roommates are present when the building official asks for permission to search the premises, when one roommate gives consent and the other objects, do not search the premises without some lawful exception to the search warrant requirement.

There are certain parties that, while they may have some possessory interest in the property, cannot consent to search. Unless the lease provides for it, a landlord may not grant consent to a government official to search a tenant's apartment. In all states, landlords may enter an apartment without consent in the case of an emergency, a water leak, or other similar exigent situation. Most leases contain a provision allowing a landlord to enter the apartment, after giving reasonable notice, to make repairs, inspect fire alarms, show the property to prospective tenants and so on. A landlord may not use these circumstances as a pretext to allow government officials to also enter the apartment.

Hoteliers cannot consent to the search of hotel rooms of lawful guests.[8] The guest has a reasonable expectation of privacy even though hotel staff can enter the room without the guest's permission in order to fulfill their duties. Like a landlord, hotel staff may not allow government officials to enter a guest room under the pretext of performing their normal duties.

In the two examples above, if the landlord or hotel staff are lawfully in the room and observe evidence of a crime, contraband, or some other incriminating evidence, they may report it to the police. The police can then use that information to obtain a search warrant.

Parents and children present on the premises can present unique issues as to who may consent to search what areas of a dwelling. The Fourth Amendment makes no distinction between an adult or child in terms of being free from unreasonable searches and seizures. An expectation of privacy is legitimate and protected if the person has a reasonable expectation of privacy and the expectation is one that society is prepared to recognize as reasonable. Society recognizes that minor children who live with their parents and rely upon them for support have a minimal expectation of privacy in their own rooms. Therefore, parents may consent to a search of their minor child's room. Where the issue becomes clouded is when an adult child, over the age of eighteen, continues to live at home. As an adult, the child is in the position to object to a search of their own room and courts will examine whether their expectation of privacy is reasonable. Courts will look at a multitude of factors to determine whether a parent can consent to the search of an adult child's room.[9] If you are ever faced with this situation where you need to enter an adult child's room and the adult child is present and objecting, it is better to not go in and instead get a search warrant.

But, may children consent to the search of their parent's home? Minor children cannot consent, and a building official should not rely on a minor child's consent to search. While an adult child living at home may consent to the search of their own room, a prudent building official will not go into the home without the parent's consent.

Trespassers may also occupy buildings without a lease, or indeed without any other kind of authority. The building official should nonetheless obtain permission before entering. In this situation, it would also be wise to check with the owner. Although a trespasser possesses very little protection under the law, both the trespasser and the owner may have a reasonable expectation of privacy in some states.

Scope of the Consent

The scope of the search of a premises will be limited by the scope of the consent given. Consent will extend to all areas to which a reasonable person under the circumstances would believe it extends. If a property owner gives consent to search the entire premises, the building official may search the entire premises. However, if the consent is to only check the circuit breaker in the basement laundry room, the building official must limit the search to that area. The scope of consent may be expanded or contracted at any time. Building officials must be cognizant of this fact. Also, consent to search may be withdrawn at any time. Once withdrawn, the building official must immediately leave or face possible claims of trespass.

Voluntary and Intelligent

Finally, the consent of the occupant must be given voluntarily and intelligently. Sometimes building officials may encounter someone who is intoxicated or appears intoxicated. In many situations an intoxicated person may still give consent to search, and any evidence discovered may be admissible. However, the prudent building official will seek permission from another person who is in a condition to consent or he will come back later.

If there is any evidence that the consent to search was coerced, then any evidence discovered may be excluded from court. It is appropriate for the building official to ask the occupant for permission to enter the premises. If permission is refused, an administrative search warrant may be sought. The official should not threaten the owner that the inspector will get a search warrant if permission is denied because that may lead to suppression of the consent search on the basis that the defendant's consent was not given voluntarily. To go any further and threaten the occupant may jeopardize use of the evidence obtained in the search. In particular, if an inspection is refused, to threaten to prosecute more actively known code violations may result in forfeiture of the evidence. The better route is to accept the decision of the occupant courteously. If the inspection is refused, other options should be considered, including the issuance of a warrant. Furthermore, always make sure that the occupant clearly understands that he or she is giving consent. If uncertainty exists concerning whether or not the occupant has consented, the building official must ask again until it is certain that consent has been obtained.

If the owner or occupant will sign a written consent, the building official should obtain one. A written consent is powerful evidence in court if the defendant contests the search.

The Plain View Doctrine

The plain view doctrine is another exception to the Fourth Amendment's warrant requirement. While consent is required to inspect a building or property, this doctrine holds that if an inspector observes a violation while at a location where he or she is legally entitled to be, no violation of the Fourth Amendment results. In other words, if the alleged violation is observable from a place where any member of the public may be, the privacy interest of the owner must be considered insubstantial; therefore, no warrant is required.

This exception is vitally important to the building official. Many violations are visible from the exterior of a building. An official may discover a number of code violations merely by standing on the sidewalk or other public right-of-way and observing the exterior of a structure. This exception also allows the building official to look through windows, provided the inspector is in a place where any member of the public may be, to discover any violations that may be present "within plain view." For example, a home has a glass front door and picture windows on either side of the front door. When standing on the porch, a place where a member of the public may reasonably be, the building inspector can see into the home. Anything seen is "within plain view." "What a person knowingly exposes to the public, even in his own home, office, or other location, is not subject to Fourth Amendment protections. However, what he seeks to preserve as private, even in areas accessible to the public, may in fact be constitutionally protected."[10] So, in our example, if the vertical blinds are down on the picture windows but the inspector can still see through the slats, whatever he now can see through the slats may in fact be constitutionally protected. If the occupant exits the premises and asks the building official to leave, the building official must immediately depart. An inspector should not attempt to inspect the rear of any property under this exception unless it backs up on a public alley.

Let's go back to our previous example where the property owner has given consent to the building official to inspect the circuit breaker in the basement. The building official is now in a place where he is legally entitled to be. While descending the stairs he notices that the steps and the handrail or guardrail are not in compliance. Because he is in a place where he is legally entitled to be, those code violations he sees while on his way to the basement can be cited for correction. If he suspects there may be other violations throughout the property and consent has not been given to search the entire property, he can use those observable code violations as a basis for a warrant to search the remainder of the property.

It is important to remember that the plain view doctrine does not merely extend to what a building official can see on the exterior of a building or from a public place. It also extends to anything the building official can see in a place where he is legally entitled to be.

Frequently, someone who is upset about a problem on his or her neighbor's property will allow the building official to view it from his or her home. Anything the inspector sees may be used as evidence, even if the building official stands at a second story window or in the backyard. Using a ladder to peer over a fence, however, is not permissible. The area surrounding a house, the curtilage, is an area in which a defendant has a reasonable expectation of privacy and is not subject to a general search. Even though the front porch is a place where a member of the public may reasonably be, it is still considered within the curtilage and could be subject to Fourth Amendment protections.[11]

The rules for commercial property are somewhat different. Those portions of a business open to the public are considered public area and are open to visual inspection without the consent of the owner. Anything observed from an airplane flying over this type of land may be used in court. Even hovering 400 feet above a partially open greenhouse was not a violation of a legitimate expectation of privacy.[12] It is important to note that the observations made from the airplane and helicopter were done in a "physically nonintrusive manner."[13]

Courts have addressed the issue of whether an inspector can enhance their own natural abilities to view something in plain view. Using a flashlight or searchlight to assist one's natural vision at night does not make an observation a search.[14] This decision was a state court case and not a unanimous decision, so be sure to check with your attorney on the use of a flashlight in your jurisdiction. Using binoculars and infrared thermal imaging devices to look inside a home are prohibited without a warrant.[15] The use of binoculars to observe "uncovered portions of a residence," or even the curtilage, may be permissible but, again, check with your attorney.[16]

An inspector who finds a violation under the plain view exception must still get a warrant in order to search other areas that are not in plain view and for which the occupant has refused consent. Citing one violation is not grounds to undertake a more thorough inspection—at least not without a warrant. In a case involving a health inspector, the failure of the inspector to secure a warrant before entering a number of units in an apartment complex led the court to reverse a dismissal of a civil rights lawsuit by a lower court. The inspector argued that the units were open and completely unsecured and therefore not reasonably within the owner's expectation of privacy. The court disagreed. Merely because the units were open and unsecured did not necessarily mean that the owner had no privacy interest in them:

> The fact that members of the public could have discovered these alleged violations by affirmatively trespassing upon [the] properties, of course, fails to legitimize an otherwise invalid search, and the fact that portions of the interiors may have been visible to tenants and their guests and invitees does not mean that [the owner] necessarily "threw open" the interiors of his premises to general public scrutiny.[17]

In short, the inspector's failure to recognize and respect the owner's Fourth Amendment rights gave rise to a valid **cause of action** against the inspector for a violation of the owner's civil rights. A cause of action is a set of facts that entitles a party to sustain an action and gives that party the right to seek a judicial remedy on his or her behalf. Out in the field, the building official must guard against the temptation of carrying an inspection further than the law will allow. Code violations that are "in plain view" do not give the building official any authority to explore the premises searching for other violations.

Emergencies

Emergency situations constitute another exception to the Fourth Amendment's general warrant requirement. While the privacy interests of the landowner may be substantial, the nature of an emergency outweighs privacy interests. In the *Jackson* case discussed earlier, a faulty wiring system was unsafe. Although the occupant consented to an inspection, if the building official had reason to believe that an emergency existed, he or she could have lawfully inspected the premises without consent or a warrant; however, the building official should rely on this exception only in very limited circumstances. Even if a building official has a reasonable belief that there is an emergency, consent should still be sought. If, after a building official explains the basis for believing that an emergency exists, consent is still not given, the official should proceed immediately to get a warrant. *Only* if the building official believes that there is an immediate danger to human life should the warrant requirement be ignored. These situations of extreme danger will certainly be few and far between. If in doubt, the warrant should be sought.

In 1978, the Supreme Court first addressed the emergency exception in depth with the case of *Michigan v. Tyler*.[18] In this case, fire and police officials, suspecting arson, conducted a number of searches while fighting a fire in a furniture showroom and after the fire was put out. All inspections were made without a warrant. The last inspection was made almost a full month after the fire had been extinguished. Tyler, the lessee of the property, was arrested and convicted of arson. The conviction was reversed by the highest court of the state of Michigan because of lack of a search warrant, and the case was appealed to the Supreme Court.

The Court broke its analysis down into three parts coinciding with the three phases of the investigation: during the fire itself; the period immediately after the fire; and a time remote from the day of the fire. It found that the fire constituted an emergency situation; therefore, no warrant is needed to enter a premises that is on fire.

> A burning building clearly presents an emergency of sufficient proportions to render warrantless entry "reasonable." Indeed, it would defy reason to suppose that firemen must secure a warrant or consent before entering a burning structure to put out the blaze. And once in a building for this purpose, fire fighters may seize evidence of arson that is in plain view.

The holding in *Camara* is similar, but the burning furniture store in *Tyler* is a graphic illustration of the "emergency" exception to the general rule requiring warrants.

The Court then held that inspections immediately following the fire can be made without a warrant. Fire officials are charged with determining the origins and causes of fire. It makes sense that they must be given a reasonable time after a fire is extinguished to do their job and make those determinations. This rationale also justifies returning to the structure within a short time period if for some reason, such as darkness or smoke, the determination could not be immediately made.

In extraordinary circumstances, a building official could rely on the same reasoning. For example, if upon an external inspection of a structure, severe structural defects were discovered indicating the possibility of immediate collapse, the building official would be within his or her rights to demand an immediate and thorough inspection of the premises. A building official, however, must use this rationale sparingly; the courts will strictly scrutinize any justifications offered for a warrantless inspection. The building official should never employ this rationale as a ruse for an otherwise invalid inspection. Aside from the fact that it is a violation of the landowner's rights, the risk is great that the court will see through the ruse. Not only will that case be lost, but the building official's credibility will be forever suspect in that court.

Finally, the Court in the *Tyler* case addressed inspections made four, seven and almost thirty days after the fire had been extinguished. Warrantless intrusions in this situation were held unconstitutional. The emergency was over; the officials had ample time within which to obtain a search warrant and failure to do so violated the Fourth Amendment. This would also be true in the area of code enforcement. As in the example above, if the building official believes that a structure is dangerous, but not of immediate concern, the failure to obtain a search warrant would be a major mistake.

Michigan v. Tyler is still law. More recently, however, the Court refined one part of its holding with its decision in *Michigan v. Clifford*.[19] Although the facts of the case are somewhat different than in *Tyler*, this case is important for its discussion of the type of warrant that must be sought. Arson inspectors entered the premises without consent or a warrant five hours after a fire had been extinguished. They claimed that they could not enter earlier because the condition of the premises was too dangerous. (This claim had helped the fire inspectors in *Tyler* to return to the scene of the fire without a warrant after it was extinguished.) In *Michigan v. Clifford*, however, the facts did not support such an explanation. Here, a work crew was on the premises during the time the arson inspectors claimed it was too dangerous to return. Furthermore, the Court recognized that the role of an arson investigator is limited to searching for signs of illegal activity. Because the investigator was not there to determine the cause of the fire, but only to look for signs of criminal intent, the Court held that the investigator needed a criminal search warrant and could not rely on an administrative warrant.

Unlike obtaining an administrative search warrant, obtaining a criminal search warrant requires demonstration of probable cause to believe that relevant evidence will be found. The general rule, then, is that the object of the search determines the type of warrant necessary. Of course, if a fire inspector is lawfully on the property with an administrative search warrant and notices evidence of criminal activity in plain view, that evidence can be used in a criminal proceeding against an arson suspect.

Heavily Regulated Businesses

For the building official, this may be the most important exception to the Fourth Amendment's general warrant requirement. As of yet, its parameters are still unclear and have not become much clearer since publication of the 1984 edition of this book. In the future, this exception may dramatically affect the day-to-day operations of building departments. The Supreme Court has frequently observed that in particular types of industries, inspections without warrants are constitutionally acceptable. In determining if a warrantless search of a business is allowed, the court will consider whether the business has a history of being closely regulated, whether there is a substantial interest by the State, whether the regulation serves a substantial interest, whether a warrantless search is necessary and whether the statute has an adequate substitute for a search warrant regarding notice, and the scope of the search. Inspections based on Occupational Safety and Health Administration (OSHA) regulations, however, are not exempt from the warrant requirement.[20]

The Third Circuit Court has held that the construction industry is one such regulated enterprise. In *Frey v. Panza*,[21] a home builder sued the municipality and its building official, alleging violation of his Fourth Amendment rights by their conducting random and warrantless inspections of houses under construction. The builder had no objection to "regularly scheduled inspections," but objected to provisions of the building code that give the building official authority to enter the structure at any reasonable hour to enforce the provisions of the code. The lower court held in favor of the building official; the appellate court affirmed.

In making its decision, the appellate court looked to the nature of the government regulation of the construction industry in the township:

> The record in this case shows that the construction industry in the township in all its phases is subject to detailed and exacting regulation by the municipality. The contractor must file plans before he begins work and he is held to the requirements of the code as his project proceeds. He is aware in advance that the work is subject to inspection without notice. The construction industry has a long history of government supervision and oversight enforced by inspection. And the statute challenged here is directed specifically and exclusively at that one industry. We note also that the ordinance limits inspections to the construction site, at reasonable hours, and for the purposes of enforcing compliance with the building code. These restrictions point toward the reasonableness of the inspection and counsel against requiring an administrative warrant.

This is a strong statement in support of the right of a building official, under the appropriate provisions of the building code, to make impromptu inspections of building sites as construction progresses. This holding, however, is not universally applicable; there are some important qualifications.

First, this is the only case that specifically deals with this issue. The Supreme Court refused to hear this case on **appeal**. This means that the Supreme Court did not issue a **writ of certiorari**. In order to have the United States Supreme Court review a lower court ruling, the Supreme Court must issue a writ of certiorari. This allows the Supreme Court to control the number of cases it hears each year and to choose which cases it wants to hear. If the Supreme Court refuses to issue a writ of certiorari, the result is that a lower court in another circuit is free to reach a different conclusion if it so desires. So far, *Frey* has stood the test of time. No other circuits have ruled against it since it came down in 1980. Because there is very little case law in this area, however, it is somewhat risky to place much confidence on such a limited amount of authority.

Second, the ruling applies only to buildings under construction. Once a certificate of occupancy has been issued, the developer has a right to expect that the construction process is finished and the structure is up to the standards of the building code and other codes. At this point, the developer's privacy interest escalates considerably, and correspondingly the government's interest in enforcing its code provisions should be low. If the building is actually occupied, whether or not it is under the authority of a validly issued certificate, this exception clearly no longer applies and the usual rules surrounding gaining entry discussed earlier in the chapter must be obeyed. When there is unlawful occupancy, the building official should pursue whatever punitive measures are available against the contractor and not against the occupant. The ordinary layperson does not understand the code requirements. The contractor is charged with knowing, understanding, and complying with code provisions and is liable when there is a violation.

Abandoned Buildings

Most building and housing codes provide authority for the demolition of buildings that are in a state of extreme deterioration. To determine whether a specific building is unfit for habitation, an inspection must be made. Usually, the building is uninhabited, and it is impossible to obtain the occupant's permission. The owner may be hard to reach or the building official may not want to ask permission for fear of refusal. It may also be inconvenient to seek a warrant for every such structure in an entire city. Most courts permit a warrantless inspection when the building is abandoned. An official can reasonably believe that those buildings where the doors and windows are open or broken out and the structure is generally in a state of extreme disrepair have been abandoned. When the building is in such a condition, the property owner has a very weak argument that he or she has a strong expectation of privacy therein. At the same time, the government has a strong interest in seeing that nuisances are abated and that dangerous structures are at least secured so that trespassers cannot enter.

Although cases around the country are generally in agreement that there is no constitutional guarantee concerning searches and seizures of abandoned property, it is always best, whenever possible, to obtain a warrant for such an inspection. This is especially true if there is some chance that the property is not abandoned. Furthermore, because different states have different standards for determining whether property has been abandoned, it is crucial to consult with the municipal attorney before entering a building believed to be abandoned.

Warrants

If none of the previous exceptions is applicable to a given case, the building official must obtain a warrant to conduct a property inspection. Fortunately, the procedure for obtaining a warrant is relatively simple, so long as all the requirements have been met.

For a warrant to be issued three requirements must be met: (1) the warrant must be issued by a neutral and detached magistrate; (2) an affidavit must be based on probable cause to believe that a violation of some code provision exists;[22] and (3) the affidavit must describe with particularity the area to be searched or inspected. When drafting the affidavit, seek assistance from your local attorney.

In the affidavit the building official must state the reason to believe there is a code violation. These reasons can include the building official's own observations, information provided by a credible witness, recent photographs, or other reliable information. The building official will state all of the reasons in the affidavit supporting the belief and present it to a magistrate or judge for signature. If the neutral magistrate is convinced, the warrant will be issued.

First, the building official must have probable cause. If the building official has some reason to believe that a violation of some code provision exists in a particular building, then the official may obtain a warrant by explaining his or her reason to a judicial officer. If a neutral magistrate agrees, the warrant will be issued.

In *Camara*, and upheld in later cases, the Supreme Court ruled that a building official need not have the same level of probable cause as a police officer in order to get a warrant. Remember, in the *Camara* case, the Court was dealing with periodic area inspections. In this type of inspection, a greater likelihood exists that a building official will discover code violations. For example, the municipality might adopt regulations that require that if more than two years have elapsed since the most recent inspection and if the building is used for industrial purposes, an inspection must be done. If the adopted regulations are reasonable, the building department may rely on the regulations to conduct inspections. If permission to inspect is refused, the building official need only demonstrate to the magistrate that the administrative guidelines are satisfied to get a warrant. It is not necessary that the building official suspect that each individual building contains a violation. Many of the buildings falling within the guidelines may have no violations at all.

Frequently, inspections are based on citizen complaints, and a warrant is sought for a single building rather than an entire area. When this occurs, the probable cause standard becomes more difficult to show. To obtain a warrant in this situation, a building official should get as much information from the complaining citizen as possible and base the application for a warrant on the citizen's statements. This requires specific proof of a known violation. The building official's reason to believe that a violation exists is based on the statement of the complaining citizen. Ordinarily, this will be sufficient. If the magistrate refuses the warrant, however, the building official may yet obtain it by simply making an inspection of the structure from the public right-of-way. Any violations in plain view may be reported back to the magistrate and serve as a basis for the issuance of a warrant to conduct a more detailed inspection. If violations are apparent on the exterior of the structure, the interior may have others. This is usually sufficient to get a warrant.

In addition to reciting the basis for probable cause, a complaint for an administrative search warrant must describe with particularity the area to be searched (or inspected) and what specifically is to be inspected. The address of the property must be specific enough so there is no mistake regarding the location. If the facts show that a particular ordinance has been violated, the section number should be included. The search warrant should contain the necessary signatures, such as those of the complainant and the judge, along with the date on which it was issued. Because the laws concerning the issuance of administrative search warrants vary from state to state, and even county to county, all building officials should consult their local attorneys when seeking these documents.

It is important to understand what can invalidate a warrant. If a warrant is found to be invalid, then any evidence discovered under the authority of the warrant will be inadmissible in court. The following three things will invalidate a warrant and all three requirements must be met: first, a false statement is contained in the warrant; second, the building official intentionally or recklessly included the false statement; and third, the false statement was material to the finding of probable cause. For example, instead of writing the address as "2414 Timberlane Dr.," the building official wrote "4214 Timberlane Dr." The house number is false; however, the mistake was simply a typo. When examining the warrant for probable cause, the house number had nothing to do with the judge's finding. Therefore, even though the warrant contained a false statement, the warrant will still be valid as the two other requirements have not been met.

Most states have statutes dealing with the issuance of administrative warrants. All building officials must work closely with the municipal attorney to ensure that state requirements are satisfied.

Some jurisdictions have criminalized aspects of their zoning and nuisance ordinances.[23] In those jurisdictions where a building official is seeking a warrant under the criminal provisions of a building code, a criminal warrant must be obtained. The requirements for the issuance of a criminal warrant are the same as that of an administrative warrant.

There are states that have combined the elements of an administrative warrant and a criminal search warrant into one and no longer make a distinction between the two. For example, Rule 40 of the Utah Rules of Criminal Procedure provides that a warrant may be issued for violations of health, safety, building, or animal cruelty laws or ordinances. The rule states:

> In addition to other warrants provided by this rule, a magistrate, upon a showing of probable cause to believe a state, county, or city law or ordinance, has been violated in relation to health, safety, building, or animal cruelty, may issue a warrant for the purpose of obtaining evidence of a violation. A warrant may be obtained from a magistrate upon request of a peace officer or state, county, or municipal health, fire, building, or animal control official only after approval by a prose-

cuting attorney. A search warrant issued under this section shall be directed to any peace officer within the county where the warrant is to be executed, who shall serve the warrant. Other concerned personnel may accompany the officer.

In Utah, the court directs a peace officer to serve the warrant but allows other concerned personnel, such as the building official, to accompany the officer. Check with your local attorney to see if your state has followed this growing trend.

Substantive Due Process

Substantive due process means that any and all legislation enacted by a government must bear some rational relationship to a legitimate governmental function. In other words, the law has to make sense. Basically, when the Supreme Court does not think that a piece of legislation is constitutional, but cannot find anything explicitly written in the Constitution that prohibits this law or regulation, it will interpret particular parts—usually the Fifth and Fourteenth Amendment—of the Constitution so that they apply to the law in question. After they determine that the law deprives people of their rights under the Constitution, legislators are on the alert that this type of law will be found by the courts to be unconstitutional in the future.

For someone who has been the recipient of adverse action by a building official, this is one of the most elemental ways of attacking the building code. For example, whenever a builder either cannot or does not want to meet one of the requirements of a building code, the easiest way to attack the code in court is to say that it does not make any sense under the circumstances of the particular development involved. Ordinarily, the building official may attempt to work out an accommodation with the builder so that an outright confrontation is avoided. Frequently, the builder will appeal the decision of the building official to a Board of Building Code Appeals. If the problem cannot be resolved in the administrative process, then a court battle may ensue.

The builder or developer challenging a provision of a local building code bears a heavy burden. First of all, the courts will ordinarily presume that the law is constitutional. That is, without some compelling proof to the contrary, the court will uphold the legislative enactment. The burden lies on the builder to disprove the rationality of the provision. Second, during the last fifty years or so, the courts have been increasingly reluctant to strike down legislation as being violative of due process unless it lacks any hint of rationality. This restrained judicial posture has evolved due to the principle of separation of powers. The judiciary believes that because the state and local legislative bodies are charged with making the law, they are better equipped to make such decisions.

For example, in *Eggert v. Board of Appeals of the City of Chicago*,[24] an owner of an existing wood-frame structure challenged the constitutionality of a law that prohibited any more than four dwelling units in a building of wood-frame construction. The court upheld the law:

> ...a city may impose reasonable building regulations for the protection of the public health and safety and...the classification adopted in such regulations must be sustained unless it is arbitrary and not reasonably related to the legislative purpose.

The court understood from the record that the purpose of the legislation was to protect against fires and to minimize the damage that would be done if one were to start. This purpose was legitimate and the court felt the means to reach it were reasonable. Because of the unwillingness of the court to interfere with the legislative process, however, most have upheld much legislation in which the connection between the challenged provision seemed to have little or no rational relationship to the stated legislative purpose.

Although there is little likelihood of a court striking down a code on constitutional grounds, this is still an area where the expertise of the building official can be decisive. In most cases, the court itself has no special knowledge in the area of building construction and land development; therefore, the ideas and policies underlying the provisions of the building code must be explained in language that the judge can easily understand. The judge must be led by the building official through the complexities of the code. The simpler the explanation, the more likely that a decision will be made in favor of the local government and the building official.

Remember that all provisions of a building code are subject to attack. Provisions requiring sprinkler systems, architect or engineer signatures, enclosed stairwells, and even certificates of occupancy have been attacked. In most of these cases, the code provisions have been upheld by the courts. One possible reason for the high rate of success in these cases may be that the judiciary can easily be persuaded of the legitimate need for governmental regulation of building codes. Unlike some other regulations, such as zoning and land use planning, the health and safety benefits of regulating the construction of buildings in a municipality are easily observable. Where the benefits of governmental regulation are so direct, the courts are slow to find fault. In general, unless the legislation is obviously unreasonable, it will not be found violative of substantive due process.

Retroactive Code Provisions

While most provisions of a building code operate prospectively, some regulations have a retroactive effect. The same constitutional standard applies; the regulations will stand if they reasonably relate to some legitimate governmental purpose. One of the more interesting cases comes from Bakersfield, California, where the city initiated suit against a property owner for failure to comply with the 1958 edition of the *Uniform Building Code*.[25] The violations included, among other things, an unenclosed interior stairway; improperly enclosed elevator shafts; other shafts and ducts containing combustible materials; inadequate separation between the boiler room and other portions of the building; and sleeping rooms connected to hallways by doors with transoms above, which had to be left open because the hallways were used as a return duct for the air-cooling system.

The defendant hotel owner maintained that the *Uniform Building Code* was unconstitutional as applied to buildings that were constructed prior to its enactment. He argued that to apply the code to his hotel deprived him of substantive due process.

The California Supreme Court disagreed: "It would be an unreasonable limitation on the powers of the city to require that this danger be tolerated *ad infinitum* merely because the hotel did not violate the statutes in effect when it was constructed 36 years ago." While the city may impose stricter standards for newly constructed buildings than for existing buildings, "the constitutional criteria to be applied in either case are whether the expenses necessarily incurred in complying with the statute and the sanctions imposed for noncompliance are reasonable in relation to the public health or safety interest being protected." The court concluded (based on expert testimony adduced at the trial) that the violations rendered the hotel a fire hazard. Naturally, there is an important public purpose in abating the hazard. The possible harm to the public was considerable. In contrast, harm to the property owner in forcing compliance was small. The court apparently believed that the improvements would increase the property value and that the owner would not suffer any great loss. Certainly, this form of harm was preferable to the outright demolition of the building, which had been approved by the court in other cases.

Some jurisdictions will uphold retroactive code provisions only in those circumstances where the building official can prove that a hazard exists. Those courts have held that the mere fact that a particular building is not up to the standards of the latest edition of the building code is an insufficient basis for the retroactive application of its provisions to the building. Usually, the courts will uphold retroactive applications if the building official can offer some reasonable explanation as to why the structure is hazardous. If a court can find any evidence to support the findings of the building official, it will most likely uphold the decision. Courts do not want to put themselves in the position of second-guessing building officials. The courts have no expertise in the area of building construction and so are hesitant to overrule the findings of an expert in the field. If no proof of the hazard can be offered, however, the courts will not hesitate to reverse.

Other courts apply a type of balancing test, especially when it is a fire code that has been revised. Unless the burden of making the changes (in other words, the cost) greatly outweighs the benefits of the improvements, the new code must be followed. Frequently, when new codes are adopted, a compliance schedule is set forth in the ordinance for existing buildings. This gives the owner time to bring the building into compliance to save the added expense.

Many jurisdictions have adopted provisions that apply specifically to existing structures. Thus, there is no doubt that the intent of the municipality is for owners to bring their structures into compliance with the updated code.

In short, the building official should recognize that each provision of any building code is subject to constitutional attack for being unrelated to any legitimate governmental purpose. Because of the very direct benefits of building codes, the courts are reluctant to strike down any provisions, unless the provisions are totally outside the bounds of reason. The role of the building official in such a court challenge is quite important. The building official will be called upon to explain, in common sense, the reasons behind any particular code provision. A clear understanding of the particular provisions of the code is definitely required.

Equal Protection Clause

The Fourteenth Amendment to the Constitution states that "No state shall...deny to any person within its jurisdiction the equal protection of the laws."

The purpose of this clause, known as the **Equal Protection Clause**, is to ensure that state governments do not arbitrarily discriminate in applying their laws to different individuals or groups of people. This clause does not, however, prohibit the state from establishing different classifications and applying different requirements or standards to each. What the clause does require is that there be a reasonable basis for the classification and the different regulation applied to each. The clause also requires that the laws be similarly enforced against all the members of the class.

The Equal Protection Clause affects building code provisions in two ways. First, it requires that the code provisions apply to people and, for that matter, to buildings that are similarly situated in substantially similar ways. For example, all residential occupancies should be subject to the same provisions of the building code. On its face, the code must treat equally structures that are similar. Second, the clause prohibits discriminatory enforcement of the code and may be raised as a defense in any enforcement actions. The defendant may claim that the building official discriminatorily enforces the code and that to allow enforcement against him violates the equal protection clause. These two concepts, facial validity and discriminatory enforcement, are described next.

Facial Validity

Facial validity means that, on its face, the words of a statute are valid; although, in reality, they may not be applicable. The Equal Protection Clause must be applied to any particular statute or ordinance very carefully because almost every law creates different classifications. For example, most building codes distinguish between the uses of structures and may impose greater restrictions on commercial than on residential structures. As long as the restrictions reasonably relate to the classifications so created, there is no constitutional problem.

Distinguishing between uses of property as a means to impose different regulations would clearly pass this test. This is another area where the expertise of the building official is important. In a court challenge, the municipal attorney must rely on the building official's ability to tell the court effectively the reasons for the different classifications. In distinguishing commercial and residential structures, as in the example above, the danger and chance of fire is greater in buildings where large assemblies of people gather. Stricter building regulations are justifiable in such a case.

Discriminatory Enforcement

Discriminatory enforcement does not look to the facial validity of the law, but rather to how that law is applied. When an individual who is found in violation of a building code raises the defense of discriminatory enforcement, he or she is claiming to be impermissibly singled out for enforcement. In the classic case of *Yick Wo v. Hopkins*,[26] a San Francisco ordinance barred the operation of hand laundries in wooden buildings, except by the consent of the Board of Supervisors. In practice, the board denied all applicants of Chinese origin while granting permits to all but one of the non-Chinese applicants. The Court held that although the ordinance has facial validity, it was administered in a discriminatory manner.

A building official must be careful to always apply the code provisions evenhandedly. If a provision is waived for one applicant, it should be waived for all others who have a similar project. The building official has discretion to employ the limited resources of his or her office in a manner believed to be most effective. For instance, certain types of residential structures may be routinely approved without plans, even though the code may require that all structures be approved only after the submission of building plans. The building code may determine that the dangers involved in issuing permits for this type of construction are minimal, that by conducting field inspections during the construction process most defects will be caught, and that the manpower saved in this area may more effectively be utilized in other areas where the dangers are greater. With this power comes a responsibility to enforce the law in a fair and nondiscriminatory manner. The building official should not change that policy in individual cases. The policy decision should be applicable to everyone or to no one at all.

The best way to avoid this kind of problem is to establish written policies for the department. In so doing, everyone in the office will know which provisions to enforce and the approved method of enforcement. The policies should be followed scrupulously.

Another means of protection for the building official arises when prosecution is made based on a citizen's complaint. Generally, if a violation is found at the reported address, the inspector should check other structures in the same vicinity for similar exterior violations. This check need not be comprehensive; a general review of the surrounding neighborhood from the street should be sufficient. If any other violations are found, those too should be prosecuted. Ordinarily, courts will not bar prosecution of one violation because of the alleged existence of others in the neighborhood, but if the inspector has already checked, his or her position in court is much more secure. It should go without saying that special favors in the enforcement process should not be tolerated.

Legal challenges based on discriminatory enforcement are rarely upheld. The courts view prosecution as a discretionary function of the building official. The formulation of a few guidelines, as suggested above, however, will greatly decrease the potential of such challenges. It is important to remember that, although most of these charges are dismissed, the safeguards outlined above will save the municipality from spending much time and money defending itself against charges of discriminatory enforcement.

Conclusion

The most important concept in this chapter is consent. In most cases the owner or occupier of a structure will be willing to submit to an inspection of the property. If not, then the building official must obtain a warrant before entry. To demonstrate probable cause, a building official must be able to produce either an administrative plan detailing the routine nature of the inspection or some indication, such as an affidavit of a neighbor, that a violation exists. Naturally, any violations that are in plain view may be the subject of enforcement action immediately. Violations in plain view may also form a basis for a search warrant. A magistrate may be willing to issue a warrant where a number of violations are plainly visible and there is cause to believe, because of the nature of those violations, that more may exist inside.

Because, in many cases, it is difficult to determine whether a property is abandoned, a building official should always get a warrant before inspecting the property.

An emergency situation is by far the most difficult to assess. On the one hand, failure to enter and inspect may result in the immediate loss of human life or damage to private property. On the other hand, a warrantless inspection may subject the building official to legal liability. Frequently in this situation, time is of the essence, and consultation with an attorney is impossible. If at all in doubt, a building inspector should obtain a warrant. There are few emergencies so severe that a brief period cannot be allotted for that purpose. If the building official truly believes that there is insufficient time to get a warrant, a record should be kept of the reasons for immediate entry. The building official should be as specific as possible in detailing why a warrant was not obtained. As a defense to a suit for damages, the building official's good faith belief in the existence of an emergency should, if at all reasonable, protect whatever actions were taken. The defense of an emergency should never be used as a pretext for a warrantless search because the probability of a lawsuit and damages is far too high.

To the building official who has neither consent nor warrant: DO NOT ENTER!

Chapter 8 Endnotes

1. It is interesting to note that in spite of this rule, the Court does not consider many searches to be "searches" under the Fourth Amendment. A government official may, without warrant search any area of a person's property where that person does not have a *reasonable expectation of privacy*. Two of the increasing number of examples of places where a person does not have a reasonable expectation of privacy are an open field and anything in plain view of the officer—even if that officer views the item by peeking through a screen door. Furthermore, it is not a search for a dog to sniff a bag for drugs, or for anyone to search garbage and then use any incriminating evidence against the defendant. Because of the increasing crime problem in this country, the trend of the Court is to make it easier for government officials to search the property of individuals in order to find evidence of criminal activity.

2. *Camara v. Municipal Court of the City and County of San Francisco*, 387 U.S. 523 (1967).

3. *Jackson v. Davis*, 530 F. Supp. 2 (E.D. Tennessee, 1981).

4. *Cranwell v. Mesec*, 890 P.2d 491 (Wash. 1995).

5. *Frazier v. Cupp*, 394 U.S. 731 (1969).

6. *Illinois v. Rodriguez*, 497 U.S. 177 (1990).

7. *Georgia v. Randolph*, 547 U.S. 103 (2015).

8. *Stoner v. California*, 376 U.S. 483 (1964).

9. In addition to age, courts will look at the living arrangements of the adult child and the parents. Factors that courts will look at include, but are not limited to, whether the child pays rent, whether there is a formal or informal rental agreement, whether the child's room has a separate lock, whether the child has taken steps to exclude others from entering the room, etc.

10. *Katz v. U.S.*, 389 U. S. 347 (1967).

11. *Florida v. Jardines*, 569 U.S. 1 (2013).

12. *Florida v. Riley*, 488 U.S. 445 (1989).

13. *California v. Ciraolo*, 476 U.S. 207 (1986).

14. *State v. Lee*, 633 P.2d 48, Utah (1981).

15. *U.S. v. Taborda*, 635 F.2d 131 (2nd Cir. 1990), *Kyllo v. U.S.*, 533 U.S. 27 (2001).

16. *Lee* at 52.

17. *Wilson v. Health and Hospital Corp. of Marion County*, 620 F.2d 1201, (7th Cir. 1980).

18. *Michigan v. Tyler*, 436 U.S. 499 (1978).

19. *Michigan v. Clifford*, 464 U.S. 287 (1984).

20. *Marshall v. Barlow's Inc.*, 436 U.S. 307 (1978), *Frey v. Panza* 621 F.2d 596 (3rd Cir. 1980).

21. Any code violation will suffice for the affidavit. It does not have to be an emergency or hazardous situation.

22. The City of Orem, Utah. The City of Orem Code, Chapter 11 Nuisances and Chapter 22 Zoning.

23. 29 Ill.2d 591 (1963).

24. *Eggert v. Board of Appeals of the City of Chicago*, 195 N.E. 2d 164 (1964).

25. *Uniform Building Code,* 1958 Edition, International Conference of Building Officials.
26. *Yick Wo v. Hopkins,* 118 U.S. 356 (1886).

Chapter 9 – Related Property Law Concepts

This chapter examines property law concepts, such as zoning ordinances and subdivision regulations.

Topics

Zoning Ordinances
Covenants
Easements
Ownership Transfer
Common Property Rights
Subdivision Regulations

Terms

abut	comprehensive zoning	encumbrance
accessory use	comprehensive zoning plan	exception
adverse possession	condemnation	expressed easement
affirmative covenant	conditional use	fixed property
affirmative easement	conditional use permit	fixtures
agent	covenant	homeowners' association
attachment	curtain wall	implied easement
bearing wall	dedication	inverse condemnation
caveat emptor	deed	lien
caveat venditor	easement	*lis pendens*
certiorari	eminent domain	metes and bounds
chain of title	encroachment	mortgage

Terms (continued)

micro zoning	planned unit development (PUD)	special use permit
negative covenant	plat or plat map	spot zoning
negative easement	plot plan	squatter
nonconforming use	possession	survey
ordinance	public easement	title evaluation
owner in arrears	public property	title search
owner persona	real estate	topography map
partition wall	real property	urban renewal
party wall	restrictive covenant	variance
permissive use	site map	warranty deed
personal property	site plan	zoning plan

Introduction

Many concepts in property law have a direct impact on the duties and functions of the building official. Zoning ordinances, covenants, easements, ownership transfer, common property rights, and subdivision regulations are only a few of the many property law concepts that should be understood. This chapter will introduce the basic doctrines of property law and outline how those doctrines interrelate with the responsibilities of a building official.

Zoning Ordinances

A zoning ordinance is a system of regulating the use and development of property within a municipality or county. When a building code is adopted as an **ordinance** by the municipality, it becomes the law. An ordinance is another name for a local law. Most building officials are familiar with a system of zoning regulations because, in most cases, the building official enforces the zoning regulations along with the building code. Sometimes the building official will be a known zoning official when acting in his or her capacity as the administrator and enforcer of the zoning ordinance.

A **zoning plan** is a document that is adopted by a municipality that provides direction and control of the development of land within its boundaries for present and future uses. Using the final version of a zoning plan is often called **comprehensive zoning**. There is usually a comprehensive zoning map that outlines the various uses into what are commonly called districts. These are broken down further into permitted or conditional uses within the district. For example, in a very simple system of zoning regulation, there might only be three different districts: residential, commercial, and industrial. Obviously, by their very names, the districts indicate what types of land uses are permitted within the boundaries of those districts. In residential districts, only residential uses would be permitted. In commercial districts, only commercial uses would be permitted. If a developer proposes a retail strip center for a parcel of land that is zoned for office/business, the permit would be denied. A **comprehensive zoning plan** is the final version of the zoning plan that is ultimately developed and completed. Comprehensive zoning is merely the outcome of using this plan.

Along with the principle uses indicated by the name of the districts, there are also permitted a number of accessory uses. An **accessory use** is normally defined as any activity that is customarily associated with, as well as appropriate, incidental, and subordinate to, the principal activity. For example, on a residential piece of property, a garage for the storage of an automobile would normally be viewed as accessory to the residential use of the property. A swimming pool located behind a residential home in a residential district would normally be considered as accessory to the residential nature of the land use. If the same swimming pool were located in a commercial district, however, and that was the only use of the particular lot in question and admission prices were charged to people who wanted to swim there, the use of the swimming pool would be considered as commercial. The primary and most positive goal of the zoning ordinance is to regulate the use of land to achieve public benefits or to maximize property value in that state or municipality. Unfortunately, zoning has also been used to exclude minority, low income, and other groups thought undesirable to the municipality.

The zoning ordinance is similar in many ways to the building code. They both permit appeals from the decisions of the administrative officials to an administrative board. The names of these boards vary from jurisdiction to jurisdiction, but because most zoning ordinances are based on state statutes, and most state statutes are based on the Standard State Zoning Enabling Act of 1926, most of the ordinances are very similar. As discussed in Chapter 4, a city or county has no power to zone or regulate unless given such power by the state legislature. If the municipal zoning ordinance in your jurisdiction has not been authorized by state enabling legislation, it is *ultra vires*, and therefore null and void.

In almost all cases, the zoning ordinance will be properly authorized to act through its zoning board. The granting of powers to the zoning board usually has three features. First, the board may consider any appeal from a decision of the zoning official. Second, the board can grant a variance to the restrictions that the ordinance imposes. Third, the board can make special **exceptions** in the ordinance itself. Variances and special exceptions are two distinctly different powers of the board in most jurisdictions and should not be confused. A **variance** is a relaxation of the strict provisions of the ordinance. The board might grant a variance when it would cause undue hardship for the owner of the land to strictly comply with the ordinance.

There are many exceptions and nuances of zoning and land use. One exception, otherwise known as a **conditional use**, is a specified use that is permitted in a designated zoning district but has to meet certain criteria or conditions for location and operation as outlined in the ordinance. These conditions provide controls to prevent the use from having an adverse effect on the surrounding residents. For example, a gas station with a car wash would be a conditional use that involves control over placement of the building, the hours of operation, noise, and landscaping. The permit that would stipulate the conditions and specific controls that have been approved for the conditional use is a **conditional use permit**. These conditions would be monitored by the municipality during construction and after occupancy has been granted. The car wash conditional use permit may state the hours of operation and the setback distance from the abutting residential property.

A day care center is another good example of a special exception. Frequently, day care centers are permitted in residential zone districts if they meet a specific set of restrictions. In granting an application for the right to have a day care center in a residential zone district, the board usually is not granting a variance, which is based on hardship, but is granting a special exception or conditional use permit.

A **nonconforming use** is defined as a structure that complied with zoning ordinances at the time it was built but no longer conforms to regulations due to the adoption, revision, or amendment of a zoning ordinance. For example, a gas station was built in an area that is later zoned as residential. The gas station is a legal nonconforming use and may remain in operation; however, if the owner decides to tear down the gas station and build some other type of business on the same plot of land, he or she will not be able to obtain a permit.

A **special use permit** is another use within a specific zoning district permitted by exception in a zoning ordinance. This type of use is also known by other names (for example, special exception, exceptional use, conditional use, etc.). Unlike simple permitted uses, a special use permit has additional conditions tied to its approval. The construction of a church or hospital may require a special use permit. **Spot zoning,** or **micro zoning**, occurs when a small parcel of land is arbitrarily selected for a zoning classification that is unrelated to the surrounding uses and zoning districts and cannot be justified based on the health, safety, or general welfare of the community. For further information, there exist many comprehensive and easy-to-understand legal treatises in these areas. Further information can be attained from the municipal attorney or by consulting a treatise.

Covenants

A **covenant** is an agreement or promise between two or more people to either do something or to refrain from doing something. A covenant in which there is an agreement between parties to do something is called an **affirmative covenant**, while a covenant in which there is an agreement to refrain from doing something is called a **negative covenant**. Although a covenant can refer to any agreement, promise, or contract, the term currently refers primarily to promises or agreements relating to real estate. A tremendous number of different types of covenants exists. This chapter, however, will limit its discussion to **restrictive covenants**.

Restrictive covenants in the area of property law consist of a provision in the deed to the property in question that limits the use of the property and prohibits certain uses. Such limitation or restriction on the use of a property is called an **encumbrance** and the owner is obligated to observe it. The rationale behind a restrictive covenant is to maintain or enhance the value of land adjacent to the land that has been restricted. Normally, such covenants are attached to a large tract of land by a developer. Before the developer subdivides the property and begins the sale of individual lots to members of the public, he or she will often have a set of restrictive covenants drafted to cover the activities that would be permitted in the area. Unless the developer expressly states to the contrary, restrictive covenants run with the land; that is, when the property owner who first purchased the land from the developer conveys that parcel to a buyer, the covenant becomes applicable to, and enforceable by, that new owner.

In addition, the builders may create a **homeowners' association**. A homeowners' association is a legally recognized entity, sometimes a not for profit corporation, made up of the owners of all the lots, who act together for the common interest pursuant to a declaration of covenants. The declaration of covenants sets forth all the restrictive covenants to be enforced on all of the lots, and the homeowners' association makes sure all members follow the restrictions.

In most cases, however, since these covenants are imposed by developers in subdivisions, the developer has no interest in continuing the restrictive covenant after he or she has sold all of the subdivisions. Therefore, a developer will usually insert an expiration date into the restrictive covenant. In most cases, the restrictive covenant will be lifted after about 25 years. Also, people whose property is affected by the restrictive covenants can agree to continue the covenants for an agreed-upon period of time, depending on their interest in restricting certain uses of the land. In many cases, changes in the conditions of a neighborhood will make a later owner unwilling to continue the covenant.

Because a restrictive covenant is essentially a contract running between property owners to maintain a certain standard of living in a neighborhood, it is enforceable by any of the parties to the contract. Therefore, any property owner who finds that another property owner is in violation of the covenant may sue the latter property owner in order to obtain compliance. If a restrictive covenant is in violation of the law, no one may enforce it. For example, if a covenant exists that restricts the use of property on the basis of race, it cannot be binding upon any property owner.[1] Checking a property's **chain of title**, which is a record of successive conveyances and deed restrictions on a particular parcel of land, will reveal any such restrictions that may exist.

A municipality, not being a party to the covenant, has no standing to bring suit to enforce the covenant; therefore, in most jurisdictions in the United States, the building official cannot enforce restrictive covenants. Of course, if the building code is more restrictive than the restrictive covenant, the building official may enforce the building code to the extent that it is more restrictive. In the case where a restrictive covenant is more restrictive than the building code, the building official may only enforce the building code provision and may not go further to enforce the more restrictive covenant.

Easements

An **easement** is a grant of an interest in land entitling a person to use land possessed by another. This simply means that while the owner of an easement across another person's property does not have a financial interest in possessing it, he does have an interest in using it for some particular purpose. The most notable easements are those for travel, either a pathway or a roadway, leading across the property of one person to the property of another. Easements may be expressed or implied. An **expressed easement** is one that is agreed upon by two parties and set out in a written instrument. An **implied easement**, on the other hand, occurs when one landowner sells a portion of his property to another, the two parcels **abut**, that is, physically touch one another, and that second owner has no other access to his property except to cross the land of another. If the owner whose property is being used as a pathway contests the use of that land in court, he or she will likely lose. In this situation, the courts will imply an easement across the property of the contesting landowner owner so that the second owner may reach his or her property.

An easement may also be affirmative or negative. The owner of an **affirmative easement** has the right to go onto the land of another and perform some type of act. In most cases, the affirmative easement allows a right-of-way to and from one's property. The owner of a **negative easement** may prevent the owner of the land in question from doing something to that land. For example, a person may own a negative easement of a portion of the view of another's land. More specifically, the easement might, for example, begin 20 feet above ground level of the other owner's land. This would prevent the other owner from building any structure that would be taller than 20 feet so that the easement owner's view would not be blocked. Negative easements are very rare. They are only permitted when they are easements for light, air, lateral support, flow of an artificial stream, scenery, or solar power. This may expand in future years.

The presence of easements on a particular parcel of land frequently becomes an issue in the enforcement and administration of building codes. One of the most common types of easement is a public right-of-way, or **public easement**. Most of the time, the public does not actually own the property beneath a highway. A highway is, in the majority of cases, an easement so that the public may travel.

In most jurisdictions, for example, if the public were to abandon a particular highway, the property underlying the highway would not be sold to a new property owner but would naturally revert to the property owners on either side of the highway property. This occurs because the state or local government did not actually own the property underlying the highway easement. It simply had a right to allow the public to pass over this property for so long as the easement was being used for travel purposes. It is important to remember that once the nature of the easement is changed or abandoned, there is no longer a right of the public to travel, and the underlying title to the property reverts back to those persons immediately adjacent to the highway.

Yet, this scenario does not accurately reflect the practice of all states. Some states do purchase the underlying property to a highway. In that situation, the state would always own the land underlying the highway regardless of whether or not the highways were being used for public travel purposes. In order to evaluate the situation regarding any particular highway anywhere in the country, the means by which the property was acquired and the history of the roadway itself must be studied. This can sometimes be a very difficult and tedious task, but it is necessary in order to know who legally owns the property in question. **Public property** is property owned by a state, municipality, or government agency for public purposes. Examples of this are state highways, parks, and government buildings.

A state or municipality can require that a private property owner relinquish some or all of his or her rights in the land so that the public may use it under its power of **eminent domain** as long as it compensates the owner for it. Federal, state, and local governments have the power of eminent domain, which means they have the power to take title of property for public use upon payment of just compensation. The government's use of its power to obtain property in this way is also known as a **condemnation** of the specified land. However, if the government does not compensate the owner, the use of the land will be considered a "taking" and held to be a violation of the Fifth Amendment.[2] In this situation, the property owner may choose to bring an **inverse condemnation** action against the government seeking just compensation for the taking.

The government is not only precluded from taking a private citizen's property without just compensation, but it is also barred from conditioning the grant of a building permit upon the property owner's agreement to allow the general public an easement to cross his or her property, unless it can show that the easement would substantially further governmental purposes related to the permit requirement.[3] Sometimes an owner of land will voluntarily transfer or appropriate land or an easement therein for use by the public. This **dedication** of land may occur by an express statement of the owner's intent or may arise by implication based on the conduct of the owner. For example, a donor may dedicate a street to a municipality for use by the general public. For dedication to be valid, the governmental authority must accept the donation of the property.

Several years ago, the Supreme Court developed a test that can help a municipality determine whether or not its easement requirements constitute a "taking" under the Fifth Amendment. In *Dolan v. City of Tigard*,[4] the court outlined the "rough proportionality" test. Under this test, no precise mathematical calculation is required to determine what constitutes a "taking." Rather, the city or municipality must make some sort of individualized determination that the land required to be dedicated to public or governmental use as set out in the ordinance is related both in nature and extent to the impact of the proposed development. Although this test is more exact than others that have come before it, applying it to particular facts has apparently caused its share of confusion. As of 1995, the Court has refused to refine or to elaborate on the test.[5]

Easements also affect the administration and enforcement of building codes by determining whether a particular lot can be built on. Frequently, a public right-of-way or easement is required to pass in front of the property in order to allow it to be built on. When this requirement arises, there is then a question as to whether a private easement is sufficient. The answer to that question depends on local interpretation. In the more well-developed areas of the country, the answer is generally no. A public right-of-way cannot be replaced by a private right-of-way for the purpose of determining whether a particular lot can be developed. In the more rural areas of this country, where public rights-of-way are rare, a private right-of-way will typically be accepted by local building code administrators in place of a public right-of-way.

Another method for acquiring title to property is to possess it for a specified period of time under specific circumstances. This manner of acquiring property is known as **adverse possession**. If the statutory requirements are met, the "**squatter**" acquires title to the property. An example of this is the Pennsylvania case of *Klos v. Molenda*.[6] The Kloses, who lived next door to the Molendas, put in a driveway, grass, and hedges along the front of their house without surveying the property. Thirty-one years later, when Mr. Molenda died, Mrs. Molenda hired a surveyor to inventory the property. The survey indicated that the property line was 30 inches closer to the Klos house than had been believed. After Mrs. Molenda dug up the grass and hedgerow, which she believed to be on her property, the court ruled that the Kloses had obtained title to the property by adverse possession.

However, the act of occupying a space that belongs to someone else is actually illegal and considered an **encroachment**. Therefore, the original property owner has the right to exclusive **possession** and control of the property as long as the statutory period has not run (typically twenty years). He or she also has the right to allow **permissive use** of the property, allowing someone to come onto the land without considering it a trespass. For example, allowing neighborhood children to take a shortcut through one's yard is a permissive use.

Ownership Transfer

This section will examine the concepts surrounding the transfer of real estate property, often called **real property** or **real estate**. Real property is defined as a parcel of land and any items permanently affixed to it, such as a house, an in-ground pool, or a fence. **Personal property** differs from real property in that it is tangible and moveable, such as a painting or a piece of furniture, and is not part of the real property sold to a real estate buyer. The buyer does, however, acquire **fixtures**, or **fixed property**, along with the purchase of a real property. Fixtures are those things that are permanently attached to the building and intended to become a part of the building. For example, the buyer of a house usually acquires the built-in kitchen cabinets and ceiling light fixtures but does not become the owner of any table lamps. A person who is the owner of any of these types of property is called the *owner persona*.

The Latin term *caveat emptor*, means "let the buyer beware." Thus, it is up to the purchaser to determine the soundness of the building prior to the finalization of the purchase or to hire a professional inspector. Conversely, *caveat venditor* means "let the seller beware." This term is used as a warning to the seller that it is illegal for a seller to fail to disclose known defects about a property. For example, an owner who is aware of underground septic or oil tanks on the property must disclose this to the prospective buyer. In a real estate transaction, a seller or buyer, or both, may choose to hire a real estate agent who usually acts as a broker. An **agent** is a person who is authorized to act on behalf of a principal, whether buyer or seller. Acts of an agent include executing deeds, and signing contracts and other documents on behalf of the principal depending on the grant of authority by the principal to the agent.

Prior to closing, the buyer, the buyer's attorney, and/or the mortgage company will want to make sure the seller actually owns the property and that there are no problems with obtaining a clear title. One way to discover any legal problems relating to a property is to order a **title search** from a title company. Among the items found in a title search report are: the legal description, the exact name of the seller, the county's tax identification number, and a listing of all **liens**, claims, or encumbrances that exist upon the property, including the name of all existing mortgage holders. A **lien** is a claim or encumbrance on a property to secure a debt or obligation.

A title search will also reveal any *lis pendens*, which are legal proceedings that may be pending in court affecting the title or ownership of the property. An example of a *lis pendens* or pending suit is a foreclosure due to nonpayment of the mortgage.

Other legal proceedings involving the property may be revealed by a title search. For example, when a building becomes dilapidated and unsafe, a building official often may petition a court to have the structure demolished. One of the most important parts of the demolition process is to have a title search performed. Anyone with a legal interest in the property will be discovered in the title search process.

To prevent the owner of the property from selling the real estate during litigation involving the owner or the property, the court may be petitioned by a plaintiff (the person who has filed the suit) to issue an **attachment**. Under an attachment, the owner is prevented from disposing of the real estate while the lawsuit is pending.

Once the title search is obtained, the buyer's attorney or the mortgage company, or both, will want to conduct a **title evaluation** to determine whether or not to finance the purchase of the property based on an examination of the title search. Most transfers of ownership of land involve a **mortgage** to finance the purchase. The mortgage is an instrument that gives the lender or seller a lien on the real estate as security for the debt incurred in the purchase of the real estate. Should the purchaser fail to stay current with his or her payment obligations under the mortgage, the purchaser is said to be an **owner in arrears**.

The seller will submit a **survey** (along with construction documents) with a legal description to identify to a purchaser or lender the exact location of a parcel of land. This is a visual rendering or map of the legal measurements of a specific parcel of land that indicates the parcel boundaries. A survey is necessary to determine compliance with local land use restrictions. The boundaries of the parcel may be described in feet and inches, or in **metes and bounds**, a way of measuring by establishing a starting point, such as a designated landmark, distances (metes), and directions (bounds) to encompass the parcel returning to the initial starting point. The survey will be reviewed for any encroachments—for example, a shed built within the required side yard setback.

Before any real estate can be properly developed, a **topography map** or "topo" must be prepared. This will show the developer the contour of the land he or she is about to build on.

There may be two maps prepared: one showing existing conditions, the other the proposed grades. This is very important because in most cases all the roads and utilities must be constructed before any buildings are erected. By knowing the existing grade elevations, the developer can install the roads at the correct elevation. Later, when the builder digs the basement for the building, he or she will know how deep it must go in order for the building to be at the correct height.

The **plat or plat map** not only gives the legal descriptions of the property by lot, street, and block number but also shows all blocks, lots, streets, and the exact dimension of each. It is available for inspection at the building department office and is used to determine exactly what parcel or parcels of land are being transferred to a new owner. This instrument is signed and certified by the preparing surveyor.

A **plot plan** is a survey that shows all utilities on the property as well as the setbacks for the proposed structure, and it is necessary for the performance of a proper plan review. A plot plan should always be included in any permit application. The building official should use the plot plan submitted to do his or her initial review and then an additional as-built plot plan before a final certificate of occupancy is issued to ensure compliance with the original plot plan.

After a survey is obtained, especially as it relates to large or complex projects, a **site map** is prepared. This is a map of the site indicating proposed construction and associated building and site work needed to prepare the parcel for construction. It is sometimes referred to as a **site plan**.

Upon completion of the sale, the buyer will receive a **deed** from the seller, which is a written legal document by which title to the property is passed. The best type of deed to obtain is a **warranty deed**. Not only does it convey ownership in the property, it promises that the buyer has good title to the property; that is, it is free from all defects in title (such as liens and encumbrances).

For commercial projects, the first page reviewed should be the **site map**. The site map will show existing conditions of the site. In many instances, proposed construction and associated buildings as well as proposed site work will be included on this map. The site map is sometimes referred to as the site plan.

Common Property Rights

There are some property rights that are shared by one or more owners and/or occupants. These are called common property rights. A **party wall** is one type of common property right. It is a structural dividing wall between two adjoining buildings or units. It is built along the common property line so that one-half of the wall lies on each property. Each property owner has a property right interest in the wall. It also functions as a firewall between the two buildings—for example, a tenant of a commercial property in a strip mall sharing a party wall with his or her neighboring tenant.

A **partition wall** is built to separate interior spaces, such as a storage area from a store. It may also separate two tenant sites from each other, such as at a town home. The code may require the partition wall to be a fire partition. However, it cannot be a **bearing wall**; it is only used for separation, not to support floors, partitions, or roof loads.

A **curtain wall** is an architectural term describing the enclosing wall or skin of a building that uniformly covers the exterior facade from floor to floor for all or a large portion of the elevation. Typically, a curtain wall is nonbearing and made of glass or other materials in large panels that are manufactured. A glass curtain wall facade of bronze-tinted glazing on three sides of a building is an example of this.

Owners of units in a condominium development may jointly own the common areas of the property. Frequently, each owner receives an undivided interest in such areas when he or she purchases the unit.

Subdivision Regulations

Subdivision regulations were developed primarily during the 1920s and 1930s as a means of controlling the future development and expansion of urban and municipal properties. Long-range urban planners began to discover during this time that the manner in which available open space was developed by private construction firms was crucial to the way the city developed overall. They realized that some control over this development pattern had to be exerted by the municipality to prevent unbridled growth and haphazard design. Consequently, subdivision authority was enacted to control this feature of municipal and urban government.

Like zoning ordinances, subdivision regulations are enacted pursuant to an enabling act. Unlike zoning ordinances, which regulate land use, subdivision regulations lay out conditions for approval of a subdivision plan. Most systems across the country work by forcing a developer, who intends to sell properties, to submit a subdivision plan to a planning commission. The planning commission reviews the subdivision plan, looking especially at: the provision for utilities, the construction of roadways through the project, the size of the lots, and any other features that may have an impact on the public—such as the dedication of a certain amount of land by the developer for a public park or school site; the commission then approves or disapproves the design. If the planning commission approves of the project, the builder may then file the "plat" in the registrar's office for his or her county and may sell the properties by reference to that plat. If the planning commission does not give its approval, the properties may not be sold as subdivided on the plan presented to the planning commission.

A **planned unit development** or **PUD** is a specialized type of subdivision that describes a large-scale real estate development project. A PUD specifies the minimum contiguous acreage and the ratios for the development of residential, commercial, and public use areas. It is unique in that it is a planned community that is developed as a single entity. Local governments often enact zoning ordinances regulating PUDs. The document that establishes a PUD is very complicated because it is so comprehensive, dealing with covenants, conditions and restrictions that regulate the use of common areas, assessments, voting rights, architectural rules and regulations, and other matters.

The building official must be aware of the existence of these plats because building permits are frequently issued for the lots very soon after the planning commission approves the plat. It is not absolutely necessary, but it is recommended that the building official review the plats prior to the issuance of a building permit. Frequently, there are separate conditions imposed on the plat that are not a matter of general building code law, but might nonetheless affect the issuance of the permit. By checking the plat before issuing the permit, the building official can ensure that all proper conditions have been met.

The enforcement of the conditions and restrictions placed on subdivision plats is generally not a matter of concern for the building official. By observing and reporting violations, however, building officials can be quite helpful to the planning commission. The planning commission and the building department must work together in order to enforce effectively and adequately the provisions of the subdivision regulations and the building code. Unfortunately, it is often the case that when these two functions are separated into two separate departments, a rivalry arises. This rivalry makes it difficult for the two groups to work efficiently together and, more dangerously, leaves some problems undetected that could and should be caught. This type of competition between municipal departments needs to be curbed and discouraged wherever it is observed.

Urban renewal is another area involving comprehensive plans. Urban renewal is generally associated with old communities that are essentially already built up. The areas are usually experiencing a decline or abandonment, or both. This includes homes becoming dilapidated and businesses moving out and leaving vacant buildings. Most often old and failing infrastructures, such as roads, sewer, and water, are associated with these areas. Urban renewal takes place when a community puts into place a plan to revitalize these depressed areas. Government funding and tax incentives often are used to encourage redevelopment of the area. In a nutshell, an old depressed area becomes new and vibrant again.

Conclusion

Numerous and varied types of regulations and laws have an impact on the function and duty of the building official. It is very difficult to keep up with not only those that already have been adopted, such as subdivision regulations and zoning ordinances but it's even more difficult to keep abreast of other regulations that are new and being tested for the first time. Regulations such as solar access ordinances and storm water management ordinances are very new, and, as yet, untried for any length of time. It is important, however, that the building official make an attempt to ensure that before a building permit is issued all the applicable regulations have been met and that all governmental entities, which are concerned with the various aspects of land use development, have been satisfied.

Chapter 9 Endnotes

1. *Barrows v. Jackson*, 346 U.S. 249 (1953); *Evans v. Newton*, U.S. 296 (1966).

2. The Taking Clause of the Fifth Amendment reads: "*...nor shall private property be taken for public use, without just compensation.*" Although the Fifth Amendment only expressly applies to the federal government, the courts have held it applicable to state and local governments under the Due Process Clause of the Fourteenth Amendment.

3. *Nollan v. California Coastal Commission*, 483 U.S. 825 (1987).

4. *Dolan v. City of Tigard*, 114 S. Ct. 2309 (1944).

5. *Parking Association of Georgia v. City of Atlanta*, 115 S. Ct. 2268 (1955), *cert. denied*. Note: The Parking Association of Georgia wanted the U. S. Supreme Court to review the Georgia Supreme Court's ruling in their case so they filed a petition for a *writ of **certiorari**. Certiorari* is simply a judicial review of a lower court ruling. Most cases cannot be appealed to the US Supreme Court as a matter of right; therefore, petitioners must petition the Court to hear their case via a *writ of certiorari*. By denying *certiorari*, the Supreme Court is refusing to hear the case. There are many reasons for not hearing a case. Because the Court can only hear a limited amount of cases, it has to turn down hundreds of petitions for *certiorari* a year. By not taking this case, however, the Court was likely implying that it felt that the "rough proportionality" test should remain good law. If it turns out that hundreds of cities are having the same problems that Atlanta did when applying the test, or if cities apply this test in vastly different ways, the Court will most likely address these problems in later years.

6. *Klos v. Molenda*, 513 A.2nd 490 (1986).

Chapter 10 – Liability for Intentional Wrongdoing

This chapter discusses intentional torts, or civil wrongs, relevant to the building code official. Legal theories and defenses are also examined.

Topics

Distinction between Governmental and Official Liability

Intentional Torts

Malicious Prosecution

Absolute Immunity

Wrongful Civil Proceedings

Abuse of Process

False Imprisonment

Intentional Infliction of Emotional Distress

Assault and Battery

Trespass

Terms

absolute immunity	false imprisonment	plaintiff
abuse of process	immunity	preponderance of the evidence
acquit	intentional tort	punitive damages
assault	license	tort
attractive nuisance doctrine	malice	tort-feasor
battery	malicious prosecution	tort liability
defense	negligence	trespass
exemplary damages	open curtilage	

Introduction

Building code officials, and indeed all Americans, have in recent years become more and more afraid of **tort liability**. Very broadly defined, a **tort** is a civil wrong, other than breach of contract, for which the court will force the wrongdoer to pay damages. A person who is at fault or causes the damage or injury bears the liability of tort. This chapter will focus on various types of intentional torts relevant to the building code official. This chapter, along with Chapters 11 and 12, should help to convince building officials that the possibility of a successful lawsuit against them is not as high as many think. Although the media makes it seem as if people with very weak cases are winning huge amounts of money in damages on a daily basis, this is not accurate. To the contrary, suits against building officials are rarely successful.

An everyday occurrence, such as a judicial enforcement of the code, can give rise to lawsuits for malicious prosecution, false imprisonment, and intentional infliction of emotional distress. These legal theories will be analyzed and separated into their various elements. Most importantly, this chapter will review the defenses the building official and his or her attorney might raise if sued for one of these torts. Familiarity with these torts should help building officials avoid committing them and, therefore, alleviate any fears of being sued.

Distinction between Governmental and Official Liability

It is important to be aware of the distinction between the building official and the local government by whom he or she is employed. The building official and the local government are two separate and distinct legal entities. A building official is a person, whereas a municipality is a corporation. Because these are two separate entities, each may be sued. This chapter will discuss some legal theories that will only be applicable to an individual, while other theories discussed will only apply to the municipality. While this book emphasizes the liability of the building official, it is still important to know about municipal liability, as it can affect the way that building officials perform their jobs.

Most of the intentional torts that will be explained in this chapter cannot be brought against the government itself. For reasons to be discussed more comprehensively in Chapter 12, the government is usually immune from those types of legal theories. Therefore, because the government itself cannot be sued, the attorney for the injured party, known as the **plaintiff**, will often look to name as defendant an agent of the government. The building official can be considered an agent of the government. Because the government cannot be sued, however, the building official cannot be sued as an agent of the government. Therefore, the plaintiff's attorney will bring a suit against the building official in his or her individual capacity. If the plaintiff prevails, the building official will be liable for damages. This seems extremely unfair, especially if the building official has committed a tort under the supervision or at the behest of the municipality.

In most cases, the government will provide **defense** counsel and will indemnify the employee if a judgment is obtained by the injured party. It would be difficult for a municipal employer to obtain employees if it did not indemnify them. To be safe, however, the building official should check any employment contract he or she may have signed. Indemnification does not give the building official free reign to commit tortious conduct. In many situations, if the government determines that the action taken by the building official is not only legally inappropriate but also in violation of the government's rules and regulations, it may refuse to represent or indemnify that official. Building officials might want to look at their employment contracts to determine whether the language discussing indemnification has any express qualifications or limitations.

Intentional Torts

Tortious or wrongful conduct can be either intentional or negligent. **Intentional torts**, as the name implies, involve conduct that the actor intended to occur. **Negligence**, on the other hand, involves conduct that was not intended to cause harm or injury but, nonetheless, did, and that conduct also breaches some duty of care imposed by the law. A person may be liable for an injury if he or she does not act with the same level of care a reasonable person would use under similar circumstances. The failure to use such care as a reasonable person would use under similar circumstances may lead to liability when an injury is involved. Therefore, a battery is considered an intentional tort, while an automobile accident, in most cases, would be considered a negligent tort. (Battery is defined later in this chapter.)

In some situations it is not very easy to determine whether certain conduct is intentional or negligent. To some extent, all actions are intentional. The relevant question focuses on whether the results were intended. Using the automobile example, if the driver of a car speeds and in so doing injures a pedestrian, that is negligence. Although the driver intended to speed, he did not intend to hit and injure the pedestrian. If the same driver speeds for the purpose of striking and injuring the pedestrian, however, the result was intended and a more serious form of liability—possibly criminal—applies.

It is important to distinguish between intentional and negligent tortious conduct because many state liability statutes, indemnification legislation, and insurance policies cover only negligent and not intentional wrongdoing.

Malicious Prosecution

The tort of **malicious prosecution** concerns the wrongful institution of criminal proceedings by one private citizen against another, resulting in damages. In recent years, however, most American courts now impose liability for malicious civil claims brought without probable cause. Because of the nature of the job, building officials are more vulnerable to these suits than others. It is not unusual for the building official to have recurring difficulties with particular individuals. Many of the people against whom the building official must bring enforcement actions might feel that he or she is bringing the enforcement proceedings solely for the purpose of harassment rather than out of any desire to see that the building code is properly obeyed. The courts recognize the seriousness of bringing a false charge. Regarding false criminal charges, there is a likelihood that the victim of the charge may have to spend time in jail. Both types of false charges involve a loss of time, money, and reputation to the victim. Because of these serious consequences, a defendant to a malicious prosecution may be found liable for high dollar amount damages. It is, therefore, important for the building official to understand what a plaintiff will need to prove in order to prevail on a claim of malicious prosecution.

There are four elements to a malicious prosecution lawsuit. The plaintiff has the responsibility of proving each and every one of these four elements. In most states, this burden of proof must be carried by a **preponderance of the evidence**. That is, the fact finder, be it a judge or jury, must conclude that it is more likely than not for each of the four elements to exist. For a successful defense, the building official must show that the plaintiff failed to carry at least one of these elements. Even if he or she cannot show that the plaintiff failed to prove an element, the building official might still have a defense for his or her actions. By closely examining the tort of malicious prosecution, the building official will see how difficult it is for a plaintiff to maintain such an action.

The elements of a malicious prosecution suit are: (1) the institution of criminal, civil, or administrative proceedings; (2) termination of the proceeding in favor of the accused; (3) absence of probable cause for the proceeding; and (4) malice or a primary purpose other than that of bringing an offender to justice. To illustrate, a building contractor is taken to court because a building she is renovating does not have the required level of fire protection in the elevator shaft. The judge **acquitted** the contractor who was able to prove that the building official had no reason to believe that the shaft was underprotected, and also proved that the building official never liked the contractor, and therefore acted maliciously.

Malicious prosecution lawsuits normally result when several unsuccessful enforcement actions are brought against the same person. If that person is repeatedly found innocent of code violations, that person will likely feel that "codes" or the "government" are out to get him or her, and will most likely react by bringing suit.

1. The institution of criminal, civil, or administrative proceedings

The first element of this legal theory must be strictly scrutinized. Some states do not allow malicious prosecution cases except for those arising out of criminal prosecutions. There are also some states that view enforcement of local governmental regulations as a civil activity. Building officials who work in those states cannot be sued for the tort of malicious prosecution. At this point, however, most states allow a suit to be brought for malicious prosecution for any kind of proceeding, whether criminal or civil. Some states even allow these kinds of suits where the proceeding was administrative. It is important to know how your state rules because many building code enforcement actions begin in front of the Board of Building Code Appeals or some other similar administrative board.

The person instituting the code enforcement proceeding will be the person who will ultimately be named as a defendant in any court suit. Also named will be the code official who signs the original warrant, citation, complaint, administrative notice, or other instrument. Additionally, the plaintiff may attempt to bring others in as defendants, as well. For example, there may be other persons in the department who may be responsible for reviewing inspection reports and making judgments regarding the institution of enforcement proceedings. A failure to check the report or to exercise good judgment in instituting such proceedings may result in their being joined as a defendant in the suit. Oftentimes, the plaintiff will also allege a civil conspiracy; this serves to increase the number of potential defendants. Under a civil conspiracy theory, anyone who helped plan or assist in the tort may thereby be rendered liable.

The private citizen who made a complaint to the building code department might also be named as a defendant in a malicious prosecution suit. Although a private citizen relies on the building official to do a full-fledged inspection, which would lead to an enforcement action, the citizen's complaint is itself the basis for the initiation of the process, making the citizen a proper defendant. If the defendant merely states what he or she believes, however, leaving the decision to prosecute entirely to the uncontrolled discretion of the building official, or if the building official makes an independent investigation or prosecutes for an offense other than the one charged by the citizen, the latter is not regarded as having instigated the proceeding. Only when it is found that the citizen's persuasion was the determining factor in inducing the building official's decision, or that the citizen gave the inspectors information that was known to be false and so unduly influenced the authorities, may the citizen be held liable.

This poses a problem. If a building official relies on the statement of a private citizen to begin enforcement proceedings without performing an independent investigation, the official may be a codefendant with that citizen in a malicious prosecution suit. The citizen may have decided to report the violation with the understanding that the building official would do a thorough investigation and only bring an enforcement action if he or she found a violation. To avoid placing the code official and a well-meaning citizen at risk of being sued, the building official should always perform a complete and independent investigation upon receiving a citizen's complaint. If a building official conducts a good investigation and makes detailed notes of his or her findings, it will be almost impossible for the employee to be found liable for damages in a malicious prosecution suit. For further protection, the building official should get the citizen to sign the complaint. This would show a court the basis for the official's investigation. A citizen, who is warned ahead of time that his or her complaint might later be used as evidence in a malicious prosecution suit, will be less likely to file a complaint that is not based in fact.

2. Termination of the proceeding in favor of the accused

The second element of this legal theory is the termination of the proceeding in favor of the party accused. In other words, the alleged code offender must be acquitted by a court or an administrative tribunal in order to have a potentially successful lawsuit. Even if the building department drops the charges or voluntarily dismisses the case, the accused may still satisfy this element. It is possible, however, to be free of liability under malicious prosecution if the code violation is dismissed only on the condition that the accused not file suit against the building official. The municipal attorney should be consulted before speaking to the accused. An attorney can draft an agreement that will hold up in court. In most cases, however, the accused will have no interest in filing a suit for malicious prosecution if the charges are dropped before they reach a court or an administrative agency's tribunal.

If the accused corrects the violation before the court date but refuses to agree not to sue for malicious prosecution, the building official has three other options to follow in order to avoid suit. First, the official could explain the situation to the judge and ask that the defendant be found guilty and that the punishment of a fine be suspended. It then appears on the record that the prosecution did not terminate favorably to the accused. On the date of the charge, the record will reflect that there did indeed exist a violation. Once this is established, no malicious prosecution lawsuit can be brought. The second option would be to ask the judge to dismiss the case but have the record reflect that the dismissal is based on prior compliance by the accused and on a joint stipulation that on the date charged, the accused was in violation of the building code section charged in the warrant, complaint, or other relevant document. The third and final option would be to obtain a release from the accused, relieving the building code department of any liability of any nature whatsoever.

3. Absence of probable cause

The third element of this legal theory is the absence of probable cause. The plaintiff has the burden of demonstrating that the building official had absolutely no probable cause to bring an enforcement action. This is very difficult for any plaintiff to do, and this is usually where the malicious prosecution charge fails. To prevail, all the building official must do in his or her defense is to demonstrate that he or she had probable cause. Although all four of the elements are important, the presence or absence of probable cause will likely decide the case.

A building official should never initiate legal proceedings without probable cause. (Remember from Chapter 8 that probable cause is defined as a reasonable ground for belief in the guilt of the party charged.) If there is some reason to believe that a violation has taken place, the defendant may be prosecuted without fearing a suit for malicious prosecution.

If the building official made a first-hand observation of the violation, there is probable cause to bring an enforcement action. As previously mentioned, testimony of citizen witnesses should not be entirely trusted. The building official should remember to take photographs and keep accurate records. Also, any photos and reports should be properly dated.

In some ways, probable cause is the easiest element against which to defend. If proper documentation is made of everything the official does in his or her capacity as building official, future legal trouble will be avoided. Another way to demonstrate probable cause is to get the advice of an attorney before bringing an enforcement action. Many state courts have held that the advice of an attorney is an absolute defense regarding the element of probable cause. In most states, an attorney's advice, whether right or wrong, is an absolute shield, provided that the building official fully discloses to the attorney all the known facts.

The court will only allow this defense if the building official was completely candid about the facts of the case when he or she consulted with an attorney.

Many building departments have attorneys assigned to them for just this purpose. The attorney must approve every case prior to the initiation of prosecution. The best way to take advantage of this resource is to insist that the attorney review the entire file, including any photographs that may be available. The attorney should also be requested to confer with the witnesses for the prosecution. Finally, a standard form should be developed for the attorney's signature approving prosecution. Alternatively, the attorney's initials on the file or the document that initiated the prosecution should suffice. If the building department does not have its own attorney, the building official may still take advantage of this defense by obtaining outside legal advice in those cases where he or she feels the judgment call is too close.

The key to showing probable cause is documentation. Everyone in a building department should be encouraged to write things down. Discretion should always be exercised, but it is generally better to err on the side of being too detailed than on the side of not being detailed enough. Many little details, which might be important to the attorneys and the judge, may not seem important to a building official.

Luckily for the defendant, the existence of probable cause is usually determined by a judge and not a jury. Judges will have a fairly uniform view as to what constitutes probable cause, whereas juries will differ dramatically. Not only will a judge's rulings be fairly consistent with each other, but a judge is trained to be more impartial than a jury and, therefore, less likely to let his or her personal feelings color the ruling.

4. Malice

The final element in a malicious prosecution case is **malice**. The plaintiff must prove that the building official acted maliciously. Unfortunately, that word is difficult to define in this context. It does not necessarily mean that the code official was motivated by hatred, spite, or ill will. When the plaintiff can show that the defendant's primary purpose in bringing an enforcement action was something other than bringing the alleged code offender to justice, malice will be found. The plaintiff may then be awarded **punitive damages**. Punitive damages can be awarded to the plaintiff who proves malice on the part of the defendant. Punitive damages are intended to punish the wrongdoer. They are often awarded as **exemplary damages**, meaning they are given in addition to damages that compensate a defendant for a monetary loss, to make an example of the wrongdoer. For example, malice will be established if the plaintiff shows that the defendant brought the enforcement action as a way to extort money from the plaintiff.

Some courts allow the presence of malice to be inferred from the absence of probable cause, the rationale being that if there was no reasonable ground upon which to believe the alleged code offender is guilty, there is no reason for the official to file an enforcement action. It is, therefore, justifiable to infer some malice on the part of the building official. If there was no legitimate reason to bring the action, then the charges were brought illegitimately. Unlike probable cause, the question of malice is to be determined by the jury.

An example

Joe Code Offender, owner of some dilapidated buildings on the east side of town, has started to do some rehabilitation work on one of his tenements. He thinks he can resell and take advantage of a historic preservation trend in the neighborhood. Unfortunately, he has neglected to obtain a building permit as required by the local building code.

The local building official, Mr. Code Enforcer, dispatches his trusty aide, Mr. Deputy Code. Mr. Deputy Code stops by the work site and informs Joe of his transgression. Joe, in a very solemn and repentant manner, promises to be at the building department the next day to get the required permit. Five days go by and Mr. Deputy Code has been so busy that he has temporarily forgotten the problem. Joe has not appeared at the department. No permit has been applied for or issued. On the fifth day, Mr. Code Enforcer asks Mr. Deputy Code what has transpired in Joe's case. Mr. Deputy Code says he will get out to the work site again that same day. He waits a day before going to the property. Joe asks for more time. Mr. Deputy Code refuses and posts a stop work order.

One week later, Mr. Code Enforcer happens to be driving by and sees ongoing construction despite the order. Once again, Mr. Deputy Code visits the scene, and this time he cannot find Joe. He writes a citation in accordance with local practice, dated that day, charging Joe Code Offender with a violation of the local building code.

Because Joe is not on the scene, Mr. Code Enforcer has another man in the department serve the citation at Joe's construction office. Unfortunately for Joe, three clients, who were waiting in his office when he is served, leave when they see he has been charged with a violation. Joe protests to the person serving the citation, "I sold that property! I pulled my men out of there last week!"

"Great argument," thinks the server, but in reply he says only, "I don't know anything about it. All I know is I'm supposed to deliver this to you." Joe becomes angry and demands that the man who served him call his boss, but the man refuses and leaves.

On the appointed date, Joe shows up in court with three attorneys. He easily shows that he has sold the property exactly five days before the date on the citation. Furthermore, he parades witnesses in front of the judge to prove that his men were not working on the building since the posting of the stop-work order. The judge dismisses the case and mumbles something about getting the wrong man. Two weeks later, Joe Code Offender files a malicious prosecution lawsuit against Mr. Deputy Code and Mr. Code Enforcer.

To determine the outcome, examine each of the four elements. Was prosecution initiated? Yes. Did it terminate favorably to the plaintiff, Joe Code Offender? Yes. Was there an absence of probable cause? This element is tricky. If he had not sold the property, the building officials would have had probable cause. Their failure to look at the ownership of the building before serving Joe, however, makes it look as if they assumed he was the owner of the property and was in violation of the code. Was there malice? This is difficult and would turn on the jury selected. There is a chance that a jury would find malice, albeit for the wrong reasons. The server's rudeness and the loss of three customers would not set well with the jurors, and they might look for a way to compensate Joe. Also, the jury might look to all of the facts to determine that Joe was, at one point, a blatant code violator.

It is undisputed that Mr. Deputy Code made a number of mistakes in this case. He did not check ownership; he did not check who was working at the site; and he put the wrong date on the citation, which is a large error. For some reason, many code personnel believe that the current date must be the one on the citation. This is not true. If the violation was observed on March 5 but not written up until March 15, the violation should be charged on the date it was actually observed. If the observation was over thirty days from the date it is written up, another inspection should be undertaken. The citation should not be post-dated. Rather, it should be made clear that on March 15 the department charged Joe Code Offender with a violation that occurred on March 5. It will save a lot of frustration later.

The building official should remember that just because a ticket was not issued on the date of the violation, a charge may still be filed anytime within the statute of limitations. If Mr. Code Enforcer had filed multiple charges against Joe, one charge may have been dismissed, but the others would have been valid, thereby lessening the chance of a civil suit. The prosecutor can always dismiss various charges as part of a plea agreement, so the building official should file all applicable charges. If Joe sold the building with existing code violations, he may have committed new offenses. This fact could be used as a bargaining chip in a civil case.

Mr. Deputy Code should have issued a ticket to the persons committing the offense on the site. If he had done so, he might have found out the contractor had changed and saved himself a lot of grief. He should have known that all responsible persons may be charged for a violation.

Absolute Immunity

In at least the state of California, public officials, including building officials, are absolutely immune from malicious prosecution cases. This was true at common law in California—that is, before the legislature acted in 1963. The principle is now codified in the California Tort Claims Act of 1963. **Absolute immunity** is a form of legal **immunity**, or protection, afforded government officials. Absolute immunity protects them from civil lawsuits so long as they are acting within the scope of their duties. In California common law, the belief was that building officials should be treated as quasi-judicial officers, and as such should be absolutely immune from liability from any action he or she takes, so long as it is in the scope of his or her employment.

The California Tort Claims Act specifically declares that:

> A public employee is not liable for injury caused by his instituting or prosecuting any judicial or administrative proceeding within the scope of his employment, even if he acts maliciously and without probable cause.

This provision protects virtually any official from a malicious prosecution suit as long as the underlying prosecution was within the scope of his or her employment. The policy underlying this act is to protect public officials from tort liability so that they may more ably discharge their duties to the public without fear of lawsuits. California's act, however, is extreme in the level of protection it guarantees. As long as California's public officials can articulate some reason why their actions fall in the scope of their employment, they are free to act maliciously. Remember that the large majority of the states do not immunize their public officials from liability when they act maliciously or without cause. Needless to say, even if a building official lives in a state that absolutely provides immunity from malicious prosecution suits, it is always better practice to refrain from acting in a malicious or arbitrary manner. If the building official is named as a defendant in a malicious prosecution suit and he or she lives in a state that does not provide absolute immunity, the official might suggest to the lawyer that absolute immunity as a defense be asserted on the off-chance that the state court of last resort will follow California's lead. If the building official's activity was outrageous, however, or this defense was already raised and rejected in that state's court in a case that has similar facts, the attorney will likely not assert an absolute immunity defense.

Wrongful Civil Proceedings

As noted earlier, malicious prosecution used to be allowed only as a result of an unsuccessful criminal prosecution. Most states, however, currently allow malicious prosecution actions to be taken as a result of civil proceedings. Although the term "malicious prosecution" can be used to describe civil suits, a more proper term would be "wrongful civil proceedings" or "wrongful use of civil proceedings." Additionally, since probable cause is a hard standard to fulfill, most US courts now impose liability for malicious civil claims brought without probable cause. This makes it easier for plaintiffs, asserting that wrongful civil proceedings were brought against them, to prevail on such a claim. There does remain a large minority of states that only impose liability on the defendant if the plaintiff can show a "special grievance," such as interference with his or her person or property by reason of the litigation. If the building official's state views code enforcement as civil in nature, it is very important to check with the municipal attorney to determine how that state rules. If he or she works in a state that allows liability to attach with no probable cause, it will be much more difficult to defend against a malicious prosecution suit than if the building official lives in a state that requires that the plaintiff show he or she has suffered from a special grievance.

Abuse of Process

Abuse of process is similar to malicious prosecution and is an appropriate action where malicious prosecution is not. So, even if a criminal or civil proceeding is brought and won with probable cause and with a proper motive, the person instituting the proceeding will be liable for abuse of process if he or she has used various litigation devices available during the course of the proceeding for improper purposes. For this cause of action to prevail, however, the plaintiff must show that the litigation was twisted to accomplish an illegitimate and unplanned for purpose. The elements of this tort are: (1) an ulterior purpose; and (2) a willful act in the use of the process not proper in the regular conduct of the proceedings. This tort occurs when the **tort-feasor** uses coercion to gain some sort of personal benefit. Basically, a person who is found liable for abuse of process is someone who has used the legal process as a threat to get something unrelated to the litigation.

In the field of code enforcement, a building official will be found liable for abuse of process if he or she brings an action against an alleged code offender for the purpose of coercing that person to surrender property. To avoid becoming a defendant in an abuse of process suit, code enforcement matters should be treated very seriously and should be kept accurately and with detailed records. It is also a good idea to take care in regard to verbal communication. A joke may be misconstrued or a careless statement misunderstood. Finally, it is important to remember that a lawsuit should never be used against a code offender as a threat to achieve any type of gain.

False Imprisonment

False imprisonment is a cause of action that allows a successful plaintiff to recover damages for the intentional and unwarranted confinement of another. If a code official arrests and confines an alleged code violator or causes an alleged code violator to be arrested or confined, the code official may be liable for false imprisonment if the accused is acquitted of the charges brought against him or her. To prevail on a claim of false imprisonment, the plaintiff must show that the building official intended to confine the plaintiff. The plaintiff may meet this burden by demonstrating that the building official knew with substantial certainty that the confinement would result from his or her actions. To prevail, the plaintiff must have been confined within definite physical boundaries. He or she must have been held within certain limits, and not merely prevented from entering certain places. It is also irrelevant to the building official's defense that there was a means of escape from this confinement if the plaintiff did not know that this escape was available. Furthermore, even if the plaintiff does know of the means of escape, he or she might still prevail on the false imprisonment claim if the means of escape was not reasonable. A means of escape is reasonable only if it would not be physically dangerous to either the plaintiff, his or her clothing, a third party, or offensive to his or her reasonable sense of decency or personal dignity.[1] Threats of harm by the defendant to the plaintiff, his or her property, or to a third party that would result if the plaintiff had left the area prescribed by defendant, would also constitute confinement.

In most cases, building officials should not worry about being found liable of this tort. If the alleged code offender was arrested in the proper manner (in other words, through use of an arrest warrant that is based on probable cause), there is no false imprisonment. Also, it is ordinarily the person serving process, such as police officers or sheriffs, who are more likely to be held liable for false imprisonment.

If the building official does actually serve process, the most important problem is the form of the document. The process server is charged with the responsibility of ensuring that the process is "fair on its face." That is, the document must substantially look as it should, including the signature of the issuing authority, who is usually a judge, and a statement of the charges. Remember, however, that regardless of whether the building official follows the proper procedure in obtaining the warrant, he or she must also serve it in an appropriate manner. A properly drafted arrest warrant is not a license to use excessive force or threats during the arrest.

Intentional Infliction of Emotional Distress

This tort may be broadly defined as the intentional or reckless infliction by extreme and outrageous conduct of severe emotional or mental distress. This claim will be sustained even in the absence of physical harm. The complained-of activity must be:

> ... so outrageous in character, and so extreme in degree, as to go beyond all possible bounds of decency, and to be regarded as atrocious, and utterly intolerable in a civilized community. Generally, the case is one in which the recitation of the facts to an average member of the community would arouse his resentment against the actor, and lead him to exclaim, "Outrageous!"

It is difficult for either the courts or the legislature to determine the precise limits of the "reasonable bounds of decency." In court, in many cases, it is up to the jury to decide. Of course, this leads to varied and unpredictable results that make it difficult to anticipate the outcome in any given case. Therefore, it is beyond the scope of this text to tell the building official how to act. The use of common sense would be appropriate. If the building official thinks that there may be a problem with his or her behavior, it is possible that a problem exists. The building official might also seek guidance from colleagues, supervisors, and municipal attorneys. It is very possible that they might have had some experience with this type of case and can guide the official's behavior so as to best avoid incurring liability.

If the building official acts consistently and records those actions, he or she has little to fear. Many of these cases are brought and dismissed. For example, a plaintiff who suffers a heart attack might claim that the building official's service of process caused it. If the service of process was not accompanied by serious threats, liability will not attach.

Assault and Battery

These are two separate torts that usually occur together. **Battery** occurs when there is an intentional infliction of harmful or offensive bodily contact.[2] It is easy to inflict offensive bodily contact. If, for example, you get angry at an alleged code offender and, grab his or her lapels or collar, you can be liable for money damages. It is very unlikely that any building department will indemnify building officials for battery, unless it is clearly in self-defense. In a situation where a building official believes his or her safety is in jeopardy, the building official should try to leave the premises before fighting back. If this action is not taken, it is likely that the building official could not sustain a claim of self-defense and will, therefore, have to pay for any damages to the plaintiff out-of-pocket.

An **assault** is the willful attempt or threat to impose injury upon another when there is the apparent present ability and intent to injure. It should be clear, then, why assault and battery usually occur at the same time. It is rarely the case that someone batters without first threatening the victim. The building official must, therefore, avoid touching the alleged code offender and must also avoid committing any action that might make the code offender afraid of being touched.

Fortunately, in many states there exists a general principal that words alone are not sufficient to constitute an assault. The courts in these states hold that the words used must be accompanied by some overt act that adds to the threatening character of the words. Even in these states, however, there may arise some cases where the surrounding circumstances are such that the words on their own are sufficient to constitute an assault.[3]

Even if the building official lives in a state that has a "words alone" rule, he or she should never be verbally abusive to an alleged code offender. It lowers the credibility and dignity of the profession. Furthermore, even if the verbal abuse was not found to be assault, the building official may still be held liable for another tort, such as intentional infliction of emotional distress.

Trespass

Trespass is a tort that may have significant impact on the duties of a building official. Liability under this theory may attach when a person intentionally enters on land under the possession of another. However, the land owner may grant permission to enter the land for a particular purpose; this is called a **license**. For example, a customer in a department store has a license to be there.

Futhermore, damages will be incurred if trespass is intentional. Even if the building official does no damage whatsoever, a jury may award a verdict in favor of the plaintiff and assess damages. Once trespass is established, the defendant is liable for virtually all consequences of the trespass, regardless of how unpredictable they may be; the fact that the defendant acted reasonable and in good faith is no defense. Liability results even if the building official honestly and reasonably felt that he or she was in the right.

An interesting variation in trespass law (sometimes referred to as **attractive nuisance doctrine**) occurs in situations where young children enter property because they are attracted there by a swimming pool or some other attractive nuisance. Here, the property owner may be held liable for injuries sustained by the trespassing children. A person who has specific conditions on his property that create a source of danger to children and attracts them to the property must take steps to prevent them from harming themselves. Consequently, building codes require property owners to provide barriers to prevent small children from gaining access to the pool.

Unless the building official has a valid defense, he or she will be found liable for trespass. There are several defenses, the most important of which is consent. If the property owner or the person in possession gives permission to enter the property, there is no trespass. The consent may be retracted at any time, however, and the right is automatically withdrawn. Remaining on the property after the property owner has asked the building official to leave is, likewise, trespass. As soon as the owner or possessor requests departure, the request must be honored.

Another defense is legal privilege. Certainly, if a valid warrant is issued and presented to the property owner, there is no trespass.

Yet another type of possible legal privilege or defense is provided by the *International Building Code*® (IBC®). Section 104.6 authorizes nonconsensual inspections at any reasonable hour:

> Where it is necessary to make an inspection to enforce the provisions of this code, or where the building official has reasonable cause to believe that there exists in a structure or upon a premise a condition which is contrary to or in violation of this code which makes the structure or premises unsafe, dangerous or hazardous the building official is authorized to enter the structure or premises at reasonable times to inspect or to perform the duties imposed by this code, provided that if such structure or premises be occupied that credentials be presented to the occupant and entry requested. If such structure or premises is unoccupied, the building official shall first make a reasonable effort to locate the owner or other person having charge or control of the structure or premises and request entry. If entry is refused, the building official shall have recourse to the remedies provided by law to secure entry.

The first part of this section establishes that right of the building official to enter the premises in order to make the permit inspections required by Section 110.3. Permit application forms typically include a statement in the certification signed by the applicant (who is the owner or owner's agent) granting the building official the authority to enter areas covered by the permit, in order to enforce code provisions related to the permit. The right to enter other structures or premises is more limited. First, to protect the right of privacy, the owner or occupant must grant the building official permission before an interior inspection of the property can be conducted. Permission is not required for inspection that can be accomplished from within the public right-of-way. Second, such access may be denied by the owner or occupant. Unless the inspector has reasonable cause to believe that a violation of the code exists, access may be unattainable. Third, building officials must present proper identification (see Section 104.5) and request admittance during reasonable hours—usually the normal business hours of the establishment—to be admitted. Fourth, inspections must be aimed at securing or determining compliance with the provisions and intent of the regulations that are specifically within the established scope of the building official's authority.

There are other circumstances where a government official may not be held liable for intentionally entering another's property. Law enforcement officials have a privilege to enter onto private property to perform their legal duties and a trespass claim will fail.[4] Also, governmental immunity statutes provide immunity from intentional trespass. Courts have found that where there is an open pathway to the front door, this is an implied invitation to members of the public to enter onto the property. Other factors that indicate the public is invited to enter the property are when a mailbox is affixed to the front of the house, there are "FedEx," "Amazon," and other deliverables at the front door and so on. Building officials may take these factors in consideration and courts will generally find an implicit invitation to come onto the property in these types of situations.

A common question and concern arises when the building official is faced with a "No Trespassing" sign. May the building official enter the property? In *Gudgel v. Anderson*, at least one court has stated that, "No Trespassing" signs are not dispositive on the issue of privacy and are only factors to be considered along with other manifestations of the desire to be left alone."[5] Those other "manifestations" include the degree to which the residence is isolated or visible from a public road or neighboring property, the use of guard dogs, fences, and gates and the amount of time the building official is on the property.

In *Gudgel*, county building officials observed what appeared to be new construction on property owned by Mr. Gudgel; however, no work permit had been issued for the new construction. Two building department officials went to the property to serve him with a stop-work order and to obtain a closer look at the project. In accordance with department policy, a uniformed police officer accompanied them. The building department first attempted to serve him personally with the stop-work order but were unsuccessful. They returned, intending to post the order on the construction itself, only to find the property posted with a "No Trespassing" sign. Despite the presence of the sign, the gate to the property was open so the building officials and officer entered the property to contact Mr. Gudgel. He refused to acknowledge whether he was the property owner and ordered the officials to leave. He even went so far as to chest-bump the police officer and threatened to get a gun if they did not leave. At that point, the officials left after having been on the property for three to five minutes.

The officials later returned to post the stop-work order. Meanwhile, the officer discovered that Mr. Gudgel was a convicted felon. Based on his assertions that he was in possession of a gun, the officer obtained a search warrant, believing Mr. Gudgel was unlawfully in possession of a gun. Upon execution of the warrant, multiple guns were found. Mr. Gudgel was charged with multiple felonies.

Mr. Gudgel argued that the evidence should have been suppressed because the information used in support of the warrant was illegally obtained. He claimed the building officials and police officer were illegally on his property in violation of the no-trespassing sign and by his requests that the officials leave his property. The court disagreed. Citing additional case law, the court said that if police officers detect something while lawfully present on areas of impliedly open curtilage, that "detection" does not amount to a search in violation of the Fourth Amendment.[6] **Open curtilage** is that area that appears to be open to the public. It includes the driveway, walkway, or any access route that leads to the residence.[7] Further, officers and building officials do not need probable cause to enter areas of open curtilage when they are there on legitimate business.

The building officials and police officer were there on legitimate business. County-adopted codes provided a right of entry for building officials to inspect and post stop-work orders. Based on those provisions of the code, entry was permissible and a warrant was not required unless entry was refused. Further, despite posted "No Trespassing" signs, the gate to the property was open and the building and area could be partially seen from the road. Finally, the officials entered the property during the day and attempted to explain their legitimate purpose for being on the property before being threatened. For all these reasons, the court found that the officials had not trespassed on Mr. Gudgel's property.

A prudent building official will always seek the advice of their attorney before entering property that is posted "No Trespassing." What the *Gudgel* case teaches us, however, is that the mere presence of a "No Trespassing" sign is not dispositive on the issue of privacy. As with all cases, the court will examine all the facts and circumstances of an alleged "trespass."

Searches to gather information for the purpose of enforcing the other codes, ordinances, or regulations are considered unreasonable and are prohibited by the Fourth Amendment to the US Constitution. "Reasonable cause" in the context of this section must be distinguished from "probable cause," which is required to gain access to property in criminal cases. The burden of proof establishing reasonable cause may vary among jurisdictions. Usually, an inspection must show that the property is subject to inspection under the provisions of the code; that the interests of the public health, safety, and welfare outweigh the individual's right to maintain privacy; and that such an inspection is required solely to determine compliance with the provisions of the code.

Many jurisdictions do not recognize the concept of an administrative warrant and may require the building official to prove probable cause in order to gain access upon refusal. This burden of proof is usually more substantial, often requiring the building official to stipulate in advance why access is needed (usually access is restricted to gathering evidence for seeking an indictment or making an arrest); what specific items or information is sought; its relevance to the case against the individual subject; how knowledge of the relevance of the information or items sought was obtained and how the evidence sought will be used. In all such cases, the right to privacy must always be weighed against the right of the building official to conduct an inspection to verify that public health, safety, and welfare are not in jeopardy. Such important and complex constitutional issues should be discussed with the jurisdiction's legal counsel. Jurisdiction should establish procedures for securing the necessary court orders when an inspection is deemed necessary following a refusal.

Remember (from Chapter 3) that if the building code is not authorized by a state statute, the privileges found within the code, which are in conflict with state law, are preempted by state law.

Conclusion

It will be rare that a building official is found liable for damages under most of these tort theories. The official should be very careful, however, to avoid maliciously prosecuting someone suspected of a code violation. Building officials should remember to always record their actions in writing and to demand that their employees do the same. All observations should be included in reports and no judicial or administrative action should be taken unless there is an inspection report to back it up.

Chapter 10 Endnotes

1. Paraphrasing from Restatement of Torts 2d, Section 36.
2. Taken from Restatement of Torts 2d, Sections 13, 18.
3. See Restatement of Torts 2d, Section 31, which provides the following hypothetical situation (paraphrased): D, a notorious gangster who is known to have killed others, phones P and tells him that he will shoot him on sight. The next day P sees D standing on the sidewalk. Without moving, D says to P, "Your time has come." In this situation, D has committed an assault.
4. *Frederique v. County of Nassau*, 168 F. Supp.3d 455.
5. *Gudgel v. Anderson*, 2008 WL 2945477.
6. *State v. Grave*, 890 P.2d 1088 (1995).
7. *State v. Maxfield*, 886 P.2d 123 (1994).

Chapter 11 – Negligent Wrongdoing

This chapter discusses the elements comprising a claim of negligence and the possible defenses and immunities that a building official might raise in response to a charge of negligence.

Topics

Elements of Negligence
Defenses
Immunities
State Tort Liability Acts
Indemnification and Insurance

Terms

absolute immunity	declaratory judgment	misfeasance
assumption of risk	duty	nonfeasance
breach of duty	joint and several liability	public duty doctrine
contributory negligence	malfeasance	qualified immunity

Introduction

As demonstrated in Chapter 10, it is quite difficult for a plaintiff to prove intentional misconduct. Because there is no intent requirement, negligent misconduct is somewhat easier to prove. It is still quite difficult, however, for a plaintiff to prevail on a claim of negligence. Furthermore, in most states, building officials are immune from liability for negligently enforcing the code. This chapter will examine the elements comprising a claim of negligence. It also examines possible defenses and immunities that a building official might raise in response to a charge of negligence. It will then discuss the importance of state tort liability acts. The chapter will conclude with a discussion of indemnification and the pros and cons of purchasing insurance against such charges.

Recall from Chapter 3 that the building official and the local government are considered two separate entities under the law. When a lawsuit is brought, the concept of **joint and several liability** allows the plaintiff to recover damages from two or more defendants. Each defendant may be responsible for the entire obligation. Any party that pays the damages may seek contributions from other responsible parties. For example, a lawsuit claiming negligence in the issuance of a building permit may be brought against the municipal township, the code official, and the code inspector or against any one of these entities for the fullest amount of the claim. The building official, however, has more of a risk of incurring liability than does the municipality. Building officials can be sued in their individual capacities and therefore are open to greater liability. While reading this chapter, keep in mind the distinction between the building official and the municipality, and the consequences that may flow to each party as a result of negligence.

Elements of Negligence

To prevail on a claim of negligence, a plaintiff must satisfy four elements. The defendant, possibly a building official, must have: (1) owed a duty to another to act according to a certain standard; (2) failed to act in accord with that standard, and, therefore; (3) breached that duty; (4) thereby causing, in the eyes of the law, an injury or damage to the other. Similar to what was required to prove intentional misconduct, the plaintiff must prove each and every element of a negligence claim by a preponderance of the evidence.

For example, if a building inspector has a legal duty to inspect every building in the manner that an ordinarily reasonable and prudent building inspector would, and he or she has not done so, the first two elements of the legal theory have been satisfied. That inspector had a duty and breached it. On these facts alone, a layperson would likely believe that this building inspector was indeed negligent. If the inspector's failure to inspect properly, however, did not cause the party to whom the duty was owed a legally recognized injury, there will be no legal liability.

The four elements of negligence will be examined next, followed by a brief discussion of two additional elements of negligence: causation in fact and public policy considerations.

The Public Duty Doctrine

The first and second elements of negligence afford the greatest protection to public officials, including building officials. A **duty**, in negligence cases, may be defined as an obligation, to which the law will give recognition and effect, to conform to a particular standard of conduct toward another. Most of these obligations are to act with the same care as a reasonably prudent person would under the same or similar circumstances. If the conduct of the defendant is below what a reasonably prudent person would have exercised, then the defendant has breached his or her duty. In tort law, the "reasonable person" standard is the most widespread.

In most cases involving building codes, however, the question is not the level of care owed, but to whom the duty is owed. If the plaintiff is not owed any duty of care by the defendant, the first element of the cause of action is missing and the case is subject to dismissal. To protect the building official, most states have adopted the **public duty doctrine**. This doctrine provides that a plaintiff who is alleging inadequate performance of a governmental activity has the burden to show that the municipality owed a duty to the plaintiff and not just to the general public when performing the activity that gave rise to the complaint. If the activity is designed for the general public, the cause of action fails for lack of legal duty to the plaintiff. Under the public duty doctrine, the courts would look to the purpose of the building code to determine to whom the building inspector owes a specific duty. Therefore, because the purpose of the building code is to ensure the safety and protection of the public at large, a plaintiff's cause of action against the building inspector will probably fail. If a building official approves a building permit for a building with faulty wiring and the building burns down, all those people whose family members were killed in the fire do not have a claim against the inspector. The courts will find that the duty was owed not only to the inhabitants of the building, but rather to every member of the public. Because the duty was not limited to the people who lived in the building, the duty element of negligence cannot be satisfied.

There are, however, two exceptions to this doctrine. The first occurs when a plaintiff can clearly establish that the building official owes a specific duty to a class of people, and the plaintiff is a member of that class. The second exception occurs when the plaintiff can show that there exists a special relationship between the building official and the plaintiff, which would cause the plaintiff to rely on the building official more than would the general public.

It is important for the building official to consult with their municipal or county attorney to determine if their state case law follows the public duty doctrine, as some states do not. Cases that have similar facts can have very different outcomes depending on the jurisdiction. For example, in Massachusetts a home buyer relied on the negligent issuance of a building permit and certificate of occupancy. The City failed to require the lot be graded to prevent low spots. After flooding and substantial damage occurred, the owners sued the town but lost. The Court found there was no special relationship between the buyer and the town upon which liability could attach.[1] Compare this to a case from the state of Washington. A town and building official were found liable in damages for negligently issuing a building permit for an apartment building when, in fact, only single residential or duplexes could be built on the property. The Court found that the city building inspector, whose job included administering zoning ordinances, had a duty to accurately inform potential buyers regarding the proper zoning classification. When the buyer justifiably relied upon the negligence of the building official to his economic detriment, the building official, in his official capacity, and town were held liable for those damages.[2]

From another Washington case, the public duty doctrine did not afford immunity to the city or its officials after the plaintiff's wife was electrocuted to death.[3] In this case, a dead raccoon was found in a stream. The cause of death was electrocution from unsafe underwater-lighting wiring in the stream. City officials were notified and sent out an inspector. A city inspector notified the property owner and for a time, electricity to the lighting system was turned off. The city took no efforts to require repair or compliance with a city ordinance. Later, the power was turned back on. The property owner's six-year-old neighbor was electrocuted while playing in the stream. His mother, plaintiff's wife, died from electrocution when she attempted to rescue her son. In this case, the Court acknowledged the public duty doctrine but found that the electrical code requirements were not only designed for the protection of the public in general but more particularly for the benefit of the neighbors residing within the "ambit of the danger involved." A special duty existed between the plaintiff and the city. Thus, liability was imposed.

Even in cases where courts once followed the public duty doctrine and afforded protection, subsequent courts and legislatures may choose to abandon the doctrine. Returning to Massachusetts in the case of *Ribeiro v. Granby*,[4] the Court found no liability after the death of a tenant from a fire in his building even though the apartment did not have a second means of egress. The town of Granby was aware that after a building remodel, the fire escape was not replaced. The town took measures to secure compliance with their town ordinances. It even went so far as to notify the building residents of the safety hazard. However, the town took no further actions to require compliance. Almost a year later, Mr. Ribeiro moved into the building but was not made aware there was no second egress. He later lost his life in a fire. In finding that no duty was owed to Mr. Ribeiro, the court stated, "we conclude that the duty owed by the building inspector was to the public at large and no special duty was owed to the decedent. To hold otherwise would cause a municipality to become substantially an insurer of each and every construction project. The tremendous exposure to liability that could result from such a decision would likely dissuade municipalities from enacting regulations designed for the protection and welfare of the public."[5]

Eight years later, however, the Supreme Judicial Court of Massachusetts abolished the public duty doctrine in light of an inconsistency created between their case law and their governmental immunity statute regarding the creation of a duty.[6] The Court stated that the evolution of the public duty doctrine has led to "inconsistent and irreconcilable parts," which leaves judges and litigants "quite incapable of predicting when and why liability will be imposed."[7]

Because case law may change with time, the prudent building official will stay abreast of those changes. This is why it is vital for building officials to stay in contact with their attorneys, especially regarding this area of the law.

Breach of Duty

Breach of duty is the third element of a negligence cause of action. It is the neglect or failure to fulfill in a just and proper manner the duties of an office. The duty owed by the building code official must in some manner be violated. If the duty is satisfied, no liability will ensue. There are essentially two ways in which a duty can be breached: by action or inaction. For example, failing to make a required inspection would be considered inaction, which breaches a duty of care. Most building code problems result from inaction. Alternatively, an inaccurate inspection would be considered an active breach of duty.

To use more legal terms, a breach of duty can result through misfeasance, nonfeasance or malfeasance. **Misfeasance** is the improper performance of some act that a person may lawfully do.[8] **Malfeasance** is the doing of an act that a person ought not to do at all.[9] **Nonfeasance** is the nonperformance of some act that a person is obligated or has the responsibility to perform.[10] Misfeasance and malfeasance are often confused, and the distinction between them is not very important. The difference between nonfeasance and misfeasance is, of course, the difference between inaction and action. These distinctions probably no longer have any validity. Years ago, liability in negligence cases was determined by which classification occurred. If misfeasance or malfeasance occurred, liability would attach, but if nonfeasance occurred, there was no liability. The theory was that liability should be imposed for active misdeeds, but not mere failures to act. In failing to impose liability on those individuals who failed to act, the courts in the past reasoned that while misfeasance is an affirmative act that creates new risk harm to the plaintiff, nonfeasance has made the plaintiff's situation no worse than if the defendant had absolutely no contact with the plaintiff. Furthermore, earlier courts were very hesitant to force individuals from harming each other. In more modern times, this difference between act and omission has largely been abandoned.

An interesting case in Tennessee occurred that was very nearly directly on point with the situation of building officials. In *State, for Use of Lay, et al. v. Clymer,*[11] suit was brought against the chief mine inspector and district mine inspector for personal injuries and wrongful death arising out of a mine explosion. State law required the inspectors to inspect every mine in each district. The plaintiffs presented proof that no inspection of the subject mine had been conducted within the statutorily mandated time period. One of the defenses was that the negligence, if any, was merely nonfeasance. The court, however, rejected this defense:

> The answer to this contention is that under the modern authorities the distinction between liability of an agent in tort for acts of nonfeasance and those of misfeasance and malfeasance, has practically been abandoned, and the courts are generally in agreement in holding that an agent is liable to third persons resulting from the violation of a duty that

the agent owes to the third person, regardless of whether the violation
be one of nonfeasance, misfeasance or malfeasance.[12]

Indeed, most states' torts claim acts make government officials, to the extent that they are liable at all, liable for omissions as well as for action. Furthermore, most states' torts claim acts, which immunize their government officials, immunize them from both acts and omissions.

Damages or Injury

The fourth element of a cause of action for negligence is injury or damage. For plaintiffs to prevail on a claim of negligence, they must have suffered some injury as a result of a duty owed specifically to them. This element is satisfied by personal injury or property damage. Although a plaintiff might claim that he or she is suffering from emotional distress as a result of the building official's negligence, the plaintiff will not prevail without showing that the emotional distress was adequately severe to require medical attention.

Causation in Fact

Although this might arguably be the most important element of negligence, it is quite complex. Many attorneys have a difficult time understanding causation; therefore, only a brief and general discussion will be provided.

There is an implicit relationship between the first four elements of negligence. The breach must cause the injury. In every negligence case, there must have been someone or something which caused the breach to occur. For example, who has caused the injury if a speeding car rams another and an improperly constructed gasoline tank explodes and kills all the occupants? Who is liable, if during an inspection, a hazardous building code violation is noted, a violation letter is written but not delivered, and a visitor in that building is killed? It is the answers to these questions that determine causation.

There is actually a two-part inquiry to determine causation. First, did the defendant's conduct in fact cause this injury? And second, as a matter of policy, should the courts impose liability? The general rule now accepted in most states is that if the defendant's conduct was a "substantial factor" in producing the injury, then legally it caused injury. Thus, more than one defendant could easily be liable for any damage. For example, both an architect and a plans examiner could be held liable for the collapse of a structure if the plans were found to be defective because the conduct of both was a substantial factor in the collapse.

Public Policy Considerations

In addition to the causation in fact problems, there may be public policy reasons not to impose liability. For example, if the injury sustained was totally unforeseeable in light of the defendant's conduct, the courts will not impose liability. A finding of total unforseeability on the part of the defendant, however, is extremely rare. Other policies that help a defendant to escape from liability include, but are not limited to, situations in which the injury is too remote from the negligence, the injury is too out of proportion to the guilt of the negligent tort-feasor; it appears too extraordinary that the negligence should have brought about the harm; allowance of recovery would place too unreasonable a burden on the negligent tort-feasor; allowance of recovery would too likely open the door for fraudulent claims; and allowance of recovery would place too unreasonable a burden on the tort-feasor.

Defenses

Contributory Negligence

Most of the common defenses to lawsuits are not easily applicable to negligence actions against building officials. The doctrine of **contributory negligence** illustrates this. The doctrine holds that if the plaintiff has been guilty of any negligence that has contributed to his injuries or damage, he is totally barred from any recovery. The building official should check with the municipal attorney to determine whether or not he or she lives in a contributory negligence state. If the owner of the premises that has been negligently inspected sued for property damage, the building official might be able to raise this defense. Suppose the owner knowingly took out a required fire wall and replaced it with an unrated wall. A fire occurs and the building is destroyed. Even though there was a negligent inspection, a court in a contributory negligence state will find that because the builder or owner was himself negligent, no liability can attach to the building official.

Now assume, however, that two business customers are hurt in the blaze. They had nothing to do with the installation of the unrated material. They did not know of any defect in the construction of the building. They cannot be contributorily negligent. Further, they may be able to sue both the owner of the property and the inspector who missed the unrated material.

Keep in mind that most of the people who sue are not at all responsible in any way for their injuries. In those cases, the contributory negligence defense would be inapplicable.

Comparative Negligence

The defense of comparative negligence acts as a partial legal defense. It will come into play only if the public duty doctrine is not followed or if any relevant immunity statutes do not afford protection. This defense reduces the amount of damages a plaintiff can recover in a negligence action, but only if it can be shown that the plaintiff was also negligent. A comparative negligence defense requires the building official show that the plaintiff was also negligent, thereby reducing the amount of damages that can be recovered by the plaintiff. For example, and using a very simplistic example, a building inspector is driving his official municipal vehicle, on his way to perform an inspection. As he approaches an intersection his attention is distracted and he does not see that the light is amber. By the time he refocuses on the road the light has turned red and he enters the intersection striking the plaintiff's vehicle that had entered the intersection. The plaintiff suffers injuries and sues the municipality and building official.

In states that have adopted the comparative negligence defense, there are varying theories that may limit or even bar recovery. The first is known as pure" comparative negligence. Under this theory, the plaintiff recovers damages based on the percentage of the defendant's negligence. In our example above, if the plaintiff entered the intersection on a green light and was then struck by the building official's truck, she was not negligent and could recover one hundred percent of her damages. Let's change the facts though, and assume the following: (1) the building official entered the intersection just as the light turned from amber to red; (2) the plaintiff entered the intersection on a red light, just before it turned green; (3) the building official is eighty percent negligent; and (4) the plaintiff is twenty percent negligent. Under a pure comparative negligence theory, the plaintiff could only recover eighty percent of her damages.

Other jurisdictions have adopted a "partial" or "modified" comparative negligence standard. One variant states that the plaintiff may only recover if her negligence is not greater than the defendants. In our example, she is only twenty percent negligent; therefore she could potentially recover all her damages. If we change the facts, she may not be able to recover any damages. Assume now, that both the plaintiff and building official ran red lights, during the two-second delay that exists to allow traffic to clear intersections. In this scenario, the plaintiff's negligence is fifty percent. Because her negligence is equal to that of the defendant, she is barred from recovering any damages.

Assumption of Risk

This defense is dependent on proof that the plaintiff knew of and understood the risk to which he was subjecting himself, yet proceeded in that course anyway. In a building codes case, establishing **assumption of risk** is almost impossible.

Let us return to the example of the owner who removed the fire wall. For assumption of risk to be a defense in this case, the owner would have had to understand the peril he or she created, appreciate the danger, and still make a choice to so proceed. As might be imagined, those elements are very difficult to prove.

Statute of Limitations

Statute of limitations are enacted by legislatures which state that a civil cause of action or a criminal case must be brought within a certain time period. The actual statute of limitations varies from state to state and from case to case. For example, personal injury and negligent homicide cases typically have a statute of limitations of four years. As with all rules, there are exceptions but if a plaintiff or prosecutor waits and files a case four years and one day later, the case will be dismissed because the statute of limitations has run, regardless of the culpability of the defendant. In Chapter 12, a detailed discussion of the federal civil rights case of *Hilda v. Brown*[13] will be introduced. Based on the same facts as the federal civil rights case, the state of Colorado filed criminal charges against a building official and another defendant. In that criminal case, we will see how the statute of limitations acted as a defense. (See case study *Hilda v. Brown*.[14])

Immunities

Assuming that the plaintiff can establish all four elements of a negligence cause of action and the building official cannot establish a defense, all is not lost. The building official may be able to take advantage of executive immunity which will protect him or her from liability. If the building official is sued, he or she may be able to claim **absolute immunity**; however, the court is hesitant to grant absolute immunity in the majority of the cases. Absolute immunity is akin to that given to a judicial officer. A judicial officer is not liable for his or her discretionary acts or omissions, even though he or she is found to have acted with malicious or other improper motives. The judicial officer must feel free to carry out discretionary functions as is seen fit without being influenced by the threat of a harassment suit.

Absolute immunity only applies to the actions that are functions of the job. For example, it is impossible to sue a judge for a decision that the judge made in court, even if it is blatantly illegal. The rationale is that society does not want a judge to feel inhibited in the decisions he or she makes. If a judge's decision is blatantly illegal, it can, or so the theory postulates, be appealed to a higher court. The decision can also be overridden by an act of the legislature. For example, a judge is not immune from liability if he or she takes bribes. This is not a function of the job of judge, so the judge is not immune from liability. In most cases, however, the line between what constitutes a function of the job and what does not is markedly less distinct. So even if a building official could establish that absolute immunity should be granted, it might be difficult to demonstrate which actions were taken in the scope of the job and which were not.

The **qualified immunity** given to lower administrative officers is much more commonly applied. The rationale behind a qualified privilege is that it is sufficient to protect the honest officer, and that the burden and inconvenience of an inquiry regarding motives far outweighs the possible evils of deliberate misconduct.

In *Rottkamp v. Young*,[15] a zoning official was sued for his failure to issue a building permit for a restaurant. The official found that the description of the activity given him by the applicant did not meet the applicable provisions of the zoning ordinance. On this point, the zoning official was overruled via a **declaratory judgment**, but the court found no tort liability:

> To fasten responsibility for damages on a public officer for the exercise of judgment or discretion in favor of one disappointed by the result would dampen the ardor of all but the most resolute, or the most irresponsible, in the unflinching discharge of their duties. In weighing the balance between the effects of oppressive official action and vindictive or retaliatory damage suits against the officer, we think that the public interest in prompt and fearless determinations by the officer, based on

his interpretation of the law and the facts before him, must take precedence. A public officer, haunted by the specter of a lawsuit, may well be subject to the twin tendencies of procrastination and compromise to the detriment of the proper performance of his duties.[16]

In defending against a charge of negligence, the building official and lower-level workers should always respond with a claim of immunity.

State Tort Liability Acts

In recent years, many states have enacted state tort liability acts. These acts determine the amount of immunity that a government official will be afforded. As was mentioned before, it is, therefore, crucial for the building official to know if his or her state has such an act and what the act says.

The acts came about as a reaction to absolute municipal immunity. That type of immunity made it very difficult for an injured or otherwise aggravated party to sue the local government. Essentially, before the acts were passed, a suit could not be brought against a municipality if it was acting in its "governmental capacity." The courts interpreted the phrase in a fairly broad manner; consequently, it was very protective of municipal corporations.

Recognizing this overly protective judge-made law, the states developed statutory substitutes. Now, if the building official resides in a state that has a tort liability act, he or she may sue or be sued only under the provisions of that act. There are often particular procedural steps that must be observed, but more importantly, the municipality, and usually its officials, can be sued only under the terms of this act. These acts have made it easier to sue the government, and have clarified the areas in which the government and its officials can face liability and under what circumstances. Although the first accomplishment is unfortunate for the municipal department, the second is quite helpful. A building official now knows with certainty whether or not he or she will be immune in a given situation. Also, with the various defenses outlined throughout this book, the building official need not be too worried about being successfully sued in the future.

The next section will briefly discuss acts passed in two states that demonstrate the benefit of the passage of these statutes. A third type of act will be mentioned because of its unusual handling of claims against employees.

DeBry v. Noble

On the issue of state tort liability, let us return to *Debry v. Noble*, addressed in detail in Chapter 6. As a result of being sued by the DeBrys, the County and Noble claimed immunity under Utah's Governmental Immunity Act ("Act").[17] The Act states that governmental entities and their employees are generally immune from liability for any injuries that result from the exercise of a governmental function.

The DeBrys claimed that building inspections were not governmental functions subject to immunity and, even if they were, the Act waived immunity. The trial court denied the DeBry's claim, ruling that inspections were indeed governmental functions, that the State had not waived immunity under the Act and that the order to vacate was not unconstitutional. The DeBrys then appealed to the Utah Court of Appeals. The Court denied their appeal.

The Court found that even where a negligent act or omission of an employee takes place, liability does not attach. In cases where an injury arises out of the "issuance, denial, suspension, or revocation of, or by the failure or refusal to issue, deny, suspend, or revoke, any permit, license, certificate, approval, order, or similar authorization," these are "core governmental functions" for which immunity is not waived and liability does not attach.[18] The Utah Supreme Court agreed with the Court of Appeals on this issue and ruled that the DeBrys failed to state a claim on this issue.[19]

California Tort Claims Act of 1963
New Jersey Tort Claims Act of 1972

The California Tort Claims Acts of 1963 and the New Jersey Tort Claims Act of 1972 are similar and are both typical of the tort liability acts across the nation. Both acts break into approximately two parts, the first of which establishes the extent of liability for governmental officials. The second discusses the liability of the entity itself.

The first point of importance lies in the definitions. The New Jersey act, for example, defines the term "public entity" to include state, county and municipal governments. A "public employee" includes an officer, employee or servant of a public entity, whether or not compensated. Note that this would protect not only the building official, but also members of the Board of Building Code Appeals (in Chapter 7). Building code officials should make sure that their job is covered under the definition of public employee. For example, if you are a state inspector and the state is not included within the definition of a public entity, you have no protection under the act, although the immunities and defense previously discussed will still apply. Since the majority of building officials work on the municipal level, and since most of the tort liability acts were specifically designed to apply to municipalities, this will probably not be a concern.

Once it has been determined that the act applies to a particular individual or level of government, the specific areas of protection can be examined. Under the California act, "A public employee is not liable for an injury caused by his adoption of or failure to adopt an enactment or by his failure to enforce an enactment."

The New Jersey act has a similar provision. This section not only protects against a suit based on the failure to adopt, or the actual adoption, of a building code, for example, but also denies an injured party the right to sue based on the official's total failure to enforce the code. This provision is unambiguous; it clearly protects the building code official if he or she fails to enforce the code. This protection may not be available in every state. It is crucial for the building official to know his or her state's tort liability act.

Another provision found in most tort liability acts offers even greater protection for building officials:

> A public employee is not liable for an injury caused by his issuance, denial, suspension or revocation of, or by his failure or refusal to issue, deny, suspend or revoke, any permit, license, certificate, approval, order or similar authorization where he is authorized by enactment to determine whether or not such authorization should be issued, denied, suspended or revoked.

New Jersey's provision is similar. Since much of what a building official does revolves around the issuance, revocation or suspension of permits, this is a critical aspect of the protection afforded by tort liability acts. Revocations are particularly troublesome, especially where the original permit was issued in error and the revocation is accompanied by a prohibition against further construction. Although building contractors are undoubtedly displeased when their permits are erroneously issued, revoked or suspended, these acts make it impossible for them to prevail on a claim against the building official.

This immunity from suit is only authorized when the building official or other public official was "authorized by enactment to determine whether or not such authorization should be issued, denied, suspended or revoked." The building official must be acting within the scope of his or her authority in taking such action on the permit. Proving that the official acted within the scope of his or her authority is usually not a problem.

It is not difficult for building officials to know when they are authorized to act. The *International Building Code*® (IBC®) provides for the issuance of a building permit in Section 105.3.1, which states:

> If the building official is satisfied that the proposed work conforms to the requirements of this code and laws and ordinances applicable thereto, the building official shall issue a permit therefore as soon as practicable.

The IBC likewise provides specific authority for the revocation of building permits in Section 105.6, which states:

> The building official is authorized to suspend or revoke a permit issued under the provisions of this code wherever the permit is issued in error or on the basis of incorrect, inaccurate or incomplete information, or in violation of any ordinance or regulation or any of the provisions of this code.

Always check the authority for a revocation or suspension of the permit. Because such broad protection is given the building code official who carefully follows the limits of his or her jurisdiction, there is no sense in exposing oneself to potential liability.

A third important provision of many of the tort liability acts offers protection for negligent inspections. California's act provides:

> A public employee is not liable for injury caused by his failure to make an inspection, or by reason of making an adequate or negligent inspection, of any property, other than the property...of the public entity employing the public employee, for the purpose of determining whether the property complies with or violates any enactment or contains or constitutes a hazard to health or safety.

New Jersey's act is similar. Notice that this provision also protects the total failure to make an inspection where one should have been made.

A final section of the California act that bears mentioning pertains to malicious prosecution:

> A public employee is not liable for injury caused by his institution or prosecuting any judicial or administrative proceeding within the scope of his employment, even if he acts maliciously and without probable cause.

Because California protected its public officials from such liability before this act was passed, this statutory provision is hardly remarkable. (See Chapter 10 for a review of malicious prosecution.) Other states have not followed California's lead, and usually will only provide immunity if the mistaken prosecution was done without malice.

Section 114.3 of the IBC, specifically provides that notice of any unlawful act be given to the alleged code offender, and that:

> If the notice of violation is not complied with promptly the building official shall request the legal counsel of the jurisdiction to institute the appropriate proceeding at law or in equity to restrain, correct or abate such violation or to require the removal or termination of the unlawful use of the building or structure in violation of the provisions of this code or of the order or direction made pursuant thereto.

The New Jersey act has some provisions that are not found in the California act. For example, New Jersey expressly protects a public official who, in good faith, attempts to enforce a statute later found to be unconstitutional. It permits the entry onto property for the purpose of inspections, which in general has the effect of immunizing the official from trespass actions. Yet, one of these additional provisions is somewhat troublesome. One of the final sections of the act dealing with the liability of employees of public entities provides that if the employee acts outside the scope of his employment, commits a crime, actual fraud, actual malice or engages in willful misconduct, he may be held liable. These terms, which obviously place a high burden on any potential plaintiff, certainly make it easy to file suit for purposes of harassment. Anyone can make the allegations necessary to go to trial, even if they are not true. The building official still must live with the suit hanging overhead and must take some time and effort away from other pressing duties and prepare for and attend the trial. Of course, no matter how good a case, there is always some chance that a jury would decide against the building official. The New Jersey act has eliminated much of the uncertainty, but the final section could very effectively be used against innocent public officials.

While the New Jersey and California acts are reflective of most states' tort liability acts, there are other acts that limit protection to the local governments and not the governmental employees themselves. This type of act encourages injured parties to seek compensation through the public employees because they cannot reach the local government.

In these types of acts, even if the local government can be sued for a particular act, the act places a cap on the amount of recovery to be paid by the municipality. After the municipality has paid the balance of the cap, it need not pay more. This is so even if its damages far exceed the cap. The plaintiff, however, remains free to recover any further amount of damage from the employee.

In conclusion, the tort liability acts serve an important function. While they attempt to make it easier for an injured party to sue both the government and its officials, they have made the law clearer as to when such liability will be imposed. Therefore, building officials now have a much better idea than ever before of when they might be held liable in tort. Furthermore, many of the prime areas of litigation are eliminated by the acts by disallowing lawsuits against officials. No liability results from the improper issuance or revocation of a building permit, the improper inspection of a building, or the institution of judicial or administrative proceedings. These are all significant benefits, and should be of great help to the building code officials in the states where they apply.

Indemnification and Insurance

Even if a building official loses a lawsuit, many municipalities have enacted ordinances that will indemnify the public official from any monetary loss he or she might suffer. Alternatively, the ordinance might provide a maximum dollar amount up to which indemnification will be provided. Ordinarily, these enactments will require that the public official acted in good faith and within the scope of his or her employment. Furthermore, they also require that any action taken must have been consistent with the regulations of the particular department in which the official worked. If the action taken was clearly against departmental regulations, the department will not indemnify the official. Only if the official acted maliciously or willfully will the government usually allow the judgment to stand without offering to help.

Many of these ordinances have established special committees to review the case to see if indemnification should be permitted. The enactments differ from municipality to municipality and must be examined carefully to ascertain whether protection for the building official exists.

Of course, building officials might decide to protect themselves by purchasing "errors and omissions insurance." This would offer protection in the situation where an error is made which could possibly give rise to liability. Since liability can be imposed for a negligent omission, the insurance also covers that type of conduct. Generally this insurance applies only to areas of specialized skill or knowledge, and if the mistake that gives rise to liability were outside the area of that specialty, no protection is afforded.

Finally, if insurance is purchased, it should not exclude coverage of civil rights actions. (See Chapter 12 for a discussion of liability that may result from civil rights action.) If a building official plans to purchase insurance, he or she should try to buy enough to cover all of the possible risks.

Criminal Negligence

Very few building officials will be charged with criminal negligence during their careers. However, it has happened in the most extreme of cases so building officials should be aware of this legal principle.

Unlike simple negligence that requires no intent, in order to convict a building official of criminal negligence, a prosecutor must prove the building official acted with a certain mental state, usually "gross negligence." Because criminal negligence is a criminal case, the prosecutor must prove her case beyond a reasonable doubt.

Gross negligence is the lack of even the slightest diligence or care on the part of the building official. Rather than act as the proverbial "reasonable person," the building official's conduct has fallen so far below that standard that his actions can be considered "gross." Proof of such "gross" negligence can include the failure to foresee and therefore allow an otherwise avoidable danger; being aware of the danger but ignoring it, displaying a gross or wanton disregard for human life; or negligence that is aggravated, culpable, or "gross." Examples of criminally negligent charges include negligent homicide, vehicular homicide, criminal negligence while driving (driving while drowsy or tired, reckless driving, texting and driving, driving while impaired) and negligent endangerment of a child.

The defenses, immunities and indemnification principles previously discussed generally do not apply to cases of criminal negligence. However, there have been exceptions. If a building official is charged with criminal negligence, the building official needs to request to be indemnified from their municipality or county. If, however, the municipal or county attorneys determine that they will not indemnify the building official, she must hire her own criminal defense attorney to represent her in the criminal case. Possible defenses include that the building official owed no legal duty to the victim, therefore the actions were not criminally negligent. Another defense has the building official show she took adequate precautions to protect the victim from harm. If the building official is found guilty of criminal negligence, the building official may be sentenced to jail or prison.

As mentioned previously in this chapter, building officials in the state of Colorado were charged with criminal negligence. That criminal case will be discussed further in Chapter 12, Case Study *Hilda v. Brown*.[20]

Conclusion

This chapter has described some basic principles surrounding the claim of negligence. The public duty doctrine was reviewed; the fact that both acts and omissions can give rise to liability has been discussed; and a brief look at proximate cause was taken. Some of the possible defenses and immunities have been examined. In particular, the qualified immunity and two state tort liability acts have been reviewed. The concepts of insurance and indemnification were briefly examined. Finally, the concept of criminal negligence was discussed and its potential ramifications.

Except in those states where the public duty doctrine has been abolished, it is still very difficult to successfully sue building officials for negligence.

Chapter 11 Endnotes

1. *Dinsky v. Framingham*, 438 N.E. 2d, 51 (1981).
2. *Rogers v. The City of Toppenish*, 596 P.2d 1096 (1979).
3. *Cambpell v. City of Bellevue*, 530 P.2d 234 (1975).
4. *Ribeiro v. Granby*, 481 N.E. 2d 466 (1985).
5. *Id.* at 613.
6. *Jean W. v. Commonwealth*, 610 N.E. 2d 305 (1993).
7. *Id.* at 504.
8. *Black's Law Dictionary* (10th ed. 2014).
9. *Id.* at 956.
10. *Id.* at 1054.
11. *State v. Clymer*, 182 S.W.2d 425 (Tenn. 1943).
12. *Id.* at 532.
13. *Hilda M. v. Brown*, 2011 WL 5220230, November 2, 2011.
14. *Id.*
15. 249 N.Y.S. 2d 330 (1969).
16. *Id.* at 334.

17. Since the DeBry lawsuit, Utah's Governmental Immunity Act has been renumbered to 63G-7, U.C.A. Any references will be made to this section of the code or to the case.

18. *DeBry v. Salt Lake County*, 835 P.2d 981, 986 (Utah Ct. App. 1992).

19. *DeBry v. Noble*, 889 P.2d 428 (Utah 1995).

20. *Hilda M. v. Brown*, 2011 WL 5220230, November 2, 2011.

Chapter 12 – Civil Rights Actions

This chapter discusses important civil rights acts of concern to building code officials, focusing particularly on the Civil Rights Act of 1871, Section 1983—deprivation of constitutional rights.

Topics

Terms

danger creation

negligent homicide

procedural due process

respondeat superior

under color of state law

urban renewal

Introduction

Until the early 1960s, federal, state and local governments were almost completely unaffected by civil rights legislation enacted after the Civil War. In 1961 and in the years following, however, the Supreme Court began to interpret heretofore untapped legislation that provided causes of action for people who suffered civil rights violations at the hands of the government. While the preceding two chapters focused on legal theories primarily brought about in state courts, this chapter will focus on the most important federal civil rights acts enacted by Congress, including the Civil Rights Act of 1871, the Fair Housing Act, and the Americans with Disabilities Act. It also includes a discussion of the Equal Employment Opportunity Commission (EEOC) issues.

As of yet, lawsuits brought under the civil rights acts have not posed much difficulty for building officials. As is true with state lawsuits and state legal theories, building officials are difficult to reach; liability against building officials is difficult (though not impossible) to establish in a federal lawsuit.

Although the federal government has enacted many civil rights statutes, this chapter will review only those that are most relevant to building officials. Because the civil rights area is a rapidly growing field of the law, and it is difficult for a layperson to stay up to date on all the current developments, it is always best to consult with a municipal attorney regarding the enactment or increased use of a particular civil rights statute.

There are a number of important defenses and immunities for any legal attacks brought under these legal theories. A building official may have federal qualified immunity just as he or she may have state qualified immunity. This type of defense protects most of the actions that a building official may take in good faith. The doctrine of ***respondeat superior***, however, may not be used as a defense in these types of cases, but for reasons that differ from those underlying the state doctrines. The doctrine states that the master or employer is liable for the wrongful acts of a servant or employee, for reasons that differ from those underlying the state doctrines.

In some cases, it may be advantageous for a plaintiff to bring suit in federal district court under a civil rights statute. If the suit is successful, that plaintiff may have his or her attorney's fees paid by the defendant, the building official. Although in most jurisdictions, the building official is indemnified by his or her employer, the fear of possibly incurring thousands of dollars in attorney's fees might force the building department to settle a case even in a situation where liability does not exist.

The Civil Rights Act of 1871 (42 U.S.C.A. Section 1983)[1]

Section 1983 is a cause of action under which a state or local government can be held liable for money damages and declaratory relief for violating the Constitution or laws of the United States while acting "under the color of state law." Some commentators have declared that "no statute is more important in contemporary America" than Section 1983.[2] Nevertheless, before 1961, the Civil Rights Act of 1871 was rarely invoked. Within the last 34 years, however, this statute has become the basis for almost all constitutional rulings arising from the actions of state and local governments and their officers.[3] The text of the statute reads:

> Every person who, under color of any statute, ordinance, regulation, custom, or usage, of any state...subjects, or causes to be subjected, any citizen of the United States or other person within the jurisdiction thereof to the deprivation of any rights, privileges, or immunities secured by the constitution and laws, shall be liable to the party injured in an action at law, suit in equity, or other proper proceeding for redress.

To establish a cause of action, two elements must be proven: (1) color of state law; and (2) a deprivation of federal constitutional or statutory rights. The courts usually refer to these two elements, and both are of considerable importance in establishing the legal theory. Although these two elements seem to be very straightforward, their meanings have evolved and expanded in response to their interpretive case law.

"Under Color of State Law"

Before the landmark Supreme Court decision of *Monroe v. Pape*,[4] "**under color of state law**" was narrowly construed. An unconstitutional act performed under the color of state law was one that was either officially authorized or so widely tolerated as to amount to a custom or usage.[5] As one might imagine, it is rarely the case that misconduct is officially authorized. *Monroe v. Pape* was the first time the Court directly considered the meaning of "under color of state law." In this case, the plaintiff, Monroe, alleged that Detective Pape and twelve other Chicago Police officers broke into his home early one morning, humiliated his entire family by making them stand naked in the living room, and ransacked every room of his home looking for evidence which would help the police to solve a recently committed murder. Monroe further alleged that he was taken to the police station, held for ten hours without arraignment, and not allowed to contact an attorney. Monroe was ultimately released, and in the end, the state filed no charges against him.

The issue before the Court was whether the actions of the police officers could be found to have occurred under the color of state law, even though the conduct was obviously not explicitly authorized by the government. The Court found that actions taken by an officer in his or her official capacity are deemed to have occurred under color of law even if they are not pursuant to an official state policy, or even if those actions violate state law. The Court concluded its ruling by stating that "misuse of power, possessed by virtue of state law and made possible only because the wrongdoer is clothed with the authority of state law, is action taken 'under color of state law' (emphasis added)."[6] In other words, if those police officers were not wearing their uniforms and badges, they could not have gone into Monroe's home without incurring both civil liability and criminal sanctions. Therefore, they should not be able to violate his constitutional rights merely because they work for a governmental entity.

The test to determine whether someone is acting under color of law is almost identical to evaluating whether state action has occurred. If there has been state action, that action was performed under color of state law. This makes sense because the Court has ruled that the private conduct is, in general, not regulated by the Constitution, so if state action has not occurred, there could be no constitutional violation.

Monroe was also important for its holding that a Section 1983 cause of action was available, even though adequate state judicial remedies were potentially available. The Court explained that this statute was intended to provide a remedy in situations where state officials prohibit practices, but provide inadequate remedies, and also in instances where state remedies are theoretically available, but are in practice unavailable. This is important because it is very likely that a state that is sued for something that one of its actors did might be unwilling to find for liability.

Establishing Municipal Liability

Monroe held that municipal governments were not "persons" under the meaning of the statute, and therefore may not be sued under Section 1983. The Court arrived at this conclusion by looking at the legislative history of the statute. In the years after the Monroe decision, however, many commentators criticized the Court's analysis of the legislative history and, likewise, criticized its decision to immunize municipal governments from the reach of Section 1983. In 1978, the Court was given the chance to change its mind.

In *Monell v. Department of Social Services*,[7] the Supreme Court explicitly overruled Monroe's limitation on municipal liability. The liability that may attach to municipal governments, however, is much less broad than what may attach to state governments. After *Monell*, municipal governments could only be sued for their own unconstitutional or illegal policies. Municipalities may not be sued for an unconstitutional act inflicted solely by its employees or agents. In other words, under Section 1983, the municipality could not be liable based on a *respondeat superior* theory. For example, if a building inspector negligently fails to send out a notice of a revocation of an occupancy permit, his or her supervisor will be free of liability under Section 1983 unless the plaintiff can show that the supervisor actively prevented the inspector from sending the notice. If the plaintiff cannot prove this, he or she can only sue the building official as an individual.

The *Monell* holding has been refined over the years. Now, there are various ways to establish an official policy or custom. The Court has found that in the absence of a written policy, even a single action by the official local legislative body constitutes an official policy. Official policy also exists when there are actions by state agencies or boards that exercise authority delegated by the state legislative bodies. Further, an action taken by someone with final policy-making authority will constitute an official policy. A determination of whether someone has final policy-making authority is a question of state law for the judge to determine. To assist in this determination, the judge should look not only to state law, but also to relevant customs or practices. A state's failure to train or supervise adequately its officers can also establish an official policy. Likewise considered an official policy is the failure to respond to repeated complaints regarding the unconstitutional conduct of the state's officers. Rather, only where the failure to train, supervise or respond to complaints reflects a deliberate or conscious choice by a state or municipality—a policy as defined by the relevant case law—can a municipality be liable for such a failure under Section 1983. This deliberate indifference standard is very difficult for a plaintiff to apply.

One final way to establish municipal liability under Section 1983 is to establish an unconstitutional custom. A custom is something that is done all the time (for example, written procedures of a municipality). Although this custom would not have received formal approval from the official legislative body, a plaintiff may try to prove the existence of a custom through repeated constitutional violations for which the officers were not discharged or reprimanded.

Deprivation of Federal Constitutional or Statutory Rights

A conduct is an action. Examples of unconstitutional conduct include illegal searches and seizures (Chapter 8) and the prosecution of a citizen without probable cause. If a building official initiates prosecution against an alleged building code offender, that official may not only face liability under the state tort known as malicious prosecution (Chapter 10), but may also face liability under Section 1983.

Procedural due process is another constitutional right a building official must be careful not to violate. Procedural due process means that parties whose rights are to be affected are entitled to be heard, and therefore must be notified. For example, if a builder has his or her occupancy permit revoked, the builder must be heard prior to the time the revocation would take effect. In some cases, however, the court will waive the procedural due process requirements. If immediate revocation is absolutely crucial to the health and safety of the inhabitants of the building, the court might waive the builder's procedural due process requirements. A building official, however, should never assume that the court will do this. Rather, always give the builder an opportunity to be heard.

In *Daniels v. Williams*[8] and its companion case, *Davidson v. Cannon*,[9] the Court held that negligent deprivations of due process rights are not redressable under Section 1983. In *Daniels*, a prisoner claimed that his freedom from bodily harm, a protected liberty interest, was denied without due process when he tripped on a pillow, which was negligently left on a staircase by a prison guard. *Davidson* concerned a prisoner's claim that prison authorities violated his due process rights by failing to protect him from attack by another prisoner. The prisoner was threatened and informed the prison authorities, but they inadvertently forgot about the messages and the prisoner was later seriously injured in an attack. The Court held that neither of the plaintiffs had a cause of action under Section 1983, and stated that, "the Due Process Clause is simply not implicated by a *negligent* act of an official causing unintended loss of or injury to life, liberty, or property...Not only does the word "deprive" in the Due Process Clause connote more than a negligent act, but we should not open the federal courts to lawsuits where there has been no affirmative abuse of power."[10] The holdings of these two cases extend to all due process claims. Now, in order to state a valid cause of action under Section 1983, a plaintiff must show that a state or municipal official intentionally violated his or her due process rights.

Immunities

Most building officials have a qualified or good faith immunity from liability under Section 1983. In 1982, the Court refined the test currently used to determine whether an officer acted in good faith. In *Harlow v. Fitzgerald*,[11] the Court held that, "government officials performing discretionary functions generally are shielded from liability for civil damages insofar as their conduct does not violate clearly established statutory or constitutional rights of which a reasonable person would have known." Therefore, if an official acts in a manner that is explicitly unconstitutional, the official will not be immune from liability, but if the official acts in a manner that is not specifically unlawful under a statute or the Constitution, the official will be immune. Further, if an official violates a statute or constitutional provision that is vague or as of yet unlitigated, the official may be immune. When in doubt whether a behavior is unlawful, it is best to consult an attorney before acting.

Although the building official can be protected by qualified immunity, the city in which that official works is not protected. In *Owen v. City of Independence*,[12] the Supreme Court held that local governments are liable even when their constitutional violations result from actions taken in good faith. Therefore, if the public official were acting pursuant to a city regulation, guideline, ordinance, statute or regulation, that official is immune from suit. The city that enacted or otherwise adopted the unconstitutional regulation or ordinance is absolutely liable in tort. It has no immunity. Thus, the city is pitted against its own public officials.

When a building official is sued under Section 1983, he or she must be somewhat careful of the municipal attorney. If the attorney represents both the city and the building official, a potential conflict of interest could arise. If the attorney seeks to show that the building official was acting pursuant to a city regulation, the court must find that the public official is immune and the city is liable. If, however, the attorney attempts to argue that the public official was acting independently and beyond the scope of the actual authority conveyed by the city regulation, the city would not be liable while the public official may be. In cases involving Section 1983, it is recommended that public officials consider hiring separate counsel from that of the city.

Case Study Hilda v. Brown[13]

While case law remains favorable towards building officials, the federal civil rights case of *Hilda v. Brown* involving a Section 1983 cause of action and its subsequent criminal case should capture every building official's attention. This case arises out of the death of the Lofgren family because of carbon monoxide poisoning while they were staying at the Lodge near Aspen, Colorado. The Lodge is a large vacation rental property. The representatives ("Plaintiffs") of the Lofgren family's estate brought a federal civil rights suit against various individuals involved with installing and servicing the HVAC system and its associated components, as well as Pitkin County Board of County Commissioners and Pitkin County Community Development Department, who issued the certificate of occupancy, and Erik Peltonen and Brian Pawl who inspected the HVAC system on behalf of Pitkin County. Collectively, Peltonen, Pawl, and the two County Defendants are referred to as the "Public Defendants." The Court will later refer to the Department and the Board collectively as "County Defendants" and Peltonen and Pawl collectively as "Individual Defendants." It is important to remember who is in which group in order to follow the Court's analysis.

Defendant Pitkin County Community Development Department ("Department"), a department of Defendant Pitkin County Board of Commissioners ("Board"), is responsible for the approval of residential construction projects, granting building permits, performing building inspections, issuing certificates of occupancy, and administering and enforcing the Pitkin County Building Code. Defendant Erik Peltonen was a building inspector employed by the city of Aspen who, by intergovernmental agreement, performed building inspections for the Department. Defendant Brian Pawl was a building inspector employed by Pitkin County.

Pertinent Facts of the Case

In 2003, the Board adopted the *International Residential Code*® (IRC®), 2003 Edition, as part of the building requirements and code of Pitkin County. Before a certificate of occupancy could be issued, all homes had to have a hard-wired carbon monoxide detector. From 2003 through 2005, permits were issued for various alterations and additions to the property. In January 2005 the Department issued a mechanical permit for the installation of a natural gas boiler. A Munchkin gas-fired hot water boiler was installed to melt snow and provide hot water to the Lodge. Installation of the Munchkin boiler required an intake vent to provide fresh air from outside, as well as an exhaust vent to remove the carbon monoxide and other gases from the residence. Plaintiffs allege that the design and installation of the intake and exhaust vents violated the manufacturer's instructions and warnings, the American National Standards, the IRC and the Pitkin County Code and building requirements.

In February 2005, the Department issued another mechanical permit for purposes of installing an HVAC system. Three gas forced-air furnaces were installed. They were supposed to be supplied with fresh air through an intake vent. However, improper installation of the vents and ductwork caused at least one of the furnaces to circulate air from the mechanical room-rather than fresh air from outside-throughout the Lodge. The plaintiffs allege that the HVAC system design and installation were improper, violating the manufacturer's instruction. They further allege that HVAC installation was in violation of the IRC and Pitkin County's Building Code.

In June 2005, Peltonen performed various inspections of the mechanical work on the boiler and the HVAC system. Pawl performed additional inspections on these systems in August 2005. Open and obvious defects to both of these systems were present at the time of these inspections and there was no carbon monoxide detector installed in the home. Despite these defects, the Lodge passed final inspection and either Peltonen or Pawl placed a tag on the gas line, which allowed the utility company to introduce natural gas service to the Lodge. The following year, in June of 2006, the Department issued a certificate of occupancy for the Lodge.

In an auction at their children's school, the Lofgren family and their friends, the MacKenzie family, purchased a five day stay at the Lodge. The Lofgrens arrived first on November 26, 2008. Their plan was to spend the Thanksgiving holiday with the MacKenzies. On the evening of November 27, 2008, it began to snow. This caused the Munchkin boiler to start up. When the MacKenzie family arrived on November 28, 2008, they found the Lofgren family dead inside one of the bedrooms. The cause of death was later determined to be carbon monoxide poisoning because of defects in the design and installation of the Munchkin boiler and the HVAC system.

Case Analysis

There were multiple causes of action brought against multiple defendants but for purposes of this discussion we will only focus on the federal civil rights Section 1983 cause of action. The Public Defendants moved to dismiss the federal civil rights claim arguing that Plaintiffs failed to state a claim for violation of their due process rights under 42 U.S.C. 1983. The Individual Defendants argued the defense of qualified immunity. The County Defendants argued that they cannot be held liable for a constitutional violation if the Individual Defendants are not found liable.

Individual Defendants' Claims of Qualified Immunity

In order for building officials to be protected against liability under a qualified immunity claim, the building officials conduct cannot have violated clearly established statutory or constitutional rights of which a reasonable person would have known. In examining a qualified immunity claim, courts will examine two elements: (1) whether a constitutional violation occurred, and (2) whether the violated right was clearly established at the time of the violation. In order to overcome the defense of qualified immunity, a plaintiff must establish both elements.

1. Did Plaintiffs allege a constitutional violation?

Plaintiffs allege that the constitutional violation occurred when the Individual Defendants conducted lax inspections resulting in a series of events that ultimately lead to the Lofgren family's death. Building officials may be subject to constitutional liability if they: (1) create a danger that results in harm to a person, even if the harm was not inflicted by the building official; or (2) if the building official has a special relationship with the plaintiff.

Because the plaintiffs acknowledged no special relationship existed between them and the Individual Defendants, they argued that the Individual Defendants were liable under a **"danger creation"** theory. The "danger creation" theory states that government actors may be liable for an individual plaintiff's safety if it created the danger that caused harm to the individual. In order to prove liability under the "danger creation" theory, a plaintiff must prove six things. First, that the government entity and individual actors created the danger or increased the plaintiff's vulnerability to the danger in some way. Second, the plaintiff was a member of a specifically defined and limited group. Third, the defendant's actions put the plaintiff at substantial risk of serious, immediate and proximate harm. Fourth, the risk was obvious and known to the defendants. Fifth, the defendant acted in a reckless manner, in conscious disregard of the known risk. Sixth, defendant's conduct, when viewed in totality, is conscious shocking. In this case, Plaintiffs failed to establish that the Individual Defendants created or increased the Plaintiff's vulnerability to the danger and that the Individual Defendants did not place the Plaintiffs at substantial risk of immediate harm.

In order to establish a Section 1983 cause of action, the conduct of the defendants must be directed at a discrete plaintiff and not to the public at large. The court found that the Individual Defendant's conduct, that of performing inspections and approving the Lodge for occupation, was directed to the public at large and not to the Plaintiffs. The Plaintiffs failed to show how the Individual Defendants created a particular danger to them or increased their vulnerability to the danger.

Plaintiffs also failed to show how the Individual Defendants created a substantial risk of immediate harm. Courts have held that for purposes of a Section 1983 claim, the conduct should pose an immediate threat of harm, which by the nature of the harm is limited in range and duration. Because the Individual Defendants performed the disputed inspections more than three years prior to the Lofgren family's death, any harm caused by the "perfunctory" inspections was not immediate.

Because Plaintiffs failed to establish sufficient facts to show that the Individual Defendants created the danger resulting in the deaths of the Lofgren family, they have failed to state a claim sufficient to support a finding that a violation of their Constitutional rights occurred.

2.   Was any constitutional violation clearly established?

As discussed above, a plaintiff must establish both a violation of constitutional rights and that the violated right was clearly established at the time of the violation. Even if Plaintiffs had shown facts sufficient to find a violation of constitutional rights, they would not have been able to show that the violated right was clearly established at the time of the violation.

The Court cited to several federal cases that held that alleged inadequate building inspections did not form the basis for a constitutional violation. For example, wrongful issuance of a certificate of occupancy and failure to adequately inspect a building before approving it for Housing and Urban Development (HUD) occupancy were not constitutional violations. A city was not held liable for a fire even though the building had been inadequately inspected the previous week.[14] Because the Plaintiffs failed to show that the Individual Defendants violated clearly established federal law, they were entitled to qualified immunity.

Liability of the County Defendants

Plaintiffs allege that the County Defendants created the danger that resulted in the Lofgren family's death, failed to adequately supervise the Individual Defendants, had inadequate policies, practices and customs and they knowingly approved a pattern of not enforcing the provisions of its building codes.

The County Defendants allegedly created the danger that resulted in the Lofgren family's death by issuing the certificate of occupancy. Similar to the discussion above, any risk arguably created was directed at the public at large and not specifically to the Plaintiffs. Further, as the Lofgren family's death occurred more than two years after the issuance of the certificate of occupancy, any danger created was not immediate. Therefore, the Plaintiffs failed to show any direct liability to the Plaintiffs.

To succeed on their claim that the County Defendants failed to adequately train their employees, Plaintiffs must prove that Individual Defendants who were supervised by the County Defendants committed a constitutional violation. As discussed above, the Plaintiffs failed to show that the Individual Defendants violated their constitutional rights. Therefore, there are no facts to support a claim of inadequate training.

The Court next examined the claim that the County Defendants had an unconstitutional policy, practice or custom of granting certificates of occupancy despite inadequate inspections. There is no allegation there was an "official enactment" resulting in unconstitutional violations. Rather, Plaintiffs allege the County Defendants had a custom of knowingly approving of the nonenforcement or selective enforcement of building codes.

Plaintiffs were unable to show any proof that the County Defendants had any notice of other lax building inspections or selective enforcement of their building codes. In fact, no proof was presented of any other instances where building code violations were ignored by the County Defendants. Therefore, because the Plaintiffs failed to prove any claim on which relief could be granted, the Section 1983 claim was dismissed.

Negligent Homicide Case

Even though the federal civil rights case was dismissed, it did not prevent the District Attorney from pursuing **negligent homicide** charges against Erik Peltonen and the owner of the plumbing and heating company.[15] For purposes of this discussion we will only discuss the case against Peltonen. In the criminal case, the county hired attorneys to represent Peltonen. They argued that because the County's implementation of the building code is involuntary, that shielded Peltonen from civil or criminal liability.[16] They also argued that the criminal statute was unconstitutional in that it was vague and did not give fair warning that an inspector could be criminally prosecuted for any alleged failure or omission in carrying out the job of building inspector.

The prosecution argued that building inspectors are not above the law. The job of building inspector carries with it a duty and responsibility to ensure that building inspections are completed in compliance with relevant city, county and state law. They further argued that Colorado's Governmental Immunity Act and County code does not give carte blanche authority to violate criminal law. Finally, the prosecution argued that there was no relevant Colorado case law or statute that said inspectors could not be held responsible for exercising their duty in a criminally negligent manner.

In the end, none of these arguments mattered or were ruled upon. The criminal case was ultimately dismissed due to a defect in the grand jury's indictment and because the three-year statute of limitations had run.[17]

This case should give every building official pause for reflection. It attracted national attention, not only for the tragic nature of the deaths but because building officials are rarely, if ever, held criminally liable in these types of deaths. It certainly generated a great deal of discussion among building officials.[18] In the civil rights case, had the Lofgren family's death occurred the first winter after the certificate of occupancy was issued, the winter of 2006–07, the court would probably have found that the "immediacy" factor of the danger creation theory had been met. However, the court may still have found that the Plaintiff's failed to overcome the protection afforded by the public duty doctrine—that the Defendants owed a duty to the public at large and not to the Plaintiffs. In the criminal case, had the statute of limitations not expired, there is no telling what a jury would have found or a judge ruled had the case gone to trial.

The take away from this case is, continue to do your job to the best of your ability as a reasonably prudent building official would do it. And, be mindful of and comply with your local and state building codes.

The Fair Housing Act

In recent years, there has been much attention paid to the millions of American citizens with some sort of physical or mental disability. In 1988, Congress amended the Fair Housing Act (FHA) of 1968 to extend its protection to handicapped persons.[19] A handicap was defined as a "physical or mental impairment which substantially limits one or more of such person's major life activities." The goal of the amendment is to overcome the stereotype that people with disabilities cannot function in "normal" surroundings and therefore need to live elsewhere. This act is of importance to the building code official because it mandates design standards for new housing with four or more units. These standards are meant to ensure general access both around common areas and within the units themselves. Some of the many requirements designers and builders of structures of more than four units must follow are: (1) doors, halls and thresholds must accommodate wheelchairs; (2) light switches, electrical outlets, thermostats and other environmental controls must also be accessible to people in wheelchairs; and (3) usable kitchens and bathrooms must be built so that wheelchairs can move about the space.

The FHA should be read together with the Civil Rights Act of 1866.[20] This act, more commonly known as Section 1982, provides that, "all citizens of the United States shall have the same right, in every State and Territory, as is enjoyed by white citizens thereof to inherit, purchase, lease, sell, hold, and convey real and personal property." Each act enhances, but does not preempt, the other.

In 1995, the Supreme Court decided *The City of Edmonds v. Oxford House, Inc.*[21] Oxford House operated a group home in Edmonds, Washington, for ten to 12 adults recovering from alcoholism and drug addiction in a neighborhood zoned for single-family residences. The City of Edmonds issued citations to the owner of Oxford House charging him with a violation of the city's zoning code. The code provides that the occupants of single-family dwelling units must compose a family, and defines family as "persons related by genetics, adoption, or marriage, or a group of five or fewer [unrelated] persons." The code did not limit the number of family members who could live in a single-family dwelling unit. Oxford House defended itself by relying on the FHA. Discrimination under the FHA includes, "a refusal to make reasonable accommodations in rules, policies, practices or services, when such accommodations may be necessary to afford [handicapped] person[s] equal opportunity to use and enjoy a dwelling."[22] The City of Edmonds then filed a suit in federal court seeking a declaration that the FHA not restrict its zoning code's family definition rule. Oxford House, along with the United States Government, counterclaimed under the FHA. They charged that the city failed to make a reasonable accommodation by refusing to permit the group home in a single-family zone.

The lower federal court ruled for the city, holding that the rule defining family was exempt from the FHA and cited an exemption found at 42 U.S.C.A. Section 3607(b)(1). This section found there to be a reasonable restriction regarding the maximum number of occupants permitted to occupy a dwelling. The court found the family definition rule to be a maximum occupancy restriction and therefore held for the City. The court of appeals reversed, however, and the Supreme Court affirmed that reversal. It found that the family definition rule was not a maximum occupancy restriction. It came to this conclusion because the rule did not have any limitation on the number of residents in the single-family home, but rather focused solely on the relationship between the parties. Under this rule, a genetically related family of 50 or more people is allowed to live together in a single-family dwelling, while a group of ten to twelve unrelated people is prevented from living together. The purpose of the FHA's exemption is meant to protect health and safety by preventing overcrowding in dwelling units. The family definition rule was found to be inconsistent with the policies underlying the maximum occupancy exemption. Occupancy limits should be based on square footage.

A growing area of litigation under the Fair Housing Act and the Civil Rights Act involves **urban renewal**. Frequently, as housing ages, the most blighted areas are multiple-family dwellings that contain subsidized rental units populated by poor persons. These dwellings are too often neglected by absentee landlords and become the site of an abnormal amount of criminal activity.

In an attempt to deal with rising crime rates and dilapidated buildings, municipalities may decide to tear down the buildings and rezone or redevelop the area. This has the effect of displacing poor people who do not have the same relocation options as other persons might have. The municipality may then face litigation over whether it has discriminated against a particular class of persons (for example, Hispanics or African-Americans) by taking action, even if the redevelopment plans are legal under state law.[23] This type of litigation is very expensive and any municipality contemplating redevelopment of this type of area should expect a lawsuit.

The Americans with Disabilities Act

In 1990, Congress continued its intervention in both the private and public sectors on behalf of disabled persons with its adoption of the wide-ranging Americans with Disabilities Act (ADA).[24] This act covers employment discrimination, public transportation, public accommodations and telecommunications. It is similar to the FHA in that it requires owners of existing public structures to make appropriate accommodations to the needs of disabled people. It also holds builders of new structures to a higher standard. It sets the design criteria for public accommodations and commercial facilities so that a disabled person can mainstream more comfortably. Included under these titles are hotels, restaurants, offices, stores and all nonresidential facilities where operations will affect commerce. It is very rare that a court will find a nonresidential facility where operations do not affect commerce. A building that falls under the ADA's coverage may get a waiver, however, if the owner can show it is "structurally infeasible" to meet the standard. People who believe that they are being discriminated against under the FHA or the ADA may seek injunctive relief and damages in federal court. They can also file complaints with the local fair housing authority.

The ADA will preempt the provisions of those building codes that are less stringent than its own requirements. As of yet, there have not been many cases arising under the ADA which would be relevant to the building official. This current dearth of litigation, however, does not exempt the building official from administering and enforcing the building code in accordance with ADA guidelines. A building official who does not follow these guidelines risks the possibility that liability will attach to him or her or to the municipality in the future.

The Attorney's Fee Award Act (Section 1988)[25]

Section 1988 is one of the most important innovations in civil rights litigation. This act allows the plaintiff to recover any expenses incurred for attorney's fees in the prosecution of the case. Therefore, if a defendant loses a Section 1983 lawsuit, the defendant may face payment not only of the actual compensatory damages awarded to the plaintiff, but of the attorney's fees as well. Frequently, the attorney's fees can amount to more than the compensation for violation of the constitutional rights of the plaintiff. For example, there is at least one instance of a prisoner's civil rights case where the prisoner was successful in obtaining a judgment roughly in the amount of $2,000. The district court judge ruled, however, that the plaintiff's attorney was entitled to fees of $9,000. Therefore, the defendant paid a total of approximately $11,000, only $2,000 of which actually went to the person who was harmed. The attorney got the rest.

This puts a building official in a bind. Frequently, the constitutional rights of a particular plaintiff are not worth much monetarily. If one considers having to pay many thousands more in attorney's fees if the case is lost at trial, therefore, there is a great impetus to settle.

Furthermore, Section 1988 only benefits the plaintiff. The building official does not have the same rights as the plaintiff. In order for the defendant to receive attorney's fees, the defendant must be able to show that the plaintiff brought a frivolous lawsuit. This is very difficult and there are few cases that have held in favor of a defendant's request for attorney's fees after a dismissal of a plaintiff's action.

Conclusion

The civil rights acts discussed in this chapter are not yet used capably by attorneys for plaintiffs against building officials. In the years to come, more and more aggrieved persons will look to the protection of federal civil rights acts to bring lawsuits against building officials. The most dangerous weapon in this arsenal is Section 1983. This provision allows anyone who has been deprived of a constitutional right to bring a lawsuit against the person who caused the deprivation. Fortunately, there are a number of defenses, the most important of which is qualified immunity. Hopefully, in most cases, the building official will have the advice of competent counsel to steer him or her clear of any obvious Section 1983 violations.

Section 1988, the Attorney's Fee Award Act can be debilitating. The expenses of an attorney can run into many thousands of dollars, and a defendant looking at the possibility of a jury verdict in federal district court may decide to settle a case just because of the existence of this one act. Therefore, building officials must continue to keep accurate records in order to protect themselves.

Chapter 12 Endnotes

1. Litigation arising under the Civil Rights Act of 1871 is more commonly referred to as Section 1983 litigation because it is codified in the United States Code as 42 U.S.A. Section 1983.

2. M. Schwartz & J. Kirklin, Section 1983 Litigation: Claims, Defenses, and Fees (2d ed. 1991).

3. The number of Section 1983 suits filed in the United States rose from 267 in 1961 to 36,582 in 1985.

4. *Monroe v. Pape*, 365 U.S. 167 (1961).

5. It is interesting to note that before 1961, the "under color of state law" language, which was so narrowly construed in Section 1983 actions, existed and was broadly interpreted in criminal statutes.

6. Monroe at 184.

7. *Monell v. Department of Social Services of New York City*, 436 U.S. 685 (1978).

8. *Davidson v. Cannon*, 474 U.S. 344 (1986).

9. *Id.*

10. *Daniels v. Williams*, 474 U.S. 328 (1986).

11. *Harlow v. Fitzgerald*, 457 U.S. 800 (1982).

12. *Owen v. City of Independence*, 445 U.S. 622 (1980).

13. *Hilda M. v. Brown*, 2011 WL 5220230, November 2, 2011.

14. *Id.*

15. Brian Pawl was charged with four misdemeanor counts of reckless endangerment connected to the deaths, but his charges were dismissed because the statute of limitations had expired.

16. Interestingly, this was an argument made in a "friend of the court" brief filed by the International Code Council as well as the attorneys for Pitkin County, the city of Aspen and the Colorado Municipal League. It was further argued that the criminal case could dramatically effect how building departments do business and "the pace of construction work would slow to a crawl." http://www.skyhidailynews.com/news/da-argues-against-dismissal-of-pitkin-county-carbon-monoxide-deaths-case/.

17. http://www.aspentimes.com/news/judge-drops-criminal-cases-in-aspen-carbon-monoxide-fatalities/.

18. Said one person: "...take heed in [the] completion of our job duties to a greater extent." Another said: "My understanding is that an inspector performing his official duties in good faith whould [sic] be immune from personal liability. I am not proposing that this be changed. I do wonder if this lack of institutional or personal liability has a negative impact on the quality of code enforcement. With no consequences for poor practices there is little motivation to address existing problems with code enforcement [sic]. What mechanisms could be created that would foster improvement?" http://www.thebuildingcodeforum.com/forum/threads/applaud-the-icc-on-this-one.5282/.

19. In 1968, Congress enacted Title VIII of the Civil Rights Act of 1968, which is more commonly known as the Fair Housing Act of 1968. This act made it unlawful to refuse to sell or rent a dwelling to any person because of race, color, religion, or national origin and was codified in the United States Code as 42 U.S.C. Section 3604. In 1974, the act was amended to prohibit discrimination on the basis of sex. Aside from prohibiting discrimination against the disabled, the 1988 amendment also prohibits discrimination against persons with children in senior citizen housing.

20. 42 U.S.C.A. Section 1982.

21. *City of Edmunds v. Oxford House*, 115 S.Ct. 1776 (1995).

22. 42 U.S.C.A. Section 3604(f)(3)(B).

23. See, for example, *Hispanics United of DuPage County v. Village of Addison*, 160 F.R.D. 681(1995).

24. 42 U.S.C.A. Sections 12101-213.

25. This act is most commonly referred to as Section 1988.

Chapter 13 – The Role of the Witness

This chapter discusses guidelines to help the building official effectively testify in court.

Topics

Fact Witness

Guidelines for Witnesses

Sequestration of Witnesses

Expert Witness

Consulting Experts

Terms

advocate

cross-examination

direct examination

discovery

expert witness

fact witness

hypothetical question

impeachment

redirect

refresh recollection

rule of sequestration

subpoena

subpoena duces tecum

voir dire

Introduction

It is very likely that, during the course of employment, a building official will be called upon to testify in court. Therefore, it is crucial that building officials know how to present themselves in administrative and judicial forums. It is usually the job of the attorney to prepare a witness for trial. Depending on the local procedure, however, the attorney handling the case may not have enough time to review thoroughly the guidelines that will help a witness testify effectively.

This chapter will help to prepare the building official for a court appearance, whether it is to testify as to specific facts or to give an expert opinion regarding certain provisions of the building code. After reading this chapter, the building official should have a good idea of how to act in the courtroom, and of the importance of working closely with a municipal or other type of attorney. This chapter will also explain how to assist effectively an attorney in the preparation of the case. Also, the process for qualifying expert witnesses will be described and examined in order to help the building official understand its importance in a jury trial. The chapter will conclude by discussing certain techniques the building official may follow when responding to cross examination.

Fact Witness

In many of the cases in which building officials or their representatives are called upon to testify, they are called upon as fact witnesses. A **fact witness** will be asked to describe circumstances that he or she has observed firsthand. Generally, cases that involve a building official as a witness will either be those that are brought to enforce a particular code section or those brought as a defense to actions for damages against the building official. In either event, the fact witness has been called in order to relate to the judge and jury the substance of what the official observed in the course of enforcing the code. In order to make sure a witness appears in court to testify on behalf of a party, a **subpoena** can be issued to order the appearance of a witness. A **subpoena duces tecum** is issued to a witness to force him or her to bring specific documents or records to a hearing.

In the majority of enforcement actions, the building official initiates the legal action. Therefore, there is no excuse for an official to fail to prepare in advance for an upcoming trial. If a department is large enough to have several inspectors, the most competent person should be assigned to a case if it is expected to end up in court as a contested manner. The most competent person is not necessarily the person with the most seniority. Rather, it is the person who has good evidence-gathering skills and who can testify clearly and convincingly. Smaller municipalities do not have the luxury of giving special assignments. The building official may also be the person doing property maintenance and fire inspections, as well as reviewing plans for new construction.

The assigned inspector should take care to follow the normal departmental procedure, which includes, but is not limited to, the preparation of any written reports. Keep in mind that in order for the inspector to become a witness later, that inspector must not only be proficient in his or her field of work, but must also be able to communicate effectively with a judge and jury. If the case is sufficiently important, it would be useful to consult with the building department's attorney for help choosing the best inspector.

To help the inspector be the best possible witness, testimonial aids are quite effective. For example, physical evidence obtained at the scene or diagrams of the property can reinforce the inspector's oral testimony. Careful consideration in developing such exhibits should be given before the lawsuit is filed. Photographs are another very effective and fairly inexpensive way of aiding testimony. Color photographs have won many a lawsuit. Again, it is always useful to consult with the department's attorney regarding the form that this testimony should take. (For a further discussion of evidence, see Chapter 6.)

All building officials should work closely with the municipality's attorney to properly prepare for trial. The attorney's role is to act as an **advocate** for the municipality; that is, to plead the cause of his or her client in court. An attorney who argues a case in court is an advocate for the party he or she represents. Sometimes the witness has to be quite vocal to get the attorney's attention. If the attorney is not responsive to the needs of the building department, the municipality should consider changing attorneys.

To prepare for a major enforcement action or a tort liability case, the building official and the attorney must frequently confer. It is important on these occasions for the building official to be entirely truthful with the attorney. The building official should inform the attorney of every fact he or she believes to be relevant to the case. Facts, even those that the official believes to be detrimental to the case, should not be omitted. Between conversations with an attorney, it is a good idea for the building official to write down every observation or recollection he or she may have concerning the issue in dispute. When speaking to an attorney, these notes will serve as a reminder of the pertinent facts, which will in turn help the attorney to present the strongest case. Only show these notes to the attorney handling the case.

As you meet with the attorney, take the opportunity to instruct him or her on the code and why it is important. Help the attorney understand why your case is deserving of attention. In many jurisdictions, the municipal attorney may not handle many code related cases. It is easy for the municipal attorney to not take these cases seriously or not give them great importance. Your job is to help them see and understand why your case is just as important as other cases they may be handling. A smart municipal attorney will appreciate any guidance you can give.

Guidelines for Witnesses

There are a number of general guidelines for a witness to follow. While on the stand, a witness must make his or her own decision regarding how to handle certain questions.

The following guidelines are not all inclusive; however, they provide a point of reference from which to begin.

1. Always tell the truth.

This is the most important guideline to remember. Many times witnesses feel they are expected to answer a certain way, and will lie to accommodate those expectations. Lying while under oath will not only most likely prove detrimental to the case, but is illegal. The easiest way to lose a case is to lie or stretch the truth, even about a seemingly insignificant detail. On **cross-examination**, the opposing attorney can easily uncover any lies or inconsistencies a witness may present in his or her testimony. If this occurs, neither the judge nor the jury will, or is obligated to, believe anything the witness has said. Therefore, not only will the lies be disregarded, but any true and possibly helpful testimony will also be disregarded. When the cross-examination serves to negate the credibility of a witness, this is called an **impeachment**. For example, a code official who relies on his or her memory rather than written records may inadvertently change his or her testimony on cross-examination compared to direct examination. This casts doubt on the believability of the witness. The opposing attorney will try to point out discrepancies between the code official's written records and his or her current testimony. If the official has testified at a previous hearing, the attorney may use the record of the previous testimony to impeach the witness. Therefore, it is always important for the code official to review all records and transcripts prior to testifying.

Of course, it can sometimes be embarrassing to answer truthfully. Opposing counsel may ask about arrests or convictions which the witness may have had or any lawsuits in which he or she has been a party. If the judge finds that the relevance of those questions is strong enough to the case at hand, he or she will require that the witness answer them. Also, the witness is almost always asked about whether he or she spoke with the attorney handling the case before he or she took the stand. When such a question is asked, the best thing to do is to tell the truth. Every attorney expects witnesses to have talked to an attorney about the case before testifying. Do not worry about trap questions. If the witness is truthful, very few things an attorney can do will damage the case. Also, if the attorney for the witness's side feels that his or her testimony has been damaged by the opposing counsel's cross-examination, the attorney will do his or her best to restore the witness's testimony on redirect. The witness should not be afraid to say he or she does not remember if that is the truth.

2. Prior to testifying, review all relevant documentation.

This includes documents that the attorney has filed with the court. It is not unusual for minor discrepancies to turn up in such documents. By reviewing the documents, the errors can be corrected, modified or explained. The witness must also be thoroughly familiar with all aspects of his or her testimony. If the witness fails to review any and all available documents, it is likely that a witness's memory will deceive him or her. The opposing attorney is trained to notice when a witness is not being sincere, or is not quite sure of the nature of the testimony. The opposing attorney will always embarrassingly call attention to any inconsistency or inaccuracy he or she detects.

The good news however, is that you may take your file or notes with you to the witness stand. Generally, you may not read from your notes but they may be used to "**refresh your recollection**." No witness is expected to remember every detail of every case. When you find yourself unsure of specific facts or details, despite having reviewed your notes before court, or when you simply forget something, let the attorney know that you do not remember the specific details of the question being asked. Tell the attorney that the answer to the question is contained in your notes. Then ask the attorney if you may refer to your notes before answering.

Typically, your attorney will then ask you a series of questions to establish a foundation for the court to show that at one time you knew the answer to the question. For example, you are asked for specific measurements of the foundation of a series of large commercial buildings you inspected the previous year. While on the witness stand, you can no longer remember the exact measurements for each building. After letting the attorney know you do not recall the exact measurements he will ask you questions such as these: "Did you conduct the inspections and take the measurements?" "Did you record those measurements at the time of the inspection?" "Do you have a copy of the inspection report with you, in your file?" "If you were to refer to your inspection report, would that help you remember the measurements?" After you have answered "yes" to each question the attorney will direct you to refer to your notes. Remember, unless the judge gives you permission, you cannot read from your notes but only use them to "refresh your recollection." After your recollection has been refreshed, look up and let the attorney know that you now remember the details of the question.

   3.   Never volunteer anything on either direct examination or cross-examination.

If opposing counsel wants to know a particular fact, he or she will ask. Be sure to answer only the questions asked. On cross-examination, the other attorney is permitted to ask what are known as leading questions. A leading question is one in which the answer is suggested in the question itself. For example, during cross-examination, an attorney may ask, "Wasn't the building foundation already laid by March 1, Mr. Building Code Official?" If the answer implied in that question is true, then the answer must be "yes." If there is some doubt on that point, the witness must clearly express that doubt in his answer. Even if the opposing counsel tries to stop the witness from elaborating on the doubt, the witness should try to say as much as he or she is able. Never allow yourself to agree to a leading question unless you are sure that it is the correct answer.

   4.   If the answer to a question is unknown, say so.

There is no crime in not knowing an answer. If the witness does not remember or, in fact, never knew a particular fact from first-hand observation, he or she should inform the opposing attorney of that fact. It is always better for the building official to admit not knowing than to guess or rely on an uncertain memory. If the building official guesses or speculates on the answer and opposing counsel produces evidence that the answer is untrue, damage to the case can be considerable.

5. Never answer a question until it is understood.

It is always best to wait a moment before responding to any question on cross-examination. By waiting a bit, the witness has a chance to analyze the question to be sure that he or she understands what is being asked. If the question is not understood, do not be afraid to ask that the question be repeated, or tell the attorney that you are not sure if you understand. The attorney will generally rephrase the question. Also, by pausing, the witness gains the chance to organize the answer. The more articulate and intelligent the answer sounds to the jury, the greater the witness's credibility will be. Finally, pausing gives the attorney time to object if the question is objectionable. At times, witnesses get so excited that they fail to give the attorney a chance to object. Needless to say, the moment the attorney begins either to speak or to stand, immediately stop speaking. If the judge sustains the objection, do not answer the question.

6. Always be polite.

No matter how great the provocation, do not get angry. Try to remain as calm as possible. Keep in mind that some attorneys purposely seek to upset witnesses in the hopes that they will reveal something in the heat of anger that they would have never revealed if they had remained calm. Remember that any anger or hostility displayed on the witness stand will only serve to help the opposing attorney.

Furthermore, never try to argue with the cross-examining attorney. The courtroom is the attorney's work place. He or she will always be more comfortable than the witness. The opposing attorney is in charge of the cross-examination, and it would be futile for the witness to try to get the last word.

7. Speak clearly and audibly.

It is crucial that the judge and jury hear the testimony. If they cannot hear the testimony, they will be less inclined to rule in the witness's favor. It is also a good idea to look directly at the jurors when answering questions. This helps them to hear and also helps to evaluate the witness's personality and demeanor. Remember that many times, it is not so much what is said as how it is said. If the witness looks and sounds confident, the judge and jurors will most likely attach greater weight to the testimony.

8. Dress neatly and appropriately.

When deciding what to wear to court, talk with your attorney. If you are testifying at a bench trial before a judge only, wearing everyday work clothes is most likely fine. Judges do not determine the facts of a case based on what you are wearing. If you are testifying in front of a jury, you need to appear professional as jurors do make decisions, perhaps unknowingly, based on the appearance of a witness. While you may not have to wear a suit and tie or dress, something more than a department issued polo shirt and jeans will be warranted. You do not need to overdress but you certainly must not underdress. This is where your attorney can advise you.

9. Be prepared.

If you are unfamiliar with court procedure, make sure that the municipal attorney prepares you for what will happen. It is important to feel comfortable before the court. Anxiety can be relieved by having some knowledge about what to expect.

10. Wait for the judge's ruling to an objection.

If either attorney raises an objection, wait until the judge rules on the motion. If the objection is sustained, the attorney will ask another question. If the objection is overruled, you may answer the question.

Your behavior in the courthouse should be restrained and dignified. Jurors cannot help but notice and take into account behavior in a hallway or outside on the courthouse steps. Every impression picked up by a juror of the building official's position in a case must be favorable. Improper conduct will do nothing but hurt the case.

Sequestration of Witnesses

One of the first questions a witness may hear upon entering the courtroom is whether the "rule" is to be invoked. The "rule" is the **rule of sequestration** of witnesses.

Simply stated, this rule requires that any witness who has not yet testified and who is not a party must be excluded from the courtroom. After testifying, the witness may stay and listen to the remainder of the proceedings.

This rule does not apply to parties, including municipal corporations. Further, corporations are theoretically inanimate and cannot be physically present in the courtroom; therefore, in some jurisdictions, the rule may allow for a representative of the corporation to sit in. Therefore, it is frequently possible to have the building official sit in for the corporation and witness all the testimony. It is always advantageous for the building official to observe the case and become familiar with the theories upon which the opposition is placing heaviest reliance. After listening to the arguments of the opposing counsel, the building official's testimony may then be more easily aimed at the positions of the opposition.

Sequestered witnesses should avoid speaking to opposing counsel during court recesses and the like. Opposing attorneys frequently try to get information from witnesses during this time. A prosecutor may not tell a witness to refrain from speaking to opposing counsel because that would be a breach of ethics. A witness, however, can choose not to speak to opposing counsel. If a witness decides to speak, he or she should be aware that anything said can be used to impeach his or her testimony (that is, to call the witness's credibility into question). Usually, the less the opposing attorney knows, the harder it is to prepare to attack the witness. Sometimes, it is in the best interest of the case to speak with the other attorney because it may hasten a plea agreement or settlement. The witness can always demand that the municipality's lawyer be present during any conference with the opposing counsel.

Expert Witness

A good **expert witness** is invaluable. A building official may often be called upon on by his or her attorney to testify as an expert witness. Every attorney wants to find an expert who knows the field thoroughly and, at the same time, can express the most complex thoughts simply and understandably to a jury of laypeople. To possess both of these qualities is extremely important and valuable. Of the two, it is more important to be able to express complex thoughts in a simple manner.

The expert witness differs from the ordinary lay or fact witness in that the fact witness cannot normally express an opinion on a given topic. The very reason for calling the expert is to obtain that expert's opinion. The expert frequently will have no connection whatsoever with the facts of a case until requested to review and comment on them. In fact, a witness who is remote from the particular issue at hand is desirable because it decreases the opportunity for opposing counsel to attack the expert as predisposed for one side or the other. Of course, in the area of building codes, a building official will probably not be able to avoid the appearance of some predisposition. This does not prevent the building official's testimony, but it may affect the credibility the judge or jury accords the opinion offered.

One of the most prevalent misconceptions regarding expert witnesses is that they must have some high level of expertise in order to qualify. Certainly, the more knowledge the better; however, there is no minimum requirement. To qualify as an expert, the witness need only have some knowledge in a particular field beyond that held by an ordinary person. No particular degree or academic background is necessary. Other ways to establish the expertise of a witness include any specialized training or experience in the field, the fact that the witness is licensed to practice or has certifications or other credentials from professional associations in the field (such as the International Code Council), that the witness has practiced in the field for a substantial period of time, that the witness has taught in the field or published articles related to the field, or that the witness belongs to professional organizations in the field. The easiest way, however, to establish the expertise of a witness is if the witness has previously been recognized by the court as an expert and has testified as an expert.

Delays often destroy useful evidence, so the first thing the expert must do is educate his or her attorney. The attorney must be made as knowledgeable as possible on the subject. It is likely that the attorney will cross-examine an opposing expert; therefore, the greater the attorney's knowledge, the greater the possibility of being successful. The attorney should strive to become as expert in the subject as the witness.

Conversely, the expert should be involved in the case as a whole. Frequently, attorneys are strapped for time; as a result, they fail to give witnesses an accurate overview of all the facts of the case. This omission is unfortunate for the lay witness and can be detrimental to testimony given by the expert. In most cases, the attorney does not know about the expert's field and may be ignorant of other areas of the same case in which the expert may be helpful. Also, to the extent that the expert understands the underlying legal theories, the expert may be able to defend himself more easily on cross-examination. The expert should insist on being briefed on the entire case and not just on the portion of the case in which he or she is expected to play a prominent role.

It is imperative that the expert meet with the attorney on a number of occasions prior to the trial date. Of course, the witness should be careful to make the attorney explain in plain language what he or she is expected to do in court. An expert must clearly understand what is expected. It is a good idea to ask the attorney to put instructions in writing so that the witness may refer to them as the case progresses.

Meetings should be held to discuss the results of investigations or research. Again, both the expert and the attorney must be sure that they understand one another. Immediately prior to trial, a final meeting should be held to prepare for trial. At this point, the attorney may have already written the direct examination questions. Witnesses should be alert to the way the questions are structured and make sure that their answers are expected by the attorney. This is especially true because a hypothetical question may frequently be used in order to ask the opinion of the expert. A **hypothetical question** is one that asks the expert to assume certain facts and to give an opinion based on such assumptions. If the case is complicated, the hypothetical question may be quite complicated. It is very useful for the attorney to write down the hypothetical question prior to asking it. Very often, if it is not written, the attorney may forget a crucial element of the hypothetical example, leading to an embarrassing answer to the question. The other questions may not be written, particularly if the attorney wishes to appear spontaneous. But in the hypothetical case, the general rule is to have it written out.

In general, the expert witness should follow all the other rules for fact witnesses. This is particularly true of the rule about avoiding undignified behavior. The jury normally accords a great deal of deference to an expert witness, so any action which might diminish that deference must be eliminated.

Usually an expert is not subject to the rule of sequestration of witnesses. The rationale for the rule of sequestration lies in the court's desire to avoid one witness from listening to another and then changing his or her story to fit the prior testimony. Since an expert does not give fact testimony, it is much less likely that his or her testimony will be changed by listening to others. It is always possible, however, for local practice to differ from the general rule. The attorney will inform the witness of whether or not the rule applies in his or her jurisdiction.

Unlike the fact witness, the expert witness needs to prepare for being qualified to testify as an expert. In some jurisdictions, this is known as *voir dire* (literally, "to speak the truth"). In this situation, *voir dire* is a preliminary examination of witnesses to prove their competency and expertise. There is considerable legal strategy involved in this area which exceeds the scope of this book. The important thing is to realize that the attorney will at the very beginning of the witness's testimony examine the witness's qualifications. The more impressive the qualifications, the better the witness looks, but there is no magic formula. It is much more important that the witness be able to communicate easily with the jury.

Not only will the attorney question the witness about his or her qualifications, but often, so will the opposing attorney. Questions of this sort are used by the opposing attorney not so much to try to disqualify the witness as an expert, but rather to point out to the jury the limitations of his or her expertise. For example, the opposing attorney might ask if whether it is true that as a civil engineer, the witness does not necessarily have a background in electrical engineering. If the witness does not have such a background, he or she should say so. There is no damage done by acknowledging limitations. Take strength from the fact that because of an expert's specialized knowledge in a particular field, most attorneys are out of their league when dealing with them. Because of this specialized knowledge, experts are dangerous witnesses to *voir dire*, and consequently, experts should feel no hesitation in admitting to their alleged "deficiencies."

Cross-examination of an expert witness is also extremely difficult for attorneys. Only when the expert is completely and obviously wrong will cross-examination be easier. Given the difficulty of cross-examinations, attorneys will usually ask simple questions that are designed to show that possibilities exist other than those supported by the witness. Normally, the expert can concede that there are indeed other possibilities. For example, the witness can admit that something other than faulty wiring caused a building to catch fire. The witness must be sure to make it clear to the court, however, that although there may be some other reason for a building fire; his or her expertise is the basis for believing that faulty wiring was the most likely cause of the fire.

Many attorneys like to ask the expert if he or she recognizes a particular book or article as an authority in the field under consideration. Before testifying, the witness should give some thought to which texts he or she is willing to recognize as authoritative. If the attorney names a text not on the list, the witness should admit that he or she does not rely upon on this text in forming opinions. If it is on the list, say so. The witness, however, should be aware that if he or she admits to relying on this text, the attorney will most likely quote some language in that text which runs counter to the opinion the witness has just expressed. To avoid being caught in this embarrassing situation, prepare for it before taking the stand.

Pretrial **discovery** will often disclose expert opinion on which opposing counsel is planning to rely. Check with the attorney to determine whether or not this information has been disclosed. If it has not been, patiently and calmly explain how and why the language quoted by the attorney does not contradict what you have said. If the witness cannot manage to provide a convincing explanation, the attorney will try to restore the testimony on redirect. While being cross-examined, an expert witness, even more than other types of witnesses, must always appear calm. The witness must also appear impartial. Because the opposing attorney will ask about the fee that the witness is receiving in return for his or her services as an expert witness, it is all the more important to convey to the jury that the witness would not so testify if he or she really did not believe the witness's testimony to be true. A good response is to say that the witness is being paid for his or her time and not the testimony. Quibbling with the attorney about insignificant details or refusing to admit an obvious fact indicates to the court that the expert witness is not truly impartial. If the judge and jury believe that the witness is not impartial, they will be less likely to believe his or her testimony.

Consulting Experts

A consulting expert is not a witness. He or she is an expert hired to help the attorney prepare for trial. Usually, consulting experts are retained only in cases of major importance. The advantage for attorneys is strategic. Retaining a consulting expert's services need not be divulged to the other side. Thus, the attorney can benefit from an expert's advice without having to share it with the opponents. A building official may serve as a consulting expert.

Consulting experts are also useful during trial. If they are seated at the table with the attorney, they can listen to the opposition's expert and help the attorney to formulate questions for cross-examination.

Order of the Court

Whether the building official has testified in a civil action or a criminal case to secure compliance with the building code, if the defendant is found liable or guilty, the court will issue some type of order that the defendant must comply with. The building official will prove invaluable to the municipal attorney if he or she helps the attorney draft the order for the court. The order should contain specific details of what needs to be done to come into compliance with the code. Citing to specific sections of the code is important. Also include reasonable timelines, due dates and when inspections will occur. By drafting these requirements ahead of time, the attorney can ask the court to adopt them and make them part of the official court record.

Having a specific, well drafted order adopted by the court can provide great advantage to the building official and the municipal attorney in the future. If the defendant fails to comply with the order, claims he did not have to do something, or even refuses to comply, it is easy to summons the defendant back to court to answer to the judge why he did not comply with the judge's order. When faced with contempt of court or the possibility of jail time, many defendants suddenly become compliant.

Conclusion

As a witness, it is crucial to remember to use common sense and to be reasonable. Speak naturally and try to communicate directly with the jury. If these simple rules, as well as the others outlined in the chapter are followed, the building official should have very few problems on the witness stand.

Appendix A

Facts about Pregnancy Discrimination

The Pregnancy Discrimination Act is an amendment to Title VII of the Civil Rights Act of 1964. Discrimination on the basis of pregnancy, childbirth, or related medical conditions constitutes unlawful sex discrimination under Title VII. Women affected by pregnancy or related conditions must be treated in the same manner as other applicants or employees with similar abilities or limitations.

Hiring

An employer cannot refuse to hire a woman because of her pregnancy-related condition as long as she is able to perform the major functions of the job. An employer cannot refuse to hire her because of its prejudices against pregnant workers or the prejudices of coworkers, clients or customers.

Pregnancy and Maternity Leave

An employer may not single out pregnancy-related conditions for special procedures to determine an employee's ability to work. However, an employer may use any procedure used to screen other employees' ability to work. For example, if an employer requires its employees to submit a doctor's statement concerning their inability to work before granting leave or paying sick benefits, the employer may require employees affected by pregnancy-related conditions to submit such statements.

If an employee is temporarily unable to perform her job due to pregnancy, the employer must treat her the same as any other temporarily disabled employee; for example, by providing modified tasks, alternative assignments, disability leave, or leave without pay.

Pregnant employees must be permitted to work as long as they are able to perform their jobs. If an employee has been absent from work as a result of a pregnancy-related condition and recovers, her employer may not require her to remain on leave until the baby's birth. An employer may not have a rule that prohibits an employee from returning to work for a predetermined length of time after childbirth.

Employers must hold open a job for a pregnancy-related absence the same length of time jobs are held open for employees on sick or disability leave.

Child Care

Leave for child care purposes is not covered by the Pregnancy Discrimination Act; however, Title VII requires that leave for child care purposes be granted on the same basis as leave granted to employees for other nonmedical reasons, such as nonrelated travel or education.

Health Insurance

Any health insurance provided by an employer must cover expenses for pregnancy-related conditions on the same basis as costs for other medical conditions. Health insurance for expenses arising from abortion is not required, except where the life of the mother is endangered.

Pregnancy-related expenses should be reimbursed exactly as those incurred for other medical conditions. No additional, increased, or larger deductible can be imposed.

If a health insurance plan excludes benefit payment for pre-existing conditions when the insured's coverage becomes effective, benefits can be denied for medical costs arising from an existing pregnancy. Employers must provide the same level of health benefits for spouses of male employees as they do for spouses of female employees.

Fringe Benefits

Pregnancy-related benefits cannot be limited to married employees. In an all-female workforce or job classification, benefits must be provided for pregnancy-related conditions if benefits are provided for other medical conditions. If an employer provides any benefits to workers on leave, the employer must provide the same benefits for those on leave for pregnancy-related conditions. Employees with pregnancy-related disabilities must be treated the same as other temporarily disabled employees for accrual and crediting of seniority, vacation calculation, pay increases, and temporary disability benefits.

Filing a Charge

The US Equal Employment Opportunity Commission has issued guidelines, including questions and answers, interpreting the Pregnancy Discrimination Act (29 CFR 1604.10). Charges of sexual discrimination may be filed at any field office of the US Equal Employment Opportunity Commission. Field offices are located in 50 cities throughout the United States and are listed in most local telephone directories under US Government. Information on all EEOC-enforced laws may be obtained by calling toll free to (800) 669-4000. EEOC's toll free TDD number is (800) 800-3302.

If you have been discriminated against on the basis of sex, you are entitled to a remedy that will place you in the position you would have been in if the discrimination had never occurred. You may be entitled to hiring, promotion, reinstatement, back pay, or other remuneration. You may also be entitled to damages to compensate you for future pecuniary losses, mental anguish, and inconvenience. Punitive damages may be available, as well, if an employer acted with malice or reckless indifference. You may also be entitled to attorney's fees. A fact sheet is available in the following formats: print, braille, large print, audiotape, and electronic file on computer disk. For further information, call the Office of Equal Employment Opportunity at (800) 669-4000 (voice) or (800) 800-3302 (TDD).

Appendix B

Facts about Sexual Harassment

Sexual harassment is a form of sex discrimination that violates Title VII of the Civil Rights Act of 1964.

Unwelcome sexual advances, requests for sexual favors, and other verbal or physical conduct of a sexual nature, constitute sexual harassment when submission to or rejection of this conduct explicitly or implicitly affects an individual's employment, unreasonably interferes with an individual's work performance, or creates an intimidating, hostile, or offensive work environment.

Sexual harassment can occur in a variety of circumstances, including but not limited to the following:

> The victim as well as the harasser may be a woman or a man. The victim does not have to be of the opposite sex.

> The harasser can be the victim's supervisor, an agent of the employer, a supervisor in another area, a coworker, or nonemployee.

> The victim does not have to be the person harassed but could be anyone affected by the offensive conduct.

> Unlawful sexual harassment may occur without economic injury to or discharge of the victim.

> The harasser's conduct must be unwelcome.

It is helpful for the victim to directly inform the harasser that the conduct is unwelcome and must stop. The victim should use any employer complaint mechanism or grievance system available.

When investigating allegations of sexual harassment, EEOC looks at the whole record: the circumstances, such as nature of the sexual advances, and the context in which the alleged incidents occurred. A determination on the allegations is made from the facts on a case-by-case basis.

Prevention is the best tool to eliminate sexual harassment in the workplace. Employers are encouraged to take steps necessary to prevent sexual harassment from occurring. They can do so by establishing an effective complaint or grievance process and taking immediate and appropriate action when an employee complains.

Filing a Charge

Charges of sexual discrimination may be filed at any field office of the US Equal Employment Opportunity Commission. Field offices are located in 50 cities throughout the United States and are listed in most local telephone directories under US Government. Information on all EEOC-enforced laws may be obtained by calling toll free to (800) 669-4000. EEOC's toll free TDD number is (800) 800-3302.

If you have been discriminated against on the basis of sex, you are entitled to a remedy that will place you in the position you would have been in if the discrimination had never occurred. You may be entitled to hiring, promotion, reinstatement, back pay, or other remuneration. You may also be entitled to damages to compensate you for future pecuniary losses, mental anguish, and inconvenience. Punitive damages may be available, as well, if an employer acted with malice or reckless indifference. You may also be entitled to attorney's fees.

A fact sheet is available in the following formats: print, braille, large print, audiotape, and electronic file on computer disk. For further information, call the Office of Equal Employment Opportunity at (800) 669-4000 (voice) or (800) 800-3302 (TDD).

Appendix C

Facts about Religious Discrimination

Title VII of the Civil Rights Act of 1964 prohibits employers from discriminating against individuals because of their religion in hiring, firing, and other terms and conditions of employment. The act also requires employers to reasonably accommodate the religious practices of an employee or prospective employee, unless to do so would create an undue hardship on the employer (see also 29 CFR 1605). Flexible scheduling, voluntary substitutions or swaps, job reassignments, and lateral transfers are examples of accommodating an employee's religious beliefs.

Employers cannot schedule examinations or other selection activities in conflict with a current or prospective employee's religious needs, inquire about an applicant's future availability at certain times, maintain a restrictive dress code, or refuse to allow observance of a Sabbath or religious holiday, unless the employer can prove that not doing so would cause an undue hardship.

An employer can claim undue hardship when accommodating an employee's religious practices if allowing such practices requires more than ordinary administrative costs. Undue hardship also may be shown if changing a bona fide seniority system to accommodate one employee's religious practices denies another employee the job or shift preference guaranteed by the seniority system.

An employee whose religious practices prohibit payment of union dues to a labor organization cannot be required to pay the dues, but the employee may pay an equal sum to a charitable organization.

Mandatory "new age" training programs, designed to improve employee motivation, cooperation or productivity through meditation, yoga, biofeedback or other practices, may conflict with the nondiscriminatory provisions of Title VII. Employers must accommodate any employee who gives notice that these programs are inconsistent with the employee's religious beliefs, whether or not the employer believes there is a religious basis for the employee's objection.

Filing a Charge

If you have been discriminated against on the basis of religion, you are entitled to a remedy that will place you in the position you would have been in if the discrimination had never occurred. You may be entitled to hiring, promotion, reinstatement, back pay, or other remuneration. You may also be entitled to damages to compensate you for future pecuniary losses, mental anguish, and inconvenience. Punitive damages may be available, as well, if an employer acted with malice or reckless indifference. You may also be entitled to attorney's fees.

Charges of sexual discrimination may be filed at any field office of the US Equal Employment Opportunity Commission. Field offices are located in 50 cities throughout the United States and are listed in most local telephone directories under US Government. Information on all EEOC-enforced laws may be obtained by calling toll free: (800) 669-4000. EEOC's toll free TDD number is (800) 800-3302. A fact sheet is available, in the alternate formats, upon request.

Appendix D

Facts about the Americans with Disabilities Act

Title I of the Americans with Disabilities Act of 1990, which took effect July 26,1992, prohibits private employers, state and local government, employment agencies, and labor unions from discriminating against qualified individuals with disabilities in job application procedures, hiring, firing, advancement, compensation, job training, and other terms, conditions and privileges of employment. An individual with a disability is a person who:

> Has a physical or mental impairment that substantially limits one or more major life activities;
>
> Has a record of such an impairment; or
>
> Is regarded as having such an impairment.

A qualified employee or applicant with a disability is an individual who, with or without reasonable accommodation, can perform the essential functions of the job in question. Reasonable accommodation may include but is not limited to:

> Making existing facilities used by employees readily accessible to and usable by persons with disabilities;
>
> Job restructuring, modifying work schedules, reassignment to a vacant position; or
>
> Acquiring or modifying equipment or devices, adjusting or modifying examinations, training materials, or policies, and providing qualified readers or interpreters.

An employer is required to make an accommodation to the known disability of a qualified applicant or employee if it would not impose an "undue hardship" on the operation of the employer's business. Undue hardship is defined as an action requiring significant difficulty or expense when considered in light of factors such as an employer's size, financial resources, and the nature and structure of its operation.

Medical Examinations and Inquiries

Employers may not ask a job applicant about the existence, nature, or severity of a disability. Applicants may be asked about their ability to perform specific job functions. A job offer may be conditioned on the results of a medical examination, but only if the examination is required for all entering employees in similar jobs. Medical examinations of employees must be job related and consistent with the employer's business needs.

Drug and Alcohol Abuse

Employees and applicants currently engaging in the illegal use of drugs are not covered by the ADA, when an employer acts on the basis of such use. Tests for illegal drugs are not subject to the ADA's restrictions on medical examinations. Employers may hold illegal drug users and alcoholics to the same performance standards as other employees.

EEOC Enforcement of the ADA

The US Equal Employment Opportunity Commission issued two regulations to enforce the provisions of Title I of the ADA on July 26, 1991. The provisions took effect on July 26, 1992, and covered employers with 25 or more employees. On July 26, 1994, employers with 15 or more employees were covered.

Filing a Charge

If you have been discriminated against on the basis of disability, you are entitled to a remedy that will place you in the position you would have been in if the discrimination had never occurred. You may be entitled to hiring, promotion, reinstatement, back pay, or other remuneration. You may also be entitled to damages to compensate you for future pecuniary losses, mental anguish, and inconvenience. Punitive damages may be available, as well, if an employer acted with malice or reckless indifference. You may also be entitled to attorney's fees.

Charges of employment discrimination on the basis of disability, based on actions occurring on or after July 26, 1992, may be filed at any field office of the US Equal Employment Opportunity Commission. Field offices are located in 50 cities throughout the United States and are listed in most local telephone directories under US Government. Information on all EEOC-enforced laws may be obtained by calling toll free to (800) 669-4000. EEOC's toll free TDD number is (800) 800-3302. A fact sheet is also available in alternative formats upon request.

Appendix E

Facts about National Origin Discrimination

Title VII of the Civil Rights Act of 1964 protects individuals against employment discrimination on the basis of national origin as well as race, color, religion, and sex.

It is unlawful to discriminate against any employee or applicant because of the individual's national origin. No one can be denied equal employment opportunity because of birthplace, ancestry, culture, or linguistic characteristics common to a specific ethnic group. Equal employment opportunity cannot be denied because of marriage or association with persons of a national origin group; membership or association with specific ethnic promotion groups; attendance or participation in schools, churches, temples, or mosques generally associated with a national origin group; or a surname associated with a national origin group.

Speak-English-Only Rule

A rule requiring employees to speak only English at all times on the job may violate Title VII, unless an employer shows it is necessary for conducting business. If an employer believes the English-only rule is critical for business purposes, employees have to be told when they must speak English and the consequences for violating the rule. Any negative employment decision based on breaking the English-only rule will be considered evidence of discrimination if the employer did not tell employees of the rule.

Accent

An employer must show a legitimate nondiscriminatory reason for the denial of employment opportunity because of an individual's accent or manner of speaking. Investigations will focus on the qualifications of the person and whether his or her accent or manner of speaking had a detrimental effect on job performance. Requiring employees or applicants to be fluent in English may violate Title VII if the rule is adopted to exclude individuals of a particular national origin and is not related to job performance.

Harassment

Harassment on the basis of national origin is a violation of Title VII. An ethnic slur or other verbal or physical conduct because of an individual's nationality constitute harassment if they create an intimidating, hostile, or offensive working environment, unreasonably interfere with work performance, or negatively affect an individual's employment opportunities. Employers have a responsibility to maintain a workplace free of national origin harassment. Employers may be responsible for any on-the-job harassment by their agents and supervisory employees, regardless of whether the acts were authorized or specifically forbidden by the employer. Under certain circumstances, an employer may be responsible for the acts of nonemployees who harass their employees at work.

Immigration-Related Practices That May Be Discriminatory

The Immigration Reform and Control Act of 1986 (IRCA) requires employers to prove all employees hired after November 6, 1986, are legally authorized to work in the United States. The IRCA also prohibits discrimination based on national origin or citizenship. An employer who singles out individuals of a particular national origin or individuals who appear to be foreign to provide employment verification may have violated the IRCA, unless these are legal or contractual requirements for particular jobs. Employers also may have violated Title VII if a requirement or preference has the purpose or effect of discriminating against individuals of a particular national origin.

Filing a Charge

Charges of national origin discrimination may be filed at any field office of the US Equal Employment Opportunity Commission. Field offices are located in 50 cities throughout the United States and are listed in most local telephone directories under US Government. Information on all EEOC-enforced laws may be obtained by calling toll free to (800) 669-4000. EEOC's toll free TDD number is (800) 800-3302.

If you have been discriminated against on the basis of national origin, you are entitled to a remedy that will place you in the position you would have been in if the discrimination had never occurred. You may be entitled to hiring, promotion, reinstatement, back pay, or other remuneration. You may also be entitled to damages to compensate you for future pecuniary losses, mental anguish, and inconvenience. Punitive damages may be available, as well, if an employer acted with malice or reckless indifference. You may also be entitled to attorney's fees.

This fact sheet is available in the following formats: print, braille, large print, audiotape, and electronic file on computer disk. For further information call the Office of Equal Employment Opportunity at (800) 669-4000 (voice) or (800) 800-3302 (TDD).

For more information about employment rights and responsibilities under the Immigration Reform and Control Act, you may call the Office of Special Counsel for Immigration-Related Unfair Employment Practices: (800) 255-7688.

Index of Terms

ABSOLUTE IMMUNITY. A policy of protecting public officials from tort liability. (Chapter 10) A high-level executive officer cannot be held liable for his or her discretionary acts or omissions. (Chapter 11)

ABUSE OF PROCESS. The improper use of various litigation devices. The elements of this tort are: 1) an ulterior purpose; and 2) a willful act in the use of the process not proper in the regular conduct of the proceedings. (Chapter 10)

ABUT. Two parcels of land that physically touch one another. (Chapter 9)

ACQUIT. To set free or release someone from a charge or accusation. To be civilly acquitted is to be found free from liability, whereas to be criminally acquitted is to be judged not guilty of a crime with which a defendant was charged. (Chapter 10)

ACT. Another name for a statutory law, and thus having the same power as a statute. (Chapter 5)

ADJUDICATION. The use of a formal legal process to resolve a dispute. (Chapter 1)

ADMINISTRATIVE ACTION. The process by which the Board of Building Code Appeals (BBCA), or any administrative agency, forms its decisions. (Chapter 7)

ADVERSE POSSESSION. Acquiring title to property for a specified period of time under specific circumstances. (Chapter 9)

ADVOCATE. To plead the cause of his or her client in court. (Chapter 13)

AFFIRMATIVE COVENANT. An agreement between parties to do something. (Chapter 9)

AFFIRMATIVE EASEMENT. Gives its possessor the right to use a portion of another's land to do some act. (Chapter 9)

AGENT. A person who is authorized to act on behalf of a principal, whether buyer or seller. (Chapter 9)

ANSWER. In a lawsuit, a written response by the defendant to the plaintiff's complaint that either denies in part or in whole the allegations lodged by the plaintiff. (Chapter 7)

APPEAL. After a decision is rendered, a party may ask a higher court to change or set aside a lower court's ruling or an administrative body's decision. Therefore, an appellate court can overrule a lower circuit court's ruling. (Chapter 8)

APPELLATE COURT. Generally, a court having the power to hear and review lower court decisions. (Chapter 8)

ASSAULT. The willful attempt or threat to impose injury upon another when there is present the apparent ability and intent to injure. (Chapter 10)

ASSUMPTION OF RISK. A defense that is dependent upon proof that the plaintiff knew of and understood the risk to which he was subjecting himself, yet proceeded in that course anyway. It is a defense against *negligence*. (Chapter 11)

ATTACHMENT. The legal process of preventing the owner from disposing of real estate **while a lawsuit is pending. (Chapter 9)**

ATTRACTIVE NUISANCE DOCTRINE. Situations in which young children enter the property because they are attracted there by a swimming pool or some other attractive nuisance. (Chapter 10)

BATTERY. An intentional infliction of harmful or offensive bodily contact. (Chapter 10)

BEARING WALL. A wall that is used to support floors, partitions or roof loads. (Chapter 9)

BREACH OF DUTY. The neglect or failure to fulfill in a just and proper manner the duties of an office. (Chapter 11)

BURDEN OF PROOF. Refers to who must prove the issue in a controversy and how much proof must be presented to an administrative tribunal or to a court of law in order to be awarded the sought-after relief. (Chapter 7)

CAUSE OF ACTION. A set of facts that entitles a party to sustain an action and gives that party the right to seek a judicial remedy on his or her behalf. (Chapter 2)

CAVEAT EMPTOR. Let the buyer beware. (Chapter 9)

CAVEAT VENDITOR. Let the seller beware. (Chapter 9)

CERTIORARI. A writ of common law origin issued by a superior court to an inferior court requiring the latter to produce a certified record of a particular case tried therein. The writ is issued in order that the court issuing the writ may inspect the proceedings and determine whether there have been any irregularities. It is most commonly used to refer to the Supreme Court of the United States, which uses the writ of *certiorari* as a discretionary device to choose the cases it wishes to hear. (*Source: Black's Law Dictionary, 6th ed.*) (Chapter 9)

CHAIN OF TITLE. A record of successive conveyances and deed restrictions on a particular parcel of land. (Chapter 9)

COMMON LAW. The body of law that developed and evolved in England from judgments and decrees of the courts and which has general application, not subject to local rules. It may also mean laws created by judges, not legislatures. (Chapter 5)

COMPLAINT. A document that initiates a prosecution or a lawsuit. It includes the parties, the nature of the claim against the defendant, and a specific demand for relief (if it is a civil suit). (Chapter 6)

COMPREHENSIVE ZONING. The outcome of using the final version of the zoning plan or the comprehensive zoning plan. (Chapter 9)

COMPREHENSIVE ZONING PLAN. The final version of the zoning plan that is ultimately developed and completed. (Chapter 9)

CONDEMNATION. The government's use of power to obtain private property for public use through its power of eminent domain. (Chapter 9)

CONDITIONAL USE. A specified use that is permitted in a designated zoning district but has to meet certain criteria or conditions for location and operation as outlined in the ordinance. (Chapter 9)

CONDITIONAL USE PERMIT. The permit that would stipulate the conditions and specific controls that have been approved for the conditional use. (Chapter 9)

CONTRIBUTORY NEGLIGENCE. A doctrine that holds if the plaintiff has been guilty of any negligence which has contributed to his injuries or damage, then he is totally barred from any recovery. (Chapter 11)

COVENANT. A written agreement between two or more parties to agree either to do something or not to do something. (Chapter 9) See also *affirmative covenant, negative covenant* and *restrictive covenant.*

CROSS-EXAMINATION. At either a trial or a hearing, an examination of a witness by the party who is opposed to the party who produced that witness. The cross-examiner cannot ask questions that are beyond the scope of what was asked on direct examination. (Chapter 13)

CURTAIN WALL. The enclosing wall or skin of a building that uniformly covers the exterior facade from floor to floor for all or a large portion of the elevation. (Chapter 9)

DECLARATORY JUDGMENT. A remedy that functions to declare explicitly the rights of the plaintiff. The plaintiff has sought this relief because he or she is in doubt as to his or her legal rights. The court's declarations bind the parties in their future actions with each other. (Chapter 11)

DECLARATORY RELIEF. It is the same as *declaratory judgment.* (Chapter 4)

DEDICATION. Land or an easement therein that is voluntarily transferred or appropriated, by a private citizen, for use by the public. (Chapter 9)

DEED. A written legal document by which title to property is passed. (Chapter 9)

DEFENSE. Evidence or arguments offered by the defendant to demonstrate or explain why the plaintiff should not prevail. (Chapter 10)

DE NOVO. A hearing that is reheld in front of a court. (Chapter 7)

DEPOSITION. A witness's testimony taken under oath prior to trial. This testimony is used in the preparation for trial. (See definition of *discovery.*)

DILLON'S RULE. States that a municipal corporation has only those powers which are (a) expressly granted to it by charter or by other state legislation; (b) implied or necessarily incident to the express powers; and (c) essential and indispensable to the declared objects and purposes of the corporation. (Chapter 3)

DIRECT EXAMINATION. The first examination of a witness taken by the party on whose behalf the witness was called. (Chapter 13)

DISCOVERY. A pretrial procedure allowing each side in a case to obtain factual information about the opposing party's case. The taking of depositions is one discovery tool. (See definition of *deposition.*) (Chapter 13)

DISCRETIONARY AUTHORITY. The granting of a modification to the code, by the building official, when there are practical difficulties encountered. (Chapter 6)

DISCRIMINATORY ENFORCEMENT. A legal concept that looks at whether some person or group was impermissibly singled out for enforcement. (Chapter 8)

DUE PROCESS. A legal procedure established by the 14th Amendment to enforce and protect basic individual rights, for example, the right to be present, to be heard and to present evidence before a judicial body. (Chapter 6)

DUTY. An obligation, to which the law will give recognition and effect, to conform to a particular standard of conduct toward another. (Chapter 11)

EASEMENT. Entitles a person to use land possessed by another. A right of way is one example of an easement. (Chapter 9) See also *affirmative easement, expressed easement, implied easement* and *negative easement.*

EMINENT DOMAIN. The government has the power to take title to property against the owner's will if the government compensates the owner. (Chapter 9)

ENABLING LEGISLATION. Express state legislation enabling local governments to enact building codes. (Chapter 4)

ENCROACHMENT. The illegal act of occupying a space that belongs to someone else. (Chapter 9)

ENCUMBRANCE. Limitation or restriction on the use of a property that the owner is obligated to observe. (Chapter 9)

EQUAL PROTECTION CLAUSE. A clause to the 14th Amendment which ensures that state governments do not arbitrarily discriminate in applying their laws to different individuals or groups of people. (Chapter 8)

EQUITABLE ESTOPPEL. A doctrine by which the municipality may be precluded by its actions, or by its failure to act, from asserting a right which it otherwise would have had. (Chapter 6)

EQUITABLE POWERS. The powers of a particular court, usually a chancery court, to fashion remedies beyond monetary damages (such as, injunctive relief). (Chapter 6)

EXCEPTION. A special use that is permitted in a particular district subject to certain conditions. A daycare center in a residential district is an example. (Chapter 9)

EXEMPLARY DAMAGES. Damages given in addition to punitive damages that compensate a defendant for a monetary loss; to make an example of the wrongdoer. (Chapter 10)

EXPERT WITNESS. A witness who has specialized experience and knowledge and testifies in order to aid the jury in understanding complicated and technical topics. (Chapter 13)

EXPRESSED EASEMENT. An entitlement for someone to use land possessed by another, which is agreed upon by the two parties and set out in a written instrument. (Chapter 9)

FACIAL VALIDITY. Means that on its face, the words of a statute are valid although, in reality, they may not be applicable. (Chapter 8)

FACT WITNESS. A witness who testifies to facts of which he or she has personal knowledge. (Chapter 13)

FALSE IMPRISONMENT. A cause of action that allows a successful plaintiff to recover damages for the intentional and unwarranted confinement of another. (Chapter 10)

FIXED PROPERTY. Articles that are permanently attached to the building and intended to become a part of the building. (Chapter 9)

FIXTURES. See fixed property.

HEARSAY. An out-of-court statement that is being introduced as the truth of the matter asserted in the statement. *Hearsay* is not admissible as evidence (subject to certain exceptions) because its validity cannot be tested in cross-examination. (Chapter 6)

HOME RULE. Results in the apportioning of power between state and local governments by providing local cities and towns with a certain amount of self government in return for accepting certain terms of the state law. (Chapter 3)

HOMEOWNER'S ASSOCIATION. A legally recognized entity, sometimes a not-for-profit corporation, made up of the owners of all the lots, who act together for the common interest pursuant to a declaration of covenants. (Chapter 9)

HYPOTHETICAL QUESTION. A question that asks an expert witness to assume certain facts and give an opinion based on such assumptions. (Chapter 13)

IMMUNITY. A legal privilege that prevents liability from attaching to the actions of certain individuals. It may be *absolute* or qualified. (Chapter 5)

IMPEACHMENT. The negating of the credibility of a witness by cross-examination. (Chapter 9)

IMPLIED EASEMENT. Occurs when one landowner sells a portion of property to another, and that second owner has no other access to his property except to cross the land of another. (Chapter 9)

INJUNCTION/INJUNCTIVE RELIEF. A judicial order prohibiting specified conduct; it may be *temporary* or *permanent*. (Chapters 4, 6)

INTENTIONAL TORT. Wrongful conduct that was intended. (Chapter 10)

INVERSE CONDEMNATION. Action taken against the government seeking just compensation for the taking of private property through the power of eminent domain. (Chapter 9)

JOINT AND SEVERAL LIABILITY. Concept allowing the plaintiff to recover damages from two or more defendants. (Chapter 11)

LIABILITY. An obligation that one is bound in law or justice to perform. (Chapter 1)

LICENSE. Land entrance permission given by the landowner for a particular purpose. (Chapter 10)

LIEN. A claim or encumbrance on a property to secure a debt or obligation. (Chapter 9)

LIS PENDENS. Legal proceedings which may be pending in court affecting the title or ownership of the property. (Chapter 9)

MALFEASANCE. The performance of some act that a person ought not do at all. (Chapter 11)

MALICE. The intentional wrongful act without just cause or excuse and with the intent to inflict some sort of injury on another. (Chapter 10)

MALICIOUS PROSECUTION. Concerns the wrongful institution of criminal proceedings by one private citizen against another, resulting in damages. (Chapter 10)

METES AND BOUNDS. A way of measuring by establishing a starting point, such as a designated landmark, distances (metes) and directions (bounds) to encompass the parcel returning to the initial starting point. (Chapter 9)

MICRO ZONING. See spot zoning.

MINISTERIAL ACT. A deed performed under the authority, policies and procedures of a superior. (Chapter 6)

MISFEASANCE. The improper performance of some act that a person may lawfully do. (Chapter 11)

MORTGAGE. An instrument that gives the lender or seller a lien on the real estate as security for the debt incurred in the purchase of the real estate. (Chapter 9)

NEGATIVE CONVENANT. An agreement in which one party promises to refrain from doing something. (Chapter 9)

NEGATIVE EASEMENT. Restricts a landowner from using a portion of his or her land that may be otherwise lawfully used. (Chapter 9)

NEGLIGENCE. Involves conduct that was not intended to cause harm or injury but which, nonetheless, did so and that also breached some duty of care imposed by the law. (Chapter 10)

NONCONFORMING USE. A structure that complied with zoning ordinances at the time it was built but no longer conforms to regulations due to the adoption, revision or amendment of a zoning ordinance. (Chapter 9)

NONFEASANCE. The nonperformance of some act that a person is obligated or has the responsibility to perform. (Chapter 11)

NULL AND VOID. Having no legal force or binding effect. (Chapter 3)

OPEN CURTILAGE. Any area that appears to be open to the public, this includes a driveway, walkway, or any access route that leads to the residence. (Chapter 10)

ORDINANCE. A local law. (Chapter 9)

OWNER IN ARREARS. When a purchaser fails to stay current with his or her payment obligations under the mortgage. (Chapter 9)

OWNER PERSONA. A person who is the owner of any fixed property or fixtures. (Chapter 9)

PARTITION WALL. A wall built to separate interior spaces. (Chapter 9)

PARTY WALL. A wall erected on an interior lot line as a common support to a structure on both sides, under different ownerships, for the benefit of both in supporting the structure. (Chapter 9)

PERMANENT INJUNCTION. A judicial order prohibiting specified conduct, which is issued after the court has heard all of the evidence in the case. (Chapter 6)

PERMISSIVE USE. Property owners' allowance of someone to come onto his or her land without considering it a trespass. (Chapter 9)

PER SE. Means "in itself." For example, negligence, *per se*, means that a person's conduct is itself negligent without considering the facts and circumstances of the behavior. (Chapter 8)

PERSONAL PROPERTY. Property that is tangible and moveable. (Chapter 9)

PLAINTIFF. A person who files a lawsuit. (Chapter 10)

PLANNED UNIT DEVELOPMENT. A specialized type of subdivision that describes a large-scale real (PUD) estate development project. (Chapter 9)

PLAT. See plat map.

PLAT MAP. A map giving the legal descriptions of the property by lot, street and block number.
It also shows all blocks, lots, streets and the exact dimension of each. (Chapter 9)

PLOT PLAN. A survey that shows all utilities on the property as well as the setbacks for the proposed structure. It is necessary for the performance of a proper plan review. (Chapter 9)

POLICE POWERS. The power of the states to adopt laws to protect and promote the health, safety, morals and general welfare of its citizens. (Chapter 5)

POSSESSION. The act of possessing. (Chapter 9)

PREEMPTION. A judicially created doctrine that says that a state may not pass a law that is inconsistent with federal law. If a state enacts such a law, the federal law will take precedence over the state law to the extent that there is conflict. (Chapter 4)

PREPONDERANCE OF THE EVIDENCE. A standard of proof. This standard is met when the evidence is of greater weight or more convincing than the evidence that is offered to oppose it. This standard is used in civil law. (Chapter 10)

PROBABLE CAUSE. A reasonable ground for belief in certain alleged facts. (Chapter 6)

PROCEDURAL DUE PROCESS. Parties whose rights are to be affected are entitled to be heard, and therefore must be notified. (Chapter 12)

PUBLIC DUTY DOCTRINE. A doctrine that provides that a plaintiff who alleges inadequate performance of a governmental activity has the burden to show that the municipality owed a specific duty to the plaintiff and not simply to the general public. (Chapter 11)

PUBLIC EASEMENTS. A public right-of-way. (Chapter 9)

PUBLIC PROPERTY. Property owned by a state, municipality or government agency for public purposes. (Chapter 9)

PUNITIVE DAMAGES. Damages that are awarded to the plaintiff who proves malice on the part of the defendant, and are intended to punish the wrongdoer. (Chapter 10)

QUALIFIED IMMUNITY. A lower-echelon public employee cannot be held liable for his or her discretionary acts or omissions. (Chapter 11)

REAL ESTATE. A parcel of land and any items permanently affixed to it, such as a house, an inground pool, or a fence. (Chapter 9)

REAL PROPERTY. See real estate. (Chapter 9)

REDIRECT. An examination of a witness by the direct examiner. The questions on redirect must be limited to the scope of the cross-examination. (Chapter 13)

REFRESH RECOLLECTION. The process an attorney will go through that allows a witness on the stand to refer to their notes to help them remember a forgotten fact. (Chapter 13)

REGULATION. A rule established by a government agency having the force and effect of law even though the rule is not set forth explicitly in the statute. (Chapter 4)

RESPONDEAT SUPERIOR. A doctrine that states that the master or employer is liable for the wrongful acts of his servant or employee. (Chapter 12)

RESTRICTIVE CONVENANT. Limits the use of the property and prohibits certain uses. (Chapter 9)

RETURN OF THE WARRANT. After serving or executing a search warrant, the official must file this document with the court acknowledging that the warrant was served on the person named in the warrant and noting the date and time the warrant was served.

REVERSE. To overturn by contrary opinion, for example, a lower court's decision. (Chapter 4)

RULE OF SEQUESTRATION. Requires that any witness who has not yet testified and who is not a party must be excluded from the courtroom. (Chapter 13)

SITE MAP. A map of the site indicating proposed construction and associated building and site work needed to prepare the parcel for construction. (Chapter 9)

SITE PLAN. See site map.

SOVEREIGN IMMUNITY. A judicially created doctrine that prevents a party from bringing a suit against a government. (Chapter 4)

SPECIAL USE PERMIT. Another use within a specific zoning district permitted by exception in a zoning ordinance. (Chapter 9)

SPOT ZONING. When a small parcel of land is arbitrarily selected for a zoning classification that is unrelated to the surrounding uses and zoning districts and cannot be justified based on the health, safety or general welfare of the community. (Chapter 9)

SQUATTER. A person who settles on land under adverse possession. (Chapter 9)

STATUTE. A law enacted by state or federal legislatures. (Chapter 3)

STATUTE OF LIMITATIONS. Set by state law, a restriction on the period of time within which a complaint must be filed. (Chapter 6)

SUBPOENA. A writ issued to make sure a witness appears in court to testify on behalf of a party. (Chapter 13)

SUBPOENA DUCES TECUM. A writ issued to a witness to force him or her to bring specific documents or records to a hearing. (Chapter 13)

SUBSTANTIVE DUE PROCESS. Any and all legislation enacted by a government must bear some rational relationship to a legitimate governmental function; the law must make sense. (Chapter 8)

SUMMARY ACTION. A stop work order that is given to abate a violation without formal court proceedings. (Chapter 6)

SURVEY. Measurements of a specific parcel of land that indicates the parcel boundaries. (Chapter 9)

TEMPORARY INJUNCTION. A judicial order prohibiting specified conduct, which is issued pending a full hearing by the court. (Chapter 6)

TEMPORARY RESTRAINING ORDER. An order issued by the court without notice to the other party and without an opportunity for the other party to be heard. (Chapter 6)

TENANT. The occupant of a building, house, apartment or land that is owned by someone else. (Chapter 8)

TITLE EVALUATION. An evaluation that determines whether or not to finance the purchase of the property based on an examination of the title search. (Chapter 9)

TITLE SEARCH. An examination of title records to determine whether the title to a property is clear. Title search reports include the legal description, the exact name of the seller, the county's tax identification number and a listing of all liens, claims or encumbrances that exist upon the property. (Chapter 9)

TOPOGRAPHY MAP. A map showing the developer the contour of the land on which he or she is about to build. (Chapter 9)

TORT. A civil wrong, other than a breach of contract, for which the court will force the wrongdoer to pay damages. (Chapter 10)

TORT-FEASOR. A wrongdoer; an individual or business that commits or is guilty of a tort. (Chapter 10)

TORT LIABILITY. Liability that is borne by the person who is at fault or causes the damages or injury. (Chapter 10)

TRESPASS. When a person intentionally enters on land under the possession of another. It connotes intrusion or invasion of private premises. (Chapter 10)

ULTRA VIRES. Literally, "beyond the powers." An entity has acted beyond the scope of its powers. (Chapter 3)

URBAN RENEWAL. Redevelopment plan put into place when a community, usually an area experiencing a decline and/or abandonment, to revitalize the area. (Chapter 9)

VARIANCE. A relaxation of the strict provisions of a zoning ordinance based on hardship. (Chapter 9)

VESTED RIGHTS. Rights that so completely belong to a person that they cannot be taken away without his or her consent. (Chapter 6)

VOIR DIRE. Literally, "to speak the truth." The examination by attorneys of prospective jurors to determine their suitability, or of the opposing counsel's witnesses to determine competence to testify. (Chapter 13)

WARRANTY DEED. A deed that not only convey ownership in a property, but promises that the buyer has good title to the property; that it is free from all defects in title, i.e. liens and encumbrances. (Chapter 9)

WRIT OF CERTIORARI. A writ allowing the Supreme Court to control the number of cases it hears each year and to choose which cases it wants to hear. (Chapter 8)

WRIT OF MANDAMUS. An order issued from a higher court requiring a private or municipal corporation or any of their officers to carry out the duties they were hired to perform. (Chapter 6)

ZONING PLAN. A document that is adopted by a municipality that provides direction and control of the development of land within its boundaries for present and future uses. (Chapter 9)

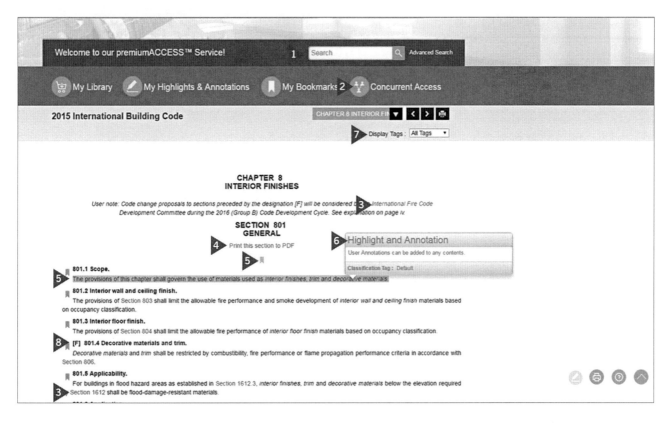

1 **Search** the current chapter or use **Advanced Search** to search across your entire set of purchased products.

2 **Concurrent user functionality** lets colleagues collaborate with shared access.

3 **Internal linking** navigates between referenced contents of the book and other purchased books in your library.

4 **Print** controls can be used to create a PDF of any section of purchased content.

5 **Bookmark** any section or subsection, define its classification, and assign a label and color to the classification.

6 **Highlight** and **Annotate**, then hover over the text to reveal a modal noting your annotation message and classification value.

7 **Display tags** enable you to filter the multiple classification tags you create. View all of them together or one at a time.

8 **Color coding** identifies changes since the previous edition of the I-Code or State Code.

1-year and 3-year subscriptions now available for:
International Codes® | **State Codes** | **Standards** | **Commentaries**
Let *codes.iccsafe.org* start working for you today!

Introducing the ICC Assessment Center, Featuring PRONTO™

All certification and testing activities are now available in the ICC Assessment Center, formerly ICC Certification & Testing.

Take the Test at Your Location

Skip the trip to the testing center for your next ICC Certification exam. Instead, take advantage of ICC PRONTO, an industry leading, secure online exam delivery service. The only proctored remote online testing option available for building professional certifications, PRONTO allows you to take ICC Certification exams at your convenience in the privacy of your own home, office or other secure location. Plus, you won't have to wait days or weeks for exam results, you'll know your pass/fail status immediately upon completion.

 With PRONTO, ICC's Proctored Remote Online Testing Option, take your ICC Certification exam from any location with high-speed internet access.

 With online proctoring and exam security features you can be confident in the integrity of the testing process and exam results.

 Plan your exam for the day and time most convenient for you. PRONTO is available 24/7.

 Eliminate the waiting period and know your results immediately upon exam completion.

#1 ICC is the first model code organization to offer secured online proctored exams—part of our commitment to offering the latest technology-based solutions to help building and code professionals succeed and advance.

Discover the new ICC Assessment Center, ICC PRONTO and the wealth of certification opportunities available to advance your career: www.iccsafe.org/MeetPRONTO

ASSESSMENT center

pronto
ICC ONLINE EXAMS

17-14661